Y0-BRH-367

DATE DUE			
Apr 18 79			
Nov 30'81			
Apr 16 82			

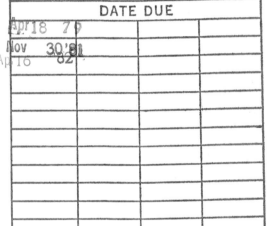

LIBRARY OF CONGRESS
SURPLUS - B
DUPLICATE

WITHDRAWN
L. R. COLLEGE LIBRARY

A SHORT HISTORY OF MODERN GREECE

1821–1956

A SHORT HISTORY OF MODERN GREECE

1821—1956

by

EDWARD S. FORSTER

THIRD EDITION
REVISED AND ENLARGED
BY DOUGLAS DAKIN

CARL A. RUDISILL LIBRARY
LENOIR RHYNE COLLEGE

GREENWOOD PRESS, PUBLISHERS
WESTPORT, CONNECTICUT

Library of Congress Cataloging in Publication Data

Forster, Edward Seymour, 1879-1950.
  A short history of modern Greece, 1821-1956.

  Reprint of the 1958 ed. published by Methuen, London.
  Bibliography: p.
  Includes index.
  1. Greece, Modern-History—1821-   I. Dakin,
Douglas. II. Title.
[DF802.F6 1977]   949.5'06   77-11620
ISBN 0-8371-9803-8

949.506
F77s
107823
Dec.1978

Copyright © *1958 Methuen & Co. Ltd.*

LIBRARY OF CONGRESS
CIP

DEC 2 2 1977

All rights reserved.

Originally published in 1958 by Methuen & Co., Ltd., London

Reprinted with the permission of Methuen & Co. Ltd., on behalf
of the Academic Associated Book Publishers Ltd.

Reprinted in 1977 by Greenwood Press, Inc.

Library of Congress Catalog Card Number 77-11620

ISBN 0-8371-9803-8

Printed in the United States of America

PREFACE TO THE FIRST EDITION

THE entry of Greece into the war in October 1940 has suggested that the present is a suitable occasion for carrying out a project which I have had in mind, and for which I have been collecting material, ever since my return from service in the Army from 1915 to 1919 as an Intelligence Officer in Macedonia and Constantinople. My interest in Modern Greece dates from my first visit to that country in 1900, which was followed by two years' residence there from 1902–4 as a member of the British School of Archæology at Athens and by several visits both before and since the war of 1914–18.

The book falls into three periods.

Part I is a summary of the story of the birth and early struggles of the Greek Kingdom and its history down to the year 1914. It makes no claim to originality and necessarily owes much to the many authors who have dealt with this period in greater detail.

Part II deals with the story of Greece during the war of 1914–18. The political events which occurred at Athens and Salonica during these years were full of dramatic interest, though their significance was overshadowed by much more momentous happenings elsewhere in Europe and Asia ; an account of what was occurring in the political sphere in Greece and its connexion with the military operations may be of interest to the general reader and, in particular, to those who spent many long months with the forces based on Salonica and must often have wondered exactly what was happening in the rest of Greece, and how it was that political events delayed for so long the advance of the Army which, after three years of waiting, achieved the glorious victory of September 1918 and drove a nail into the coffin of the

Central Alliance. After a year spent as an Intelligence Officer in the field, I was attached from 1916 to 1918 as British representative to a bureau of the French G.H.Q., which was in close touch with the political activities of General Sarrail and his successors, and thus had the opportunity of gaining some first-hand knowledge of what was happening in that sphere. The account here given of this period is an abbreviated version of an account which I wrote immediately after my return to England in 1919.

Part III deals with events in Greece from the Armistice in 1919 down to the Italian invasion of Greece in October 1940. It was a period of constant political change in Greece which seems to necessitate a year-by-year treatment of events. Such interest as is offered by the history of the earlier years is provided by the struggle between the Monarchists and Republicans and by the attempts of the Balkan States to patch up their differences and form an Entente which might act as a single Power and present a united front to possible outside aggression. Towards the end of the period the interest increases as the crisis comes nearer ; and an attempt has been made to describe the reactions of Greece to the course of events in Europe in which she herself eventually became involved. More attention has been paid in this part of the book to economic matters, which assumed an importance which they lacked in the earlier periods.

A final chapter gives some personal impressions of the modern Greek people.

Any one who writes about the events in Greece during the years following 1914 has to make up his mind whether he supports the Royalist or the Venizelist party. Much has been written on both sides and, in particular, much skilful propaganda has been used in the attempt to prove that King Constantine was a martyr and M. Venizelos an unscrupulous adventurer ; but an impartial survey of the evidence has brought the conviction that M. Venizelos was right in the drastic measures he took to bring Greece into the war on the side of the Allies and that the results have justified his policy.

The Bibliography at the end of the book forms a record of the more important books which I have consulted and will, I hope, be a guide to those who wish to supplement what is necessarily a very brief account of the events which it attempts to chronicle. In Part III I owe a debt of gratitude to the admirable publications of the Institute of International Affairs, which are a mine of accurate and authoritative information, to the files of *The Times*, and to the historical summaries in the *Annual Register*. I would recommend those who desire more detailed information about the Greek people and about Greek political personalities to consult the writings of Dr. William Miller, who is the historian *par excellence* of modern Greece in this country.

The spelling of place and personal names gives rise to difficult problems ; I have tried, perhaps at the expense of consistency, to use those forms which I think will be most familiar to my readers.

I have to acknowledge with thanks the help of my colleagues, Professor G. R. Potter, who read my MS. and made many valuable suggestions ; Mr. W. S. Maguinness, whose careful scrutiny of the proofs has been of great service ; and Messrs. A. M. Woodward and F. E. Tyler, who have given me advice. I have also to thank my neighbour, Mr. Charles Boot, for the loan of numerous books from his library at Thornbridge Hall.

EDWARD S. FORSTER

March 31, 1941

PREFACE TO THE THIRD EDITION

IN preparing the third edition of this book, I have retained the late Professor Forster's account of the years 1940–45 and I have made each section of the *Epilogue* of the second edition a separate chapter. All I have done is to delete the concluding paragraphs in which the author looks back on the events of the war years and states the problems of post-war Greece. The author's account of the years 1940–45, though written by May 1945, is very adequate and it would be difficult to improve upon it in the space available. I have, however, added one or two notes supplementing the account in the light of more recent knowledge and linking it up with the new Chapter XXVI dealing with Greece during the post-war years. Finally, I have transferred the chapter, *The Greeks of To-day*, to the end of the book, having merely deleted the last sentence and having added a few remarks to round off the book, using chiefly a form of words from the original concluding paragraph to Chapter XXIII. Should the reader seek a fuller and contemporary account of the Greeks of to-day, I can recommend him the excellent volume, Francis King, *Introducing Greece* (1956).

CONTENTS

PART I

GREECE FROM THE TURKISH CONQUEST TO THE OUTBREAK OF THE WAR OF 1914-18

PART II

GREECE DURING THE WAR OF 1914-18

PART III

GREECE FROM 1918 TO 1957

MAPS

Drawn by Stephen J. Dernie

TO

H. S. F.

AND

A. S. F.

PART I

GREECE FROM THE TURKISH CONQUEST TO THE OUTBREAK OF THE WAR OF 1914-18

CHAPTER I

THE GREEKS UNDER TURKISH DOMINATION AND THE GROWTH OF NATIONAL SENTIMENT

THE modern kingdom of Greece owes its origin to two main causes : primarily, to the spontaneous impulse of the Christian population of the Ottoman Empire, and, secondarily, to the practical sympathy of Great Britain, France, and Russia.

The origin of the Greek kingdom.

The preservation of Greek national sentiment throughout the dark ages of Turkish rule is one of the most remarkable phenomena of modern history. The conquering Turk found Greece an easy prey. The gradual decline of the Byzantine Empire had led to decay and stagnation in its outlying territories. Further, since the time of the Fourth Crusade, which had turned from its main object, the recovery of the Holy Land, to conquer Constantinople, there had been Frankish feudal principalities in the Greek lands, whose misrule and incessant quarrels had reduced the Greek inhabitants to a state of miserable servitude. The Turkish armies after the conquest of Macedonia and Thessaly, where their rule was firmly established some years before the close of the fourteenth century, obtained a footing in Central Greece in 1396. The complete subjugation of Greece was, however, delayed by the danger which threatened the Turks from the Mongols ; and the Byzantine Empire, making a final effort before its own end came, succeeded in destroying Frankish rule in the Peloponnese in 1430. After the fall of Constantinople in 1453 the conquest of Greece was not long delayed, the Peloponnese being finally reduced in 1466—the year in which the Parthenon at Athens became a Turkish mosque—and Euboea

The Turkish conquest of Greece.

in 1470. Mohammed II, after deliberately exterminating

The Turkish system in Greece. the remaining Frankish lords and the Greek notables, handed over their lands to his own veterans and established the Turkish system of *timars*, or fiefs, held for life as the reward of distinguished military service. Under this system the Greek cultivator remained on his lands paying a fixed revenue to his overlord, who in his turn was under the obligation of giving his personal service to the Sultan and providing a band of followers varying according to the size of his fief. Every unbeliever was also compelled to pay the *haratsh*, or poll-tax, from which all Moslems were exempt.

The Janissaries. Mohammed also imposed the blood-tribute of Christian children, one-fifth of the males being collected every four years and carefully educated as Mohammedans, thus providing the Sultan with a standing army and a devoted body of household slaves. These forcibly Islamized Christians for two centuries formed the chief basis of the Sultan's personal authority and of the military superiority of the Ottoman Empire. These measures effectually subjected Greece to the Turkish domination and abolished the last traces of the political system inherited from Imperial Rome by the Empire of the East, and the political history of Greece became merged in that of its Ottoman rulers. The Hellenic race during this period sank so low in the social scale and became so reduced in numbers that he would have been a bold prophet who had foretold that it could ever lift up its head again.

The Ottoman Empire, under the direction of a series of able and energetic sultans, reached its culminating point in the reign

The zenith of the Turkish Empire. of Suleiman I, the Magnificent (1520–1566), who ruled from Buda-Pesth to the Persian Gulf and threatened Austria, while his navies menaced countries as far apart as Spain and India. The seventeenth century marks the beginning of the decline of Turkey, which may be dated from the unsuccessful siege of Vienna in

The beginning of its decline in the seventeenth century. 1683. In Greece a Western Power, Venice, again asserted itself, and it was in the bombardment of the Acropolis at Athens by the Venetians in 1687 that a cannon-ball landed in a Turkish powder magazine in the Parthenon and caused an explosion, which partially destroyed it. The

Peace of Carlowitz in 1699 gave the Venetian Republic the rule of the Peloponnese, which it retained until 1715, when the Turks won it back again. But the great days of the Ottoman Empire were over and henceforward, instead of being a Central European Power, it became a definitely Eastern Power, and Europe was freed from the menace of a Turkish invasion.

The only Christian administrative authority which was not abolished by Mohammed the Conqueror was the Greek Church.

The Greek Church under Turkish rule and its preservation of Greek nationality. The Patriarchate of Constantinople was left undisturbed, and the Patriarch was the head not only of the ecclesiastical body but also of the Greek community, and was the representative of the Greek nation in its dealings with the Ottoman Government. Such questions as those regarding inheritance and marriage were referred not to the civil courts but to the ecclesiastical tribunals. The great mass of Greeks, however, was scattered in isolated communities engaged in agricultural pursuits. Here the parish priest and the head-man of the village decided ordinary judicial cases between Christians, holding a kind of court in the church with the notables of the village, including doubtless the schoolmaster, as assessors. This semi-ecclesiastical communal system did much to keep alive the sentiment of nationality. The debt of the Greek nation towards the parochial clergy and the schoolmasters during the dark ages of the Turkish domination is one which cannot be overestimated ; more than any other classes they contributed to keeping alive the flame of Hellenism and national patriotism amongst the agricultural population during the long centuries of Ottoman rule.

The decline of the Turkish Empire which set in during the later part of the seventeenth century had the effect of improv-

The decline of the Ottoman Empire. ing the position of the Christian population. The gradual breakdown of the administration loosened the hold of the Central Government in the more distant portions of the Empire, while the growing power of the neighbouring Christian peoples forced the Ottoman Government to conciliate the goodwill of its Christian subjects. In the agricultural regions money payment finally took the place of personal service and the Greek peasant became in many districts practically the free owner of the land which he tilled.

In the urban communities the improved position of the Greeks allowed their intellectual superiority to assert itself in
The Greeks as Turkish civil servants. two spheres, the official and the commercial world. The Ottoman Government no longer carried on campaigns against the great Christian powers of Europe, with whom its relations became more and more those of diplomacy. A career was then opened for which the Greek with his keener intellect and imagination was much better fitted than the Turk. There thus arose the important class of Greek officials in the service of Turkey, who had received the name of Phanariots from the quarter of the capital in which the Patriarchate is situated. Though at first they were employed only in secretarial duties, their aptitude for affairs marked them out for more important posts. The celebrated Grand Vizier Achmet Kyöprülü after the conquest of Candia in 1669 created for his Greek secretary, the Chiot Panagiotakis, the post of Dragoman of the Porte, a position which rapidly became one of great political importance. A similar position, that of Dragoman of the Fleet, was afterward created in the service of the Capitan Pasha, who was charged with the administration and the collection of taxes in the Islands of the Ægean. Alexander Mavrocordatos, also a native of Chios, succeeded Panagiotakis and gained great credit for his conduct of the negotiations which led to the conclusion of the Peace of Carlowitz in 1699. The creation of the positions of Voivodes, or Christian rulers, of Moldavia in 1712 and Wallachia in 1716 gave the Phanariots further opportunities of distinction, and the holders of these offices naturally chose their subordinates from among their own nation.

The Phanariot influence was partly good and partly bad. It was good in that the Greeks, through the important positions
The Phanariot Greeks. occupied by numerous members of their community, exercised an enormous influence throughout the Ottoman Empire, and the whole nation gained vigour from the improved conditions under which it lived. Moreover, the necessity for literary instruction which was required for official duties acted as an impulse to education. This education, moreover, was essentially Hellenic and did not

merely aim at producing competent officials but disseminated a
more general type of culture. Even the great Phanariot princes
found time to be men of letters as well as administrators.[1] On
the other hand, the Phanariot officials were naturally closely
attached to the ruling power in Turkey, and it was to their interest
to support the existing state of affairs, which gave them wealth
and enabled them to live in luxury. It is, however, to their
credit that their position as servants of the Ottoman Government
did not lead them to adopt either the Turkish language or the
religion of Islam ; they were, without exception, staunch apostles
of Hellenism.

Just as the declining vigour of the Ottoman gave a fresh
scope to the Greek in the sphere of official life and diplomacy,
Greek trade so in another field the indifference and contempt
under the Turks. which the Turk has always felt for commerce
gave the Greek genius an opening of which it
was not slow to avail itself. Even as early as the period immediately following the Turkish conquest, the strong government of
the early Sultans had given a scope to the commercial activities
of his Greek subjects and a considerable trade was carried on
with Italy and even with Spain. Greek commerce naturally
benefited from the prestige enjoyed by the Turks throughout
Europe until the end of the sixteenth century, although it had
The Jews in to meet the competition of the numerous Jews
Turkey. expelled from Spain by Ferdinand and Isabella
at the end of the fifteenth century, whom the
Ottoman Government allowed to settle in Turkey, especially
in Constantinople and Salonica, and to whom it extended
its protection. But the unsettled conditions which ruled
in the seventeenth century, the prevalence of piracy, and
the increasing maladministration of the Ottoman Empire
restricted enterprise and gradually extinguished much of the
Extension of commerce with the outside world which Greek
Greek trade in industry had built up. Further, the Venetians
the eighteenth during their occupation of Greece established
century. monopolies in their own favour which materially
damaged Greek commercial interests. The
eighteenth century, however, saw a marked revival of

---

[1] For example, Alexander Mavrocordatos wrote *Moral Essays* and a
Treatise on the Circulation of the Blood.

Greek trade, especially in its second half, when commercial treaties concluded between Russia and Turkey gave the Greek merchant the protection of the Russian flag. During the period of disturbance throughout Europe which followed the French Revolution, the Ottoman Government for a long time managed to preserve its neutrality, and Greek merchants were enabled to make enormous profits. During this period the foundations were laid of the great carrying trade which is one of the principal *Rise of Greek* industries of Modern Greece. The Greek *communities* merchant soon realized that his enterprise could *outside the Otto-* find a scope outside Turkey, and wealthy *man Empire.* commercial houses grew up not only at Odessa, Moscow, Trieste, and Venice but even in London.[1] This rise of Hellenic communities in foreign countries had an important influence, in that it impressed upon many Greeks that a great future lay before their nation if it could win for itself a Greece freed from the Turkish domination. The Greek resident abroad also became familiar with ideas of liberty, such as found no encouragement in the land of his birth.

The improved condition of the Greek race in Turkey in *Types of Greek* the eighteenth century may be illustrated by *communities* taking several types of Greek communities. *under the rule* In southern Greece Hydra, Psara, and Spetsai *of Turkey.* formed a group of islands whose ships carried on a lucrative trade and which formed the training ground of the Greek fleet of the War of Independence. In northern Greece the town of Ambelakia on the Peneus was *Hydra, Psara,* an important manufacturing centre, famous for *and Spetsai.* its dyed thread, and had direct commercial relations with Western Europe. Amongst the islands of the Ægean, Chios, which has produced some of the most distinguished sons of Modern Hellas, was a highly flourishing *Ambelakia.* community, celebrated not only for its silk and cotton goods but also for its literary culture, and enjoyed the right to collect its own taxes, the Greek

[1] The princely generosity of Greek merchants and bankers settled in other countries in supporting the national interests of Greece with their personal fortunes is probably without parallel in any other nation. Numerous examples might be quoted from the time of the Greek War of Independence down to the present day.

authorities paying the Ottoman Government a fixed annual sum
Chios. which was shared on an equitable basis among
the families of the island. But perhaps the most
remarkable of all the Greek communities in Turkey was the
town of Aïvali, or to call it by its Greek name Cydonia, on the
Aïvali. west coast of Asia Minor, opposite to Mitylene,
which in 1740 was established as an independent
Greek municipality from which Turks were excluded by a
special *firman* of the Sultan and was famous for its spacious
public buildings, its educational institutions, and the wealth and
culture of its inhabitants. But the description of a few communities does not give a true idea of the peaceful penetration
of Hellenic influence throughout the Ottoman Empire, where
not only the greater part of the trade but practically all the
learned professions were in the hands of the Greeks.

The growing importance of the Greek element in the
Ottoman Empire could not fail to attract the interest of the
neighbouring powers of Europe. To Russia
Russian in particular the Greeks were bound by the
sympathy for the tie of a common religion, and during the
Greeks in eighteenth century the fact that there were
Turkey. frequent conflicts between the Russians and
the Turks inspired in the minds of the Greeks a hope that Russia
might assist them in their aspirations for freedom. Many
Greeks entered the Russian service and acquired influence with
the ruling powers there. In 1770 a project was formed by
Gregory Orloff, a favourite of Catherine the Great, for establishing an independent principality in Greece. In April of that
year a Russian fleet appeared off the coast of
The rising in Laconia and the whole of the Peloponnese rose
the Peloponnese against its masters. The rising, however, was
in 1770. abortive and was suppressed chiefly by Albanian
troops, who remained in the country and became a terror not
only to the Christian but also to the Moslem population. The
internal disorder which resulted led to the increase of the important class of outlaws known as Klephts ('brigands'), who
took to the mountains and lived in open rebellion against the
Ottoman authorities. They were destined to play a great part
in the War of Independence, and the ballads which tell of their
doings are among the most precious heirlooms of the Greek

race, breathing as they do an ardent patriotism combined with a delicate sentiment and chivalry which makes them unlike anything else in literature.[1]

In spite of the failure of the rising of 1770 the seed of revolution was sown, though conditions in Greece itself and the state of public opinion in Europe were not yet favourable to its growth. It is to the French Revolution that we must attribute the final impulse which led to the achievement of Greek Independence. The ideas of liberty which it inspired, not only encouraged the Greeks to hope that freedom was at hand for all the oppressed nations of the earth, but also gave rise to a growing sympathy among the free peoples of Europe with those races which were still in bondage, and, in particular, a desire to do something for the country where freedom had had its birth. The ferment caused by these new ideas produced a literary renaissance amongst the Greeks. The leader in this movement was Adamantios Coraes, who was born at Smyrna in 1748 and was not only a literary apostle of modern Hellenism but also one of the most distinguished classical scholars of his day.[2] In 1803 he read in Paris before a learned society a 'Memoir on the Present State of Civilization in Greece,' in which he insisted on the imperative necessity for Greek national emancipation, and issued to the Greeks his Σάλπισμα πολεμιστήριον, a spirited appeal to revolution. Constantine Rhigas (1753–98) had already written his stirring national songs, which hold a high place in modern Greek literature, and had founded a society which was the prototype of the celebrated Hetairiai (literary and political unions), which rapidly sprang up in every Hellenic community. The most famous of these which became *par excellence* the National Hetairia was founded by four Greek merchants at Odessa in 1814. It soon became an immense organization which extended wherever Greeks were to be found and was believed to have embraced

The effect of the French Revolution.

The Greek literary renaissance.

Coraes.

Rhigas.

The Hetairia.

---

[1] Numerous collections of klephtic ballads have been made, the best known being those of Fauriel and Passow.

[2] A good account of Coraes is to be found in Platon E. Drakoulis, *Neohellenic Language and Literature* (Oxford, 1897), pp. 48 ff.

200,000 members, who adopted mysterious signs and ceremonies not unlike those of the Freemasons and described themselves as the agents of an Unknown Power which in due time should deliver Greece from the Turkish yoke.

Meanwhile the Greeks had been brought into contact with Great Britain through the protectorate established by that Power in the Ionian Islands in 1815. Here, though the inhabitants did not enjoy all the liberty which they might have desired, they at least experienced the advantages of an equitable administration of justice and the encouragement of industry and commerce. At the same time the presence of a British administration in the Ionian Islands helped to familiarize educated opinion in Great Britain with the aspirations of the Greek nation and the problems to which they gave rise. Remarkable evidence of the interest in Greece taken by individual Englishmen is to be found in the large numbers of travellers who visited the country at the beginning of the nineteenth century in the course of the ' Grand Tour ' undertaken by many rich young Englishmen as part of their education.[1] These travellers returned to their native land with the impression that the internal state of Turkey could not much longer remain as it was.

The British in the Ionian Islands.

We have now briefly reviewed the condition of the Greeks under the Ottoman domination and traced their rise from a state of subjection till they formed an important element in the Turkish Empire, assisting in its administration and carrying on the greater part of its trade, inspired, however, by a strong feeling of nationality and a desire for liberty. We have further seen how from the middle of the eighteenth century onwards circumstances had brought the Greek race into contact with the Christian countries of Europe, in particular with Great Britain, France, and Russia, with the double result of strengthening in the mind of the Greeks their aspirations for freedom and of inspiring the sympathy of friends who would help them when the moment came to strike a blow for liberty.

Summary.

[1] It was to this class that many of those Philhellenes belonged, who placed their personal services and fortunes at the disposal of the Greeks during the War of Independence.

CHAPTER I

THE GREEK WAR OF INDEPENDENCE:
GREECE UNDER KING OTHO (1821–64)

THE first attempt at revolt was made in 1821, when the Hetairia appointed as its leader Alexander Ypsilanti, member of a well-

The abortive rising under Alexander Ypsilanti.
known Phanariot family which had produced several Princes of Wallachia and Moldavia, and who was himself an officer in the Russian army. With an insignificant following he raised the standard of revolt in Moldavia and apparently expected a general rally of the peasantry to the Greek cause. He received no support from the Rumanian population, who had chafed under the Phanariot rule, and his rising was quickly

The Revolution proclaimed in the Peloponnese.
suppressed. Simultaneously, however, the revolution broke out in the Peloponnese and marked the beginning of the glorious War of Greek Independence. On 6th April 1821 Germanos, Archbishop of Patras, unfurled the national standard at the monastery of Hagia Lavra near Kalavryta, a day which has always been celebrated throughout the Greek world as a Greek Independence Day.

This is no place to rewrite the history of a war which has been the subject of graphic contemporary accounts, which have

The Greek War of Independence.
told of the great deeds of Kanaris and his fire ships, of the heroic death of Marco Botzaris, and of the feats of Odysseus the Klepht and countless others. A brief outline of the chief events must suffice.

The movement spread rapidly and was joined by the islands, especially Hydra and Spetsai, which provided the insurgents with a useful fleet, and by Central and Northern Greece. The Turks replied to the rising by a massacre of Greeks at Constantinople, including the Patriarch, Gregory V, who was hanged on Easter Day in the gate of the Patriarchate. Similar scenes were enacted in Macedonia, Thrace, and elsewhere, which only served to widen the breach, the Greeks in exasperation retaliating on the Turkish population in Greece.

The early years of the war saw the balance of success inclining in favour of the insurgents, whose courage attracted to their ranks a large number of foreign Philhellenes. *Early successes of the insurgents.* A change for the worse occurred towards the end of 1824, when the Sultan Mahmoud II induced his vassal Mehemet Ali, Pasha of Egypt, to invade the Peloponnese with an Egyptian army under the command of his son Ibrahim. *Quarrels amongst the Greek leaders.* Quarrels and even fighting broke out amongst the Greek leaders, and the trained Egyptian army was able to inflict serious defeats upon its adversaries. But several magnificent incidents such as the defence of Mesolongi, where Byron had died in April 1824 and which fell into Turkish hands in April 1826, appealed to the imagination of Europe and increased the sympathy felt for the Greek ideal of freedom. *Sympathy of Russia, Great Britain, and France.* In Russia popular feeling demanded that the cause of Orthodox Christianity should not be allowed to perish. The Tzar Nicholas I, who succeeded the weak and vacillating Alexander in November 1825, was not unwilling to take action, while in England and France strong sympathy was felt for the Greek cause to which they had already given many volunteers.[1] At the same time the reconciliation of the rival parties in Greece, who met and elected Count John Capodistrias as President in April 1827, seemed to augur greater unity in the insurgent armies—a promise, however, which was not destined to be fulfilled.

In July 1827 a Triple Alliance was concluded between Russia, Great Britain, and France, who undertook to mediate between the Turks and the Greeks. An armistice was *The Triple Alliance undertakes mediation.* proclaimed, which was accepted by the Greeks but refused by Turkey. An Allied fleet, therefore, set sail for Greek waters under the command of Admiral Codrington and made a demonstration off the west

[1] Sir Richard Church and Lord Cochrane, one of the greatest seaman Britain has ever produced, took over the commands of the Greek Army and Fleet early in 1827.

coast of the Peloponnese. Though there had been no intention
The Battle of   of engaging the Turks, the action of the Otto-
Navarino.   man commander in firing on a man-of-war's
boat sent to parley precipitated a battle in which
the Turkish fleet was annihilated at Navarino on 20th October
1827. This victory of the three Allied Powers set the seal upon
Greek freedom.

In the following spring the Russo-Turkish war broke out,
but the troops of Ibrahim Pasha remained in the Peloponnese
The end of   until the threat of the arrival of a French force
the war.   under General Maison compelled them to
evacuate the peninsula. The last engagement
with the Turks took place in September 1829, when Demetrios
Ypsilanti, the brother of Alexander Ypsilanti who had first
raised the standard of revolt in 1821, defeated a retiring Turkish
force in a narrow defile between Thebes and Livadia. In the
same month the Peace of Adrianople was concluded between
Russia and Turkey, which expressly recognized the independence
of Greece.

Early in the following year the London Conference of the
Allied Powers discussed the establishment of the new state,
The Conference   issuing its protocol on 3rd February 1832. The
of London.   new Greece was restricted to the Peloponnese,
Central Greece, and the Islands of the Cyclades,
the northern frontier being drawn from the Gulf of Arta to the
Gulf of Volo.[1] It thus excluded much territory which could
The boundaries   not be described as anything but Greek, in
of the new state.   particular Thessaly, Crete, Samos,[2] and the
Ionian Islands. It was a settlement which left
the majority of Greeks outside the pale of freedom and
failed to satisfy the essential principles of nationality. It
was in vain that the plenipotentiaries announced that 'the
Greek question was irrevocably settled'—subsequent history
has another tale to tell; but at least it was a beginning and
the nucleus of an independent Greek State had at last been
formed.

The crown of Greece was first offered to Prince Leopold of

---

[1] See map on p. 149.

[2] From 1832 onwards, Samos was ruled by a Christian governor as an
independent Principality under the suzerainty of Turkey.

Saxe-Coburg, who later became King of the Belgians, but after
some hesitation he refused it. The choice was
a wise one, and it is interesting to speculate what
would have been the result of his acceptance.
Meanwhile in Greece affairs became more and
more disordered, and opposition to the autocratic rule of Capodistrias increased until, on 9th October 1831, he was assassinated
at Nauplia by two members of the powerful Mainote clan of
Mavromichalai. The subsequent condition of anarchy was such
that the Allied Powers saw the necessity of setting up some
form of government and chose as king Prince Otho of Bavaria,
son of Louis I, who was known as an ardent Philhellene. It is
interesting to note that the choice of a Bavarian prince was
dictated in part by the feeling that Germany could never have
any possible *locus standi* for interfering in the affairs of Greece
and that the selection was an absolutely neutral one.

Otho of Bavaria chosen king of Greece.

Otho was in his seventeenth year when the throne was
offered to him, but it was nearly a year before he arrived at
Nauplia early in 1833, accompanied by swarms
of Bavarian officials and attended by Bavarian
troops. His arrival was hailed by the more
sanguine of his subjects as the beginning of a new era for Greece.
As he was not yet of age personally to assume the rule of his
new kingdom, a Council of Regency was established. This
consisted of three Bavarians, an arrangement which effectually
excluded the Greeks from any real share in the government.
The promised National Assembly, which was to draw up the
Constitution, was never summoned. Every department of the
administrative and educational system was filled with Germans.
The administration was entirely centralized, and no advantage
was taken of the communal system which already existed and
might well have been used for local self-government in a country
of which the physical features necessitate numerous isolated
communities. The financial state of the country, with the load
of debt incurred during the war, was hopeless from the beginning,
and oppressive taxation drove many of the peasants to take to
the hills, and brigandage became once more a serious danger.
The free expression of popular opinion was curtailed by the
muzzling of the Press. The disputes which arose between the
members of Council of Regency only made confusion worse

The Bavarian Regency.

confounded. For allowing such a state of affairs to arise the three
Allied Powers cannot be entirely acquitted of blame ; they had
brought the infant state into being and were morally responsible
for its upbringing until it could stand alone.

In 1835 King Otho came of age and took over the government at Athens, whither the capital had been transferred from
Otho comes Nauplia in the previous year. He determined to
of age. govern the country himself and presided in
person over the deliberation of the Cabinet.
In spite of the strong recommendations of Lord Palmerston and
Sir Robert Peel he consistently refused to grant a Constitution.
German influence was still predominant and caused growing
discontent. The desire of the Greeks of the ' enslaved ' territories
for inclusion in the kingdom of Greece gave occasion in 1841
to a rising in Crete, but the revolt was suppressed by the Turks,
and the failure of the Government to support this national
The Revolution movement added to the unpopularity of Otho's
of 15th Sept. rule. Finally, on 15th September 1843, a blood-
1843. less revolution took place, which forced Otho
to yield to the desire of his people for a constitutional régime and for the dismissal of the Bavarian clique.
A new Ministry entirely composed of Greeks was formed, and
it was agreed that a National Assembly should be summoned,
by whose decisions the King consented to abide.

Thus at last Greece was freed from foreign domination and
took its place among the constitutional states of Europe. The
Bavarian *camarilla* had not only failed to administer the government and finances of the country but had prevented the Greeks
from acquiring the apprenticeship in the art of statesmanship
which the young nation so much needed.

In spite of misgovernment, Greece had already made no little
progress, both commercially and intellectually, since the founda-
Progress of tion of the kingdom. The national aptitude of
Greece under the Greeks for the sea had led to the increase of
King Otho. the Greek mercantile marine and to the growing
importance of the ports of Syra, the Piræus, and
Patras, while the currant and silk industries had made material
progress. In 1837 the University of Athens was founded and
immediately became an important centre for the propagation of
Hellenic culture and a training ground for the learned professions

of which full advantage was taken by the Greeks of 'unredeemed' as well as free Hellas.

The National Assembly met in November 1843. It is interesting in view of subsequent events to note that Greeks from Thessaly, Macedonia, and Epirus took part in it. The details of the Constitution, which Otho swore to obey on 20th March 1844, do not concern us here, since it was superseded by that of 1864, which forms the real charter of popular liberties in Greece. It may be noted, however, that it established two chambers, a Lower House (*Βουλή*) and a Senate (*Γερουσία*), and that it declared the Orthodox Church of Greece to be autocephalous and administered by a Synod of Archbishops.

The Constitution of 1844.

Party faction, brigandage, and financial difficulties continued to afflict the country. In 1847 the British Government demanded the payment of the interest which was in arrears on the guaranteed loan; while it was undoubtedly within its rights, the other two Powers abstained from doing the same, and the British action was regarded as unfriendly. Other difficulties arose over the claims of a certain Don Pacifico and other British subjects.[1] Further, on the outbreak of the Crimean War, Greece found Great Britain and France, two of the Powers who had brought about the recognition of her independence, ranged against the third, Russia, and actually supporting Turkey, the hereditary enemy of Hellas. The bond of a common religion decided the sympathies of Greece in favour of Russia. Otho, enthusiastically seconded by his queen, Amalia, placed himself at the head of a national movement for the extension of Greece ; and unsuccessful, and indeed hopeless, attempts were made to seize Thessaly and Epirus. Otho, like Constantine at a later date, failed to reckon on the importance of the command of the sea, and the result of his ill-timed movement was that the Anglo-French fleet occupied the Piræus from 1854 to 1857. It may be admitted now that the Crimean War, though due to other causes, resulted, as far as the Balkan States were concerned, in prolonging the power of Turkey to repress nationalism and liberty in the Nearer East. The fact, however, remains that the attempt to profit by the disagreement between the Powers which had helped her in the

The Crimean War.

[1] The details are given by W. Miller, *The Ottoman Empire*, pp. 179 ff.

past only brought Greece into a humiliating situation, whereas a restrained attitude of neutrality would have placed her in the debt of Great Britain and France. Be that as it may, this abortive attempt to increase her boundaries was evidence of the irrepressible enthusiasm of the Greeks for the freedom of their ' enslaved ' brethren—an enthusiasm that has more than once refused to listen to counsels of inaction which would have better served the cause of Hellenism.

The fortunes of Greece were never so low as in the years which followed the Crimean War. The state was bankrupt, *The abdication of* brigandage was rife, the army was disaffected, *King Otho.* and risings occurred in several parts of Greece, while the popularity which Otho had gained by his championship of national expansion was fast declining. Matters came to a head in 1862, when Otho had for a second time to face a popular revolution. This time he bowed before the storm and abdicated after having occupied for nearly thirty years a position for which he had no real qualifications.

The right of the Greeks thus to take matters into their own hands was even at the time generally recognized in Europe. The words used by Earl Russell, the British Foreign Minister of the day, in a letter to the British Minister at Athens, are worth quoting : ' During a long course of years the British Government endeavoured to impress on King Otho the mistaken nature of the system of government which he pursued, and the necessity of adopting a system better calculated to conciliate the affection and confidence of his subjects and to promote the prosperity of Greece. The kingdom of Greece having, by the transactions of 1832, been acknowledged as an independent State, the people of Greece are entitled to exercise the rights of national independence ; and one of the rights which belong to an independent nation is that of changing its governing dynasty upon good and sufficient cause. Her Majesty's Government cannot deny that the Greeks have good and sufficient cause for the steps they have taken.' These words show a genuine appreciation of the right of the Greek nation to decide its own destiny and must have helped to heal the wounds caused by the treatment of Greece by Great Britain and France during the Crimean War.

Of Otho himself the Greeks of to-day have learned to judge

less harshly than their forefathers who deposed him. If he had

The Greek estimate of King Otho. given Greece an heir to the throne, born in Greece and brought up in the Orthodox Faith, his subjects might have forgiven him much. He was indefatigable in visiting every part of his kingdom and making himself personally familiar with his subjects and the conditions of their lives. The unpardonable faults which caused his downfall were his refusal to satisfy the legitimate desire of the Greeks for a democratic constitution and his interference in matters which should have been left to the decision of a responsible Greek Government.

The question of a successor to the throne became the immediate pre-occupation of the whole nation, who fixed upon

The throne of Greece offered to Prince Alfred (Duke of Edinburgh). Prince Alfred of Great Britain, Duke of Edinburgh, second son of Queen Victoria, as their choice. It was made clear, however, that the understanding arrived at between the Three Powers in 1830 excluded from the throne of Greece all members of the reigning houses of these Powers. In spite of this, when the matter was put to the democratic test of a plebiscite, Prince Alfred received the overwhelming majority of 230,000 out of 240,000 votes. It is interesting to note that only 93 votes were cast in favour of a republic and only 6 in favour of a Greek. In view of the

Prince William George of Denmark chosen king. impossibility of the acceptance of the crown by Prince Alfred, the British Government undertook to find a king for Greece, thus taking upon itself a responsibility which made Great Britain in a special manner answerable for the future welfare of the country. The choice fell upon Prince William George, second son of Prince, afterwards King, Christian of Denmark. The recent marriage of his sister, the Princess Alexandra, with the Prince of Wales was a close tie with Great Britain, while his subsequent marriage with the Grand Duchess

The Ionian Islands ceded to Greece by Great Britain. Olga of Russia, daughter of the Grand Duke Constantine, was a bond with another of the Protective Powers. The National Assembly acquiesced in the choice of the British Government all the more readily in that it was announced that the Ionian Islands would for the future belong to their rightful owners and form part of the Greek kingdom.[1] This concession, the justice of which had been recognized ever since the visit of Gladstone to the Islands on a special mission in 1858, was a happy augury for a reign which was to see other important accessions to the territory of the Greek kingdom. The Three Powers also undertook each to remit £4000 a year from the interest of the loan of 1832, which was to be added to the new king's Civil List.

Prince William George of Denmark, who arrived at Athens on 30th October 1863 and ascended the throne as King George I,

The accession of King George I. was, like his predecessor, only seventeen years of age at the time of his accession. The National Assembly had already been sitting for some months framing the new Constitution, but it was only on 28th November 1864 that its work was finished and the new

The National Assembly. King took the oath. This Constitution forms one of the most democratic documents ever drawn up and fixed the limits of a constitutional monarchy which King George religiously observed throughout his long reign.

A large majority in the National Assembly voted in favour of the abolition of the Senate set up in 1844, and the Chamber

The Constitution of 1864. of Deputies (βουλή), therefore, became supreme in the State. Its members were to be elected by direct, secret, and universal male suffrage. It expressly stated in the Constitution that the deputies represented the nation and not the districts for which they were elected, and their numbers were to be determined in proportion to the population of each constituency. No deputy might be elected until he had completed his thirtieth year, and he must be a native of the district he represented or have resided and enjoyed political rights therein for two years.

The most interesting portions of the Constitution are those which lay down the position of the sovereign. The Royal

The nature of the monarchy. prerogatives were strictly limited so as to preclude the possibility of such intervention in both political and judicial affairs as had characterized the rule of King Otho. The form of government thus set up has been well described as a Monarchical Democracy. The

[1] See map on p. 149.

sovereign is the head of the State, not by the divine right of kings but by the will of the people whose servant he is.   Though possessing both legislative and executive powers, he could exercise them only through his Ministers and was thus a passive organ of the State in the administration of public affairs and a channel for the transmission of the will of the people.   In such a constitution the personal influence of the sovereign has no place, and any arbitrary interference by the Crown in the affairs of the nation is the negation of the essential principles of democracy ; the will of the people expressed through their elected representatives is the only source of power in the State.

A few other points in the Constitution of 1864 may be noted.   Local self-government was established on a system resembling that of the Code Napoléon ; the freedom of the Press was asserted and guaranteed ; the independence of the Orthodox Church of Greece was again proclaimed in terms almost identical with those used in the Constitution of 1844 ; and, while nothing was said as to the religion of the new King, it was enacted that the heir to the throne must be a member of the Orthodox Faith.   Finally, it was laid down that a revision of the Constitution could only be contemplated, if, after a period of ten years, the Chamber in two successive legislatures voted by a majority of three-quarters of its members in favour of the reconsideration of specified provisions.

By this Constitution Greece at last obtained, after more than forty years of independence, a régime under which she could be governed by Greeks for the benefit of Greeks.   Henceforward the Greeks of the Greek kingdom were masters in their own house, but it was still a house from which a majority of the national family was excluded.

CHAPTER III

THE REIGN OF KING GEORGE I DOWN TO THE
ANNEXATION OF THESSALY (1864–81)

IT was not without reason that King George I assumed the title not of 'King of Greece', which had been borne by his pre-decessor, but of 'King of the Hellenes'. This title embodies the aspirations of the Greeks for the incorporation in Free Hellas of all their 'unredeemed' brethren, which is the keynote of Greek history from 1864 onwards. The problem of en-slaved Greece cast its shadow over the first fifty years of the new reign, and the powerlessness of the nation to attain its ideals did much to hamper internal progress. The inclusion of Thessaly was, as we shall see, the only addition made to Greece during this period. She had won her liberty and her democratic con-stitution, but, until the rise of M. Venizelos, she produced no statesman capable of leading the nation along the path of national expansion.

The problem of the unredeemed Greeks.

The position of Greece as a small state under the protection of greater Powers forced her to fix her attention on international politics, and in particular the doings of the 'Concert of Europe', rather than on her own internal affairs and material progress. At the same time the barrier of Turkey stretching from the Adriatic to the Ægean effectually cut her off by land from the rest of Europe.[1] The Turkish Empire had been apparently on the point of dissolution for so many genera-tions that it seemed scarcely worth while to cultivate a garden which might at any time be converted into a larger domain. The problem was further

Greece under the Protection of the Powers.

The rise of Bulgaria.

---

[1] The fact that Greeks leaving their native lands for France or England still talk of going to *Europe* is an excellent illustration of their feeling of isolation from the civilized world, caused by the barrier which formerly existed across their northern frontier.

complicated by the rise of the other Balkan nationalities and, in particular, Bulgaria, with their own ideals and plans for national expansion and their own intrigues to enlist the sympathy and help of the Great Powers. A brief summary of the principal events which affected Greece during this period will best illustrate the difficulties which the country had to face.

There is probably no district which is so essentially Greek as the island of Crete. Its occupation by the Venetians from the *The Cretan question.* Fourth Crusade down to 1669 may have resulted in a slight infusion of Western European blood, but its isolated position saved it from any Slav or Albanian admixture. The Turks made no attempt to found settlements in the island and were never more than an official class and an army of occupation. Even the Cretan Moslems are Greeks by race and have retained the Greek language, in spite of their conversion to the religion of Islam. That such an island should feel the strongest possible sympathy with the Free *Risings of 1841 and 1858.* Hellas and a desire for union with her was only natural, and we have seen how in 1841 Crete rose in insurrection. Another rising had taken place in 1858, which ended without much bloodshed in the recall of the Turkish Governor and the promise—the Porte was ever lavish of promises—of some degree of local self-government.

The appeal to the Powers, 1866. In 1866 a petition was presented by the Christians of Crete complaining of financial oppression and generally of the maladministration of the island. This was followed later by an appeal to the Sovereigns of the Protective Powers for union with Greece or, failing that, some measure of political reform. The British Government, which had received reports from its consular authorities in the Ionian Islands representing the inhabitants as having suffered as the result of the cession of these islands to Greece, refused to support the union of Crete with Greece. At the same time the Porte was not indisposed to encourage an armed rising which *The Cretan Assembly at Sphakia.* might serve as an excuse for handing back the control of Crete to Egypt, to which it had been subject as recently as 1840. Egyptian troops were sent to the island, and various concessions were promised if the Cretans would consent to

3

union with Egypt. So far were they from accepting that a Cretan Assembly held at Sphakia proclaimed the independence of Crete and its union with Greece. There was strong Greek sympathy for the cause of their suffering brethren, but the King and his Prime Minister, Boulgaris, realized that Greece was from a military standpoint quite incapable of going to war with Turkey, and they could only assume an attitude of benevolent neutrality. Volunteers, however, flocked from Greece, and the island was divided into three military districts; but the tide of success

The defence of Arkadion.
soon turned against the insurgents. The heroic defence of the monastery of Arkadion, near Retimo, where at the moment of its capture the Abbot fired the powder-magazine and involved both the defenders, who preferred death to defeat, and their assailants in a common destruction, inspired Europe with a sympathy for the Cretan cause and modified the attitude of the Governments of the Protecting Powers. France even proposed to allow the Cretans to decide their own destiny by a plebiscite, and Russia supported her; but Great Britain refused to consent. Meanwhile the insurgents still held out, and their enemies, though they were able to spread fire and the sword through many parts of the island, had themselves suffered such heavy losses that the Sultan became anxious for a settlement and sent his

The 'Organic Statute of 1868'.
Grand Vizier to reorganize the administration of Crete. His proposals were embodied in the 'Organic Statute of 1868', which nominally gave the Christians a larger share in the government and temporarily lightened the load of taxation. The resistance of the Cretans still continued, and the assistance sent to them from Greece almost precipitated a war between Greece and Turkey, for which many Greeks were anxious and which was only averted by a change of government. Finally a conference of the signatories of the Treaty of Paris met to consider the Greco-Turkish question. The Greek Foreign Minister submitted a statement of the wrongs of the Greek nation and demanded a settlement of the Cretan question and a rectification of the boundaries of Greece. The only result was that the Porte agreed to suspend the measures which it had inaugurated against its Greek subjects, while the Greek Government undertook to forbid Greek subjects to take up arms in favour of their 'en-

slaved' brothers. The Cretan insurgents, seeing that they could no longer count upon Greek support, gave up the struggle and the solution of the Cretan question was again postponed.

It was not long before another event occurred which, though not directly concerned with the Greek kingdom, had a grave effect upon Greek national interests. Ever since *The Creation of* the Turkish conquest, the Patriarch of Con- *the Bulgarian* stantinople had been the head and representative *Exarchate.* of all the Christian subjects of the Porte. But the growing sentiment of nationality amongst the Bulgarians, largely fostered by Russian propaganda, chafed against a system which subjected them ecclesiastically to a Greek authority. The Turks, who had hitherto placed all the Christians in their Empire in a single category under the comprehensive title of Rûm, welcomed any quarrels, ecclesiastic or otherwise, which might create divisions among them ; as long as the Christians were busy with their own dissensions, they were hardly likely to combine against their common oppressor. When the Patriarch refused to listen to any demand of the Bulgarians for a separate ecclesiastical organization, the Sultan was appealed to and on 28th February 1870 issued a *firman* constituting the Bulgarian Exarchate, which, like the Patriarchate, was to have its head-quarters at Constantinople. The sphere over which the Exarch was to hold ecclesiastical sway was not limited to the Vilayet of the Danube, which afterwards became the Principality of Bulgaria, but extended also over the Vilayets of Adrianople, Salonica, Monastir, and Kossovo.

The result of the establishment of the Exarchate was to set up a rival ecclesiastical system in regions whose religious affairs had been for centuries administered by the *The perversion of* Patriarchate, and to place in the hands of the *the Exarchate to* Bulgarians an instrument which they were not *political ends.* slow to pervert to political purposes. For a period of forty years nothing so much tended to perpetuate Turkish misrule in Macedonia and render reform impossible as the dissensions between the Patriarchal Church and the Exarchate and political propaganda under the disguise of religious enthusiasm.

Not many years elapsed before a train of events was started

in the Balkan Peninsula which ended by again indirectly involving

The Russo-Turkish War of 1877.

Greece. The Slavonic provinces of the Ottoman Empire had hitherto shown themselves less eager than Greece to assert their rights, but in 1875 a rising occurred in Herzegovina and another in Bulgaria which eventually led to the Russo-Turkish War of 1877. The Greeks had at first remained passive spectators,

Excitement in Greece.

but, as events proceeded, the growing sympathy shown for the cause of Bulgarian independence could no longer leave them unmoved. In 1876 meetings were held throughout Greece urging the Government to take measures to press for the rights of Hellenism in view of the possibility that the Powers would enforce a Balkan settlement. In June 1877 a party truce was declared at Athens and the ablest politicians of all parties combined to form a Coalition Government under the presidency of the aged Admiral Kanaris, one of the heroes of the War of Independence. The Foreign

M. Trikoupis restrains the Greeks.

Minister, Charilaos Trikoupis, afterwards a distinguished Premier, approached the British Government and expressed the willingness of the Cabinet to use all its influence to prevent the rising of Greek subjects of the Ottoman Empire, provided that, when the time came for a Balkan settlement, the claims of Greece should be taken into serious account. Though no promise of territorial expansion was accorded, an undertaking was given that the claims of Greece should be given the same consideration as those of the other Christian nationalities. The Greek Government, therefore, refused to accept a Russian invitation to join in the struggle and share the spoils. However, the victorious advance of the Russians inevitably caused a popular movement throughout Greece in favour of war and brought about the resignation of the Coalition Government. The new Govern-

Risings in Thessaly, Epirus, and Crete.

ment, in which M. Koumoundouros was Prime Minister, not only encouraged risings in Thessaly, Epirus, and Crete but announced the dispatch of Greek troops to the Greek provinces of Turkey. Meanwhile the victorious Russians were at the gates of Constantinople (February 1878) and an armistice was proclaimed. The Greek troops who had been sent to occupy Thessaly were, therefore, recalled, but the movement in that province was already far advanced and was only checked by British intervention and the promise that Greek interests should be supported. Hostilities in Crete were similarly brought to a close by British mediation.

On 3rd March 1878 a Treaty between Russia and Turkey was concluded at San Stefano, just outside Constantinople. This

The Treaty of San Stefano.

Treaty, which was subsequently supserseded by the Treaty of Berlin, absolutely ignored the claims of Greece. Its most important feature is that it sought to establish a 'Greater Bulgaria', comprising not only Bulgaria proper and Eastern Rumelia but the whole of

The claims of Greece ignored.

Macedonia, with the exception of Salonica and Chalcidice, as far as the Lakes of Ochrida and Prespa, thus extending from the Danube and Black Sea to the Albanian Mountains. Ethnologically and geographically it was an impossible settlement. For Greece its most serious effect would have been to extinguish for ever the just claims of the Macedonian Greeks. Amongst other absurdities it would have left Salonica in Turkish hands but without the adjoining territory, and made Albania, Thessaly, and Epirus detached fragments of territory under Turkish rule. The Treaty of San Stefano was an attempt at an essentially Slav [1] settlement such as could not be tolerated by any impartial judge ; unfortunately its impossible provisions have ever since remained the Bulgarian national ideal and have encouraged the Bulgars to aspire to a position in the Balkans to which neither ethnological nor any other considerations entitle them.

It soon became apparent that the Treaty of San Stefano was an arrangement which Europe could not ratify, and the British

The Powers refuse to ratify the Treaty of San Stefano.

Government insisted on reopening the whole question of the Balkans and exacted from Russia an agreement to modify the pretensions of Bulgaria. This demand was dictated no doubt chiefly by the desire to prevent Russia from making Bulgaria a protectorate, and it was supported by Austria, which could not remain a disinterested spectator while an arrangement was being made to block her path to Salonica.

[1] The Bulgars are, of course, not Slav by blood but an Asiatic people akin to the Huns, Avars, and Finns ; their language, however, being Slavonic, they were naturally included in the Pan-Slav programme of Russia.

At this juncture Bismarck exhibited himself in the new rôle of a peaceful mediator and proposed that the Powers should

The Congress of Berlin.

meet in conference on the neutral ground of Germany and discuss the Treaty of San Stefano. After some delay on the part of Russia, the Congress of Berlin met on 13th June 1878, under the Presidency of Bismarck himself, and set itself to settle the affairs of the Balkan Peninsula practically without consulting the peoples whose destiny it took upon itself to decide.

The details of this Conference and its conclusions are so familiar that it will only be necessary here to note those provisions which directly or indirectly concerned Greece. Lord Salisbury, in fulfilment of the desire of the British Government that Greece should not suffer for her observance of neutrality during the Russo-Turkish War, pleaded for the admission of the Greek delegates and pointed out that, while Bulgaria enjoyed the championship of Russia, Greece had no one to support her claims. He was only able, however, to procure that the Greek representatives should be allowed to state their case without taking any part in the deliberations of the Congress.

The Congress of Berlin, while recognizing the complete independence of Serbia, Rumania, and Montenegro, reduced

The claims of Greece ignored.

the Great Bulgaria of the Treaty of San Stefano to a small self-governing Principality tributary to the Sultan between the Danube and the Balkan Mountains and created to the south of it, between the Balkan and Rhodope Mountains, another state under the title of Eastern Rumelia under the direct authority of the Sultan but enjoying ' administrative autonomy '. As regards Greece, the Sultan and the King of the Hellenes were to come to an understanding for the modification of the frontier of Greece, and, if they failed to reach an agreement, the Powers undertook to mediate between Greece and the Porte. But for the moment nothing was done regarding the extension of the northern frontier of Greece, while Crete was definitely left under Turkish dominion, the Porte again undertaking to put into force the Organic Statute of 1868. Thrace, Macedonia, Epirus, and Albania, which remained under Turkish rule, were promised a new form of administration, the details of which were to be decided by special commissions. The Porte, however, took care never to carry out these provisions, and its misrule, especially in Macedonia, was destined to be a constant source of trouble and discredit to the Powers who permitted it to continue.

The only possible source of satisfaction which a Greek could feel in contemplating the results of the Congress—beyond the vague promise of a rectification of the northern frontier of Greece—was the fact that the ' unredeemed ' Greeks of Macedonia still remained under Turkish rule, or rather misrule, from which they might one day be delivered, instead of being handed over to Bulgaria, from whose clutches they would never have been released. Thus the feeling of the Greeks, who had hoped for so much, was one of profound disappointment, while the failure of Great Britain to secure any satisfaction for them tended to lower British prestige in their eyes. Moreover, *The British occupy Cyprus.* the revelation of the agreement between the British Government and the Porte, by which Great Britain was allowed to occupy Cyprus, where the majority of the population was Greek, and in return guaranteed the Asiatic possessions of Turkey against invasion, could not leave Greece unmoved.

The settlement of the Balkans laid down in the Treaty of Berlin nominally remained the Charter of the Peninsula until the formation of the Balkan Confederacy in 1912, but its provisions were on several occasions violated with impunity both by the Signatory Powers and by the Balkan States when it suited their convenience to do so.

It was three years before Greece could obtain a settlement of the question of her northern frontier. The Porte had nothing *The question of the northern frontier of Greece.* to gain by a speedy solution and the discussion dragged on until the accession to power of Gladstone's ministry of 1880, which was hailed by the Greeks as a good omen in view of his championship of the Greek claims to the Ionian Islands. A Conference was held in Berlin in June of that year at which the British and French delegates proposed a solution which would have gone far towards satisfying Greece, since it suggested a frontier extending from the ridge of Olympus on the east to the River Kalamas on the west and would have included Jannina. M. Trikoupis on behalf of Greece eagerly accepted the proposal, which was hailed with general enthusiasm. The Porte, however, refused its consent, whereupon the Greek Army was mobilized. Meanwhile a change of government in France turned the scale against the Greeks, and a consequent difference of opinion between the French and British Governments regarding the Greek frontier question stiffened the opposition of the Porte. In the end the question was decided by a Conference held at Constantinople in 1881, at which Lord Goschen, the British delegate, did his utmost to obtain Preveza and the Olympus frontier for Greece. But Turkey resolutely refused to cede the former, and Greece could not risk hostilities. The frontier was, therefore, eventually drawn from a point a little north of the historic Vale of Tempe to Arta on the Ambracian Gulf.[1] By this arrangement Greece received the rich plain of Thessaly and a small portion of Epirus. It was a settlement of which it may be said that it might have been much less advantageous, and would have been so but for the support accorded to Greece by the British Government.

The Conference of Constantinople, 1881.

The annexation of Thessaly.

Crete, which, as we have seen, was left by the Treaty of Berlin in Turkish hands, was offered by the Porte to Greece in return for the abandonment of her claims to Thessaly, but the Greek Government naturally preferred to increase its territory on the mainland. Crete had, therefore, to be content with another promise of the enforcement of the Organic Statute of 1868. This time the Porte realized the necessity of making some concessions, and these were embodied in the 'Halepa Pact',[2] which established a form of Parliamentary Government and a General Assembly. Moreover, the appointment of Photiades Pasha, a Greek by race though a Turkish subject, and a man of considerable administrative ability, did much to conciliate the Christians of Crete, and his long period of rule was one of comparative calm. In 1889, however, another disturbance occurred, which had its origin in the political strife between the parliamentary parties, one of which, to embarrass its opponents, inopportunely brought forward a proposal for union with Greece. This gave rise to

Crete.

[1] See map on p. 149.
[2] So called from the suburb of Canea where most of the foreign consulates were situated.

collisions between the Christian and Moslem inhabitants, where-upon the Porte reduced the numbers and powers of the Assembly, thus to a large extent annulling the provisions of the ' Halepa Pact '. Thus the Cretan question, which ought to have been settled once and for all by the Berlin Treaty, dragged on and was destined to cause more trouble and bloodshed before its final solution.

CHAPTER IV

THE REIGN OF KING GEORGE I FROM 1881 TO 1908

DURING the fifteen years which followed the annexation of Thessaly Greece was mainly occupied with internal questions.

Greece under the leadership of Trikoupis. The expenses of placing the army on a war-footing in order to support the Greek claims had greatly added to the burden of debt. Fortunately in Charilaos Trikoupis modern Greece possessed for the first time a statesman of real ability, whose long premiership, which began in 1882, did much to restore, at least temporarily, the financial position of Greece. For a period of twelve years he guided the helm of the state except for intervals when his rival, Theodoros Delyiannis, managed to oust him from power. From 1883 until his retirement in 1895 Greek politics were a duel between these two men, the one a genuine statesman, the other a clever parliamentarian. To Trikoupis it is due that the policy of road and railway construction was inaugurated, which has done so much to assist the exploitation of the country ; and the confidence which he inspired attracted foreign capital with which to develop to some extent the mineral resources of Greece. That he was unable to achieve more than he did was due to the fact that his rival was always ready to pander to the ' jingoism ' of his fellow-countrymen and took every opportunity of thwarting the policy of better relations with Turkey, which Trikoupis regarded as necessary if Greece was to consolidate her financial position.

The only external event which affected Greece during these years was the Union of Eastern Rumelia with Bulgaria and

Union of Bulgaria and Eastern Rumelia. the subsequent recognition by the Powers in 1886 of this practical violation of the Treaty of Berlin. It gave rise to intense excitement at Athens, where there was a national feeling that any aggrandisement of Bulgaria should be accompanied by territorial concessions to Greece, so that the balance of power

in the Balkans might not be disturbed. Delyiannis, who was in
Excitement at Athens. office at the time, raised a large loan and proceeded to mobilize the Greek Army. After
several times warning Greece against undertak-
ing hostilities against Turkey, the Powers, with the exception
of France, established a blockade of the Greek coast which
The blockade of Greece. lasted for two months. This led to the fall of
the Delyiannis Cabinet, and the ministry which
succeeded it put an end to the mobilization,
which had only added to the Greek debt without obtaining any
advantage, and Trikoupis shortly afterwards returned to power.

In 1893 disputes with Turkey again gave Delyiannis the
opportunity of mobilizing the Greek Army and incurring further
debt, with the result that Trikoupis was again recalled to office.
This time, however, finding the restoration of Greek credit a
task which was beyond his powers, he retired from politics in
1895 and died in voluntary exile from the country for whose
best interests he had struggled for so many years. It was not
long before the removal of his restraining influence had a
disastrous effect upon Greece.

In 1896 fresh trouble began in Crete, where the appointment
of a Christian governor was a signal for attacks by the Moslems
on the Christian population. The latter formed
Crete. a Committee with definitely political aims, a
proceeding which only served to widen the gulf between the
two religious parties in the island. In the summer of 1896 a
serious affray occurred in Canea which induced the Porte to
promise reforms, including European commissions to reorganize
the gendarmerie and the judicial system ; but, as usual, nothing
was actually done—partly no doubt because the attention of the
Powers was distracted from Crete by the Armenian massacres in
Constantinople. The state of affairs in Crete, therefore, became
worse and worse, sanguinary encounters again taking place early
in 1897.

In Greece, where Delyiannis was again Premier, sympathy
for the cause of the Cretan Christians became more and more
Greek troops land in Crete. intense, until in February Greek troops under
Colonel Vassos landed in the island with the
express purpose of carrying out its annexation
to Greece, whereupon the Powers intervened and occupied

Crete with an international force. But anti-Turkish feeling in Greece, fomented by a newly-formed ' National Society ', was now aroused to such a pitch that nothing would satisfy it except war with Turkey. King George, in view of the evident resolve of his people, publicly associated himself with the national demand. The prospects of success, however, were hopeless from the first. Whereas the Turkish Army had been recently re-organized by a German mission, Greece both from a military and from a financial point of view was unprepared for war, while the presence of the naval forces of the Powers in Greek waters prevented any real use being made of the Greek fleet, which might have achieved some success, such as the occupation of some of the Turkish islands, or at any rate prevented the transportation of Turkish troops from Asia Minor to Salonica. Again, no co-operation could be expected from the other Christian peoples of the Balkan peninsula, who were warned against interference by the Austrian and Russian Governments and conciliated by timely concessions on the part of the Porte. Nevertheless the Greeks flew at the Turks, ' as if the bird of Athena should fly at the eagle '. The ' Great Idea ' has always induced the Greek patriot to throw prudence to the wind on the slightest provocation, and there was no statesman strong enough to oppose the irresistible impulse of popular excitement.

In April Greek irregulars crossed into Macedonia and a few days later Turkey declared war. The four weeks which followed

Turkey declares war on Greece. saw the complete defeat of Greece. Hostilities took place in two theatres of war. In Epirus the Greeks crossed the frontier and engaged the Turks at Pente Pigadia, thus preventing an advance on Arta. On the Thessalian frontier Edhem Pasha, advancing through Elassona, after forcing his way through the Melouna Pass, successfully engaged the Greek forces, who offered a strong resistance, at Reveni. Thus the northern portion of the Thessalian

Defeat of the Greeks. plain fell into Turkish hands and Larissa was occupied after the Crown Prince Constantine's army had fled from it in hopeless disorder. At Velestino, however, Colonel Smolenski, the only Greek com-mander who distinguished himself, repulsed the Turks in a first engagement, but in a second attack the enemy won the day. Other defeats took place on the historic battlefield of Pharsala and at Domoko, which opened the Phourka Pass and the road into Central Greece.

Meanwhile intense excitement reigned in Athens, and King George was never so near losing his throne. The political situation was only saved by the intervention of M. Demetrios Rallis, the leader of the Opposition, who hurled himself into the breach and assumed the Premiership. Greece was only saved from disaster by the Powers, who brought about an armistice on 20th May. The Turks remained in occupation of Thessaly for some months, until a peace was concluded in December, under which Thessaly was restored to Greece, though a slight modification of the frontier gave certain strategic points to Turkey. Greece was also forced to pay an indemnity of £4,000,000, and an International Financial Commission was established at Athens which took over the Government monopolies and the harbour-dues of the Piræus and guaranteed the payment of the war indemnity and of the interest on the National Debt of the country. Thus, though the rash enthusiasm of the nation had brought it into a humiliating position, materially Greece lost little. The result for the future King Constantine was, however, serious, since he was, perhaps not without some justice, made a scapegoat for the disgraceful flight from Larissa, and he lived for many years under a cloud of unpopularity which was never entirely dispelled until the Balkan War of 1912. The position of the future Queen Sophia was also rendered far from pleasant by the fact that officers of the army of her brother, William II of Germany, had trained the victorious Turkish Army and had actually taken part in the operations against Greece.

The Powers rescue Greece.

The disgrace of the Crown Prince.

Meanwhile Crete, which had been the original centre of trouble, remained in the occupation of the six Powers, until in 1898 Germany and Austria withdrew as not being vitally interested in the Cretan question. The island was divided into districts controlled by British, French, Russian, and Italian troops, Candia being assigned to the British and garrisoned by a battalion of infantry. In September 1898, however, after a rising against the British had occurred at Candia, in the course of which the British vice-consul was murdered, it became obvious that a

Crete under the control of the Powers.

radical settlement of the Cretan question could no longer be
delayed. In November, therefore, the last Turkish soldiers

*Prince George of
Greece as High
Commissioner
in Crete.*
were dispatched from the island and a National
Government formed with Prince George of
Greece as High Commissioner, though the
suzerainty of the Sultan was expressly recognized.
A Constitution was drawn up and the Cretan
Assembly met for the first time in 1899. Crete had thus at last
achieved autonomy, of which the outward and visible signs
were a Cretan flag and a coinage and postage-stamps of her
own. The only thing lacking was union with the Mother
Country.

The history of Crete during the nineteenth century provides
an excellent example of Turkish methods of misgovernment.
The policy of dividing the island into two hostile camps constantly
making attacks on one another, and the continual refusal to do
more than issue, under external pressure, *firmans* and statutes,
which, though they would have done much to redress the
existing grievances, were never carried out, perpetuated an
intolerable state of affairs and could not fail to excite the indignant
sympathy of Greece. It was a policy from which Turkey had
nothing to gain and which made it certain that Crete must
finally be severed from the Ottoman Empire.

The Governorship of Prince George, which was originally
an appointment for three years, eventually lasted for eight

*Venizelos as a
Cretan statesman.*
years. The chief interest of these years is that
they first brought into prominence a statesman
who was destined not only to mould the future
policy of Greece but also to become one of the most striking
figures in the political world of Modern Europe—Eleutherios
Venizelos. He was born in 1864 in Crete, but was the descendant
of a Greek family of the mainland ;[1] his grandfather had fled
to Crete from Athens before the War of Independence in order
to escape from Turkish tyranny. He was educated at Syra and
afterwards at the University of Athens, whence he returned to
his native island and soon made his name at the Cretan bar.

---

[1] It is necessary to insist on this point in view of a rumour, which obtained
a wide circulation, that Venizelos was not a Greek at all but of Jewish descent,
his name being a corruption of Ben-Israel—a derivation which will hardly
stand the test of philology.

He took an active part in the revolt against Turkey in 1896, and, when Crete became autonomous, quickly made his mark in the Cretan Assembly, becoming Minister for Foreign Affairs and Justice. When Prince George showed an inclination to take too much power into his own hands, he met with a resolute resistance from Venizelos, who placed himself at the head of a party of opposition, which eventually seceded to Therissos, where it set up a Provisional Government and proclaimed the union of Crete with Greece. Thus for the first time Venizelos was driven to become a rebel against absolutism—a step which he was destined to repeat in far graver circumstances. The insurgents maintained themselves until the winter of 1905–6 *The Resignation* and carried on a guerilla warfare, until the *of Prince George.* Powers intervened and Prince George was obliged to resign. He was succeeded in 1906 by M. Alexander Zaïmis, a conservative politician who had gained credit as Premier at the time of the conclusion of peace after the Greco-Turkish War. Under Zaïmis' régime Venizelos became the leading statesman of Crete and the idol of his fellow-countrymen in spite of his opposition to any premature agitation for union with Greece. His career as a statesman in Crete was an admirable preparation for the larger political sphere in which he was destined to play a leading part.

The years which immediately followed the conclusion of peace after the Greco-Turkish War present no striking incidents *Greece under the* as far as the internal history of Greece is con-*premiership of* cerned. The chief political leader of this period *M. Theotokis.* was M. Georgios Theotokis, who had formerly served under Trikoupis. It was a period of internal development and in particular of the growth of the larger towns—Athens, the Piræus, Patras, and Volo, which rapidly became an important outlet for the agricultural produce of the rich Thessalian plain.

An external problem, however, in which Greece was vitally interested was rapidly reaching an acute stage—the Macedonian *The Macedonian* question. The growing sentiment of nationality *question becomes* in the Balkan States had naturally induced the *acute.* various nations to look for new spheres of influence which might eventually be added to their domains, and Macedonia offered a suitable field for their operations. The Hellenes remembered that Macedonia had long formed part of the Byzantine Empire, while the Serbs and Bulgarians recalled the shorter periods when a Serbian or a Bulgarian Emperor had ruled there. Ever since the Turkish conquest, however, the Sultan had misruled a medley of races— Greek, Turkish, Serbian, Bulgarian, Vlach, Jewish, and Albanian —some of them inextricably commingled.

For the first four centuries of the Turkish domination the chief bond of union between the Christian nations of Macedonia had been the fact that all came under the ecclesi-astical jurisdiction of the Greek Patriarchate, and that such culture as existed was Hellenic. But the establishment of free nationalities in the Balkans and the apparently impending dissolution of the Ottoman Empire in Europe gave rise everywhere to a growing desire to ' redeem ' the still enslaved Christians, and the first step of each nation was to stake out its claims in Macedonia. It was a proceeding upon which Turkey looked with a not unfavouring eye, since, as long as the various nationalities quarrelled among themselves, they were unlikely to combine against the common enemy. The most striking example of the playing off by the Porte of one nation against another was the concession already mentioned of the Bulgarian Exarchate as a rival to the Greek Patriarchate.

Racial rivalry in Macedonia.

To the Greek, who is apt to fix his attention on the events of bygone history rather than on the hard facts of the present, it was obvious that Macedonia was a Greek land. The abortive Treaty of San Stefano, however, had envisaged a ' Greater Bulgaria,' which became the ideal of the Bulgarian Imperialists, who drew fresh encourage-ment from the ease with which Eastern Rumelia had been annexed. The Bulgars, therefore, claimed the whole of Macedonia, including all the Ægean coast (except Chalcidice, which was too obviously Greek), and extending as far as Lake Ochrida on the west and Monastir on the north. Greece naturally claimed Southern Macedonia, while Serbia demanded ' Old Serbia,' which included parts of Northern and Central Macedonia. Thus the claims of Greece and Serbia did not clash, while Bul-garia, which aimed at a Balkan hegemony and sought to drive

Greece.

Bulgaria.

Serbia.

a wedge between Greece and Serbia, came into conflict with
Rumania. both these nations. Then Rumania, not to be
outdone, discovered that the nomadic Koutzo-
Vlach shepherds were their long-lost brothers and became their
champion ; and the Porte welcomed, as a new element of
discord, a theory which was never likely to lead to a demand
for annexations from a state which was not co-terminous with
Macedonia. In the process of time, under Turkish rule, the
Slav-speaking population of Macedonia had become ' Macedonian ' rather than definitely Bulgarian or Serbian and was
therefore regarded as a legitimate prey by Bulgaria, whose
propaganda was first in the field. There were thus two main
pairs of rivals in Macedonia, the Bulgarians and Serbs striving
to win to their side the Slav-speaking population, and the
Greek Patriarchists and the Bulgarian Exarchists struggling to
maintain the numerical superiority of the two churches and, as
a result, of their respective nationalities. At first the struggle
was waged mainly on ecclesiastical and scholastic lines, and
the Bulgarian educational propaganda, which had obtained a
start over its rivals, managed by questionable methods to attract
much of the youth of Macedonia to its schools ; but the Bulgars
showed that the policy might in the future become less pacific
by the brutal manner in which they treated the Greek minority
Bulgarian in Eastern Rumelia after its annexation in
propaganda. 1886. The success of the Bulgarian propaganda
is shown by the fact that numerous pupils of
the Bulgarian schools in Macedonia were induced to migrate to
Bulgaria, where many of them attained to important positions
The Bulgarian and set themselves to agitate in favour of their
Committee. Macedonian brothers. In 1890 they formed a
Macedonian Committee at Sofia, of which the
watchword was ' Macedonia for the Macedonians ' and which
addressed a petition to the Powers asking for the establishment
of an autonomous Macedonia under a Governor at Salonica who
should belong to the ' predominant nationality ', that is, of course,
Bulgaria. When this petition produced no result, armed bands
were sent across the frontier into Turkey, one of which burnt
the Moslem village of Dospat. Though it failed to produce the
effect for which they had hoped, the action of the Macedonian
Committee showed that in the future force would be resorted

4

to rather than guile for the Bulgarization of Macedonia. Meanwhile in the ecclesiastical sphere the Porte pursued its usual policy of granting concessions which would serve to intensify racial hostility. In 1890 the Sultan allowed Bulgarian bishoprics to be founded at Ochrida and Uskub, and a few years later at Veles and Dibra. In 1896 a similar concession was made to Serbia by the permission to establish a Serbian bishopric also at Uskub.

The defeat of Greece by Turkey in 1897 and the consequent unwillingness of the Porte to pay any further attention to the *Bulgarian* grievances of its Greek subjects emboldened the *comitadjis.* Bulgarians to resort to more drastic measures for converting the Macedonian Greeks to the Bulgarian cause. Bands of *comitadjis* were formed at Sofia and sent over the border to institute a reign of terror, and from 1897 to 1904 they had matters their own way, massacring prominent Greeks, priests, and schoolmasters and burning the villages and crops of all who refused to accept Bulgarian nationality. In 1903 Austro-Hungary and Russia found themselves obliged, as the Powers most interested, to demand the application of a scheme of reform, under which Hilmi Pasha was appointed Inspector-General of Macedonia ; but the uselessness of this measure was illustrated by the increased disturbances which in the summer of that year led to the most considerable rising that had yet taken place in Macedonia. By 1904 the position of the Greeks in Macedonia had become so serious, and so little attempt had been made to impress upon the Sultan the necessity *Greek* for taking drastic measures to restore order, *comitadjis.* that a number of Greek officers and other patriots realized that the only way of saving their brothers in Macedonia was to equip armed bands to deal with the Bulgarian *comitadjis.* This naturally served to increase the confusion of the unhappy province, Greeks fighting against Bulgarians and both against the Turkish irregulars, who, being unpaid and ill-fed, indiscriminately plundered all the Christian nationalities ; but at least the action of the Greek bands arrested to some extent the progress of Bulgarian propaganda and encouraged the Macedonian Greeks not to despair altogether of the national cause. It was during these struggles that a Greek officer, Paul Melas, was killed under circumstances which raised him to the rank of a Greek national hero.

As a result of a meeting between the Tzar of Russia and the Emperor of Austria the so-called ' Mürzsteg Programme ' was

The ' Mürzsteg Programme '.
issued in September 1903, which included a proposal for the establishment of an international gendarmerie in Macedonia ; but it was some time before the financial details were settled, and the scheme was not ratified until 1907. Foreign officers, however, began to arrive in 1904, the Drama district being assigned to the British, Serres to the French, Monastir to the Italians, Salonica to the Russians, and Uskub to the Austrians. But their efforts did little to arrest the interracial struggle, which called for much more radical remedies. In 1905 the British Government, in view of the unwillingness of the Sultan to carry out reforms, persuaded the other Powers to join Great Britain in a blockade of Mitylene and forced the Porte to agree to the recognition of the financial experts who had been sent to Salonica by the Powers.

It is interesting to note that, while the other Powers were striving to find a settlement of the Macedonian question, Germany

Germany culti-vates Turkish friendship.
refused to co-operate and set herself to cultivate Turkish friendship. In 1898, at a time when the other rulers of Europe looked askance at Abdul Hamid as the author of the Armenian massacres, William II and his consort visited him at Constantinople on their theatrical journey to the Holy Land, and Germany as a reward obtained the further concessions for the proposed Bagdad railway. In return Germany deliberately flattered and supported the Sultan, and, by refusing to send officers for the international gendarmerie and to join the other Powers in the blockade of Mitylene, encouraged Turkey to regard Germany as its only friend and to employ every device to avoid carrying out the demands of the other Powers. Thus German influence contributed to the continuance of the reign of terror and bloodshed in Macedonia.

But a new movement was destined soon to arise in Macedonia, due to causes other than the grievances and disputes of the Macedonian Christians, and was to lead eventually to a solution of the Macedonian question very different from the policy of internal reform contemplated by the Powers.

CHAPTER V

THE YOUNG TURK REVOLUTION AND THE
BALKAN LEAGUE (1908–12)

THE Young Turk Revolution of 1908 affected the Greeks both by its results in Macedonia and by its indirect influence upon the

The Young Turk Movement. internal politics of Greece. Its details belong to the history of the Ottoman Empire rather than to that of the Hellenic kingdom. It was the result of an underground movement which had long been smouldering and finally burst into flame at Salonica. Of its organizers some were exiles who had been expelled from Turkey for their opposition to the Hamidian régime, but the prime movers were unscrupulous adventurers, many of them not of Ottoman blood,[1] who were inspired as much by personal ambition as by motives of patriotism. They obtained ready aid, especially in finance, from the Jews and Judæo-Moslem Dunmehs [2] of Salonica, where the masonic lodges were hotbeds of propaganda ; and it was not long before the loyalty of the army was undermined. On 24th July Enver Bey and his fellow-members of the 'Committee of Union and Progress' proclaimed the constitution in Macedonia and the two Mace-

Abdul Hamid restores the Constitution. donian Army Corps threatened to march on Constantinople. Abdul Hamid could only bow before the storm and issue an Irade restoring the constitution, which had been in abeyance since 1878, and summoning an elected chamber of 280 members. The new movement was welcomed with enthusiasm not only in Macedonia, where all the conflicting nationalities indulged

[1] Enver was son of a renegade Pole, Talaat a Bulgarian gipsy, and Djavid a Dunmeh.

[2] This curious sect, which includes some of the most prosperous merchants of Salonica, consists of Islamized Jews. Their doctrines are somewhat obscure, but, while outwardly practising Mohammedanism, they retain certain Jewish ceremonies.

in an orgy of reconciliation, but also in Western Europe,

The Revolution welcomed in Macedonia. where the granting of an elected chamber was regarded as the panacea of all political troubles, and the Macedonian question seemed automatically to have found its solution. The foreign governments, however, took the opportunity of the momentary disorganization of the Ottoman Empire to further their own ends—Austro-Hungary formally annexing Bosnia and Herzogovina, and Ferdinand of Bulgaria proclaiming himself ' Tsar of the Bulgarians ', a title which was in itself a challenge to the rival peoples of the Balkans as recalling the old Bulgarian Empire which had temporarily enjoyed a rule far wider than the modern State.

Elections were immediately held, with the result that, in spite of attempts at coercion on a large scale, eighteen Greek

The Turkish elections. deputies were elected, while four seats were won by Bulgarian subjects of the Sultan. The new Chamber was opened by Abdul Hamid, who solemnly declared his intention of ruling henceforward as a constitutional monarch. But his long reign was almost at

The counter-revolution and the deposition of Abdul Hamid. an end ; on 12th April 1909 a counter-revolution broke out in Constantinople, no doubt under the auspices of the Sultan, and when the news of it reached Salonica, the Committee of Union and Progress decided that the Macedonian Army Corps should march upon the capital to uphold the Constitution. On their arrival fighting took place in Constantinople and Abdul Hamid was deposed and relegated to a villa outside Salonica, where he remained until the Balkan War. His successor, Mohammed V, who had passed his life in enforced seclusion and had no knowledge of affairs, was an easy tool in the hands of the Committee. In the disturbed condition of the Ottoman Empire the army, the only organized body in the state, naturally tended to become more and more powerful, and the fact that its organization had long been in the hands of the Germans, who accepted the new régime without any protest against its anti-Christian bias, opened the door for the German penetration of the whole Ottoman Empire.

In Macedonia the effect of the Revolution was for a time to arrest the interracial strife, and the *comitadji* warfare came to an end ; at the same time it forestalled, as no doubt it was intended to do, any coercive measures which might be contemplated by the Powers. But it became obvious before long that the new constitution was a mere pretence as far as the Christian subjects of the Porte were concerned, since the Young Turks soon showed themselves even more intent than Abdul Hamid himself upon maintaining the supremacy of the Moslem element and carrying out with still greater thoroughness the policy of 'Ottomanizing' the Christian population. Amongst other measures which were directly opposed to the interests of the Christians were the attempt to introduce universal taxation throughout the Empire, thus annulling privileges which had been enjoyed for centuries—for example, by the Albanians—and the imposition of military service upon the Christians and Jews. In the European provinces the closing of Christian schools and other measures for suppressing the non-Moslem element led to a reconciliation between the Greeks and Bulgarians of Macedonia and Thrace with the object of combining against the Young Turks in the election of 1911. An arrangement was made whereby eight of the eleven seats allotted to the Christians of Macedonia were to be occupied by Greeks and four only by Bulgarians, while in Thrace three seats were allotted to Greeks and one only to Bulgarians. This agreement, which received the blessing of the Œcumenical Patriarchate and the Bulgarian Exarchate, is interesting as an official admission by the Bulgarians that the Greeks enjoyed a numerical superiority over the Bulgarians of Macedonia in a ratio of 8 to 3 and in Thrace in a ratio of 3 to 1. It is also of importance as pointing to the possibility of a more general *rapprochement* between the two nations, which was afterwards to be realized in the Balkan League.

The effect of the Revolution in Macedonia.

The Young Turk policy of 'Ottomanization'.

The Greeks and Bulgarians combine for the election of 1911.

We may now turn to the effect of the Young Turkish Revolution upon the kingdom of Greece. It was only natural that the Greeks of the autonomous state of Crete should regard the beginning of a new régime in Turkey and the difficulties which had arisen between the Porte and Austro-Hungary and Bulgaria as a favourable moment for throwing off once and for all the trammels of Ottoman suzerainty.

The effect of the Young Turkish Revolution on Greece.

M. Zaïmis, the High Commissioner of Crete, happened at the time to be absent from the island, where a meeting of the Chamber
Crete proclaims its independence. was held and a proclamation issued declaring the union of Crete with Greece. A committee of five members, one of whom was M. Venizelos, was formed to carry on the government in the name of King George. The Athens Cabinet, in which M. Theotokis was then
The dilemma of M. Theotokis. Premier, was thus placed in an awkward dilemma. If it satisfied the aspirations of the Cretans, it might offend the Protecting Powers as well as incur the hostility of Turkey ; whereas if it failed to do so, national feeling not only in Crete but also in Greece would be outraged, and a golden opportunity might be lost for ever. It is not improbable that, if the Greek Government had taken the bolder course of admitting Crete to the Greek kingdom before the fall of Abdul Hamid, all might have been well. The
The Greek Government's ' correct ' attitude. Premier, however, preferred the more correct attitude of declaring that the Greek Government could take no official cognizance of the action of the Provisional Government in Crete, and matters remained for many months in a condition of deadlock. When the military party had finally asserted itself in Turkey and had inaugurated its nationalistic policy, it was tempted to cover the mistakes of its domestic administration by diverting public attention to foreign politics. The question outstanding with Austro-Hungary and Bulgaria had been settled to Turkey's disadvantage, but the Cretan question was still undecided. Extravagant demands were therefore formulated, which even included a modification of the conditions of autonomy granted to Crete in 1898. The result was still further to exasperate public opinion in Greece, and M. Theotokis felt obliged to resign on 17th July 1909. He was succeeded by M. Demetrios Rallis, who, however, found it necessary to postpone a dissolution, since a new election would place him in the difficulty of having to choose between excluding the deputies who would certainly be elected in Crete and so alienating public sympathy, or risking hostilities with Turkey if he decided to admit Cretan representatives to the Chamber. Towards the end of July the Powers finally withdrew their troops from Crete, whereupon the Cretans hoisted the Greek flag at Canea. An exchange of

notes ensued, in which Turkey lodged a protest, while the Greek Premier disavowed any intention of departing from a correct attitude. The offending flag was eventually removed by a party of marines landed by the Powers, and all danger of hostilities was finally dissipated by a declaration of the Powers to the Porte that the Macedonian and Cretan questions were not merely difficulties to be adjusted between the Ottoman and Greek Governments but matters of European concern.

Meanwhile the growing conviction of the Greek public that the cause of Greek nationalism was being betrayed gave *The 'Military* rise to increasing irritation against the leaders of *League' at Athens.* the political parties. In May 1909 some of the younger military officers formed a 'Military League', which has been described as a second-hand imitation of the Committee of Union and Progress and which soon became the rallying point of opposition to the politicians. On two points it may be urged that the Leaguers had some show of justice on their side in demanding reforms ; firstly, the organization of the Greek Army had made practically no progress since its disastrous exhibition in the Greco-Turkish War, and, secondly, the constant changes of government with the attendant evils of the 'spoils system' had long prevented any real consistency of national policy. In August the League formulated its demands, and, on the refusal of the Premier to accede to them, the members of the League, numbering over 500 officers, left Athens under the leadership of Colonel Zorbas and established a camp near the city. Thereupon M. Rallis resigned and was succeeded by M. Kyriakoulos Mavromichalis. The new Premier adopted an attitude favourable to the Leaguers, who broke up their camp and, returning to Athens, made demands which included the reorganization of the army and navy and the exclusion of the Royal Princes from all military and naval commands. Meeting with a strong element of opposition in the Chamber, the Leaguers threatened to occupy the building with troops ; but the execution of this threat was forestalled by the *The Greek* King, who consented to the removal of the *Princes removed* Crown Prince from his post of Commander-*from the services.* in-Chief and his other sons from their positions in the army and navy. Meanwhile the junior officers of the navy demanded the removal of a number of their

superior officers and, when they failed to obtain satisfaction,
The League organized a mutiny. Finally, the League went
coerces the so far as to coerce the Chamber into passing
Chamber. a number of measures under threats of force
and to demand the dismissal of members of
the Cabinet. The condition which affairs had now reached in
Greece involved the negation of all free government, and a
state of chaos had resulted which almost amounted to revolution,
while the dynasty seemed to be tottering to its fall.

Fortunately a solution of the crisis was possible to which all
parties agreed, namely, the summoning of M. Venizelos from
Venizelos Crete, where he had proved himself to be
summoned from possessed of high qualities of statesmanship.
Crete. The policy of the League had been purely
destructive ; what was now required was
constructive statesmanship, and M. Venizelos was indicated as
the man for the task. Seldom have the man and the opportunity
been so well fitted to one another. From his first arrival he
inspired general confidence ; for none could fail to recognize in
him the ideal patriot who cared for nothing but his country's
good. The support accorded by King George I to the man
who had contributed more than any one else to the deposition
of his son Prince George from the position of High Commissioner in Crete, is one of the many services which that king
rendered to the land of his adoption. M. Venizelos immediately
Venizelos insists insisted on the necessity of summoning a
on a National National Assembly to revise the Constitution.
Assembly. The League was dissolved, and the Assembly
held its first sitting on 14th September 1910,
but the discussions which arose as to whether its functions could
legally be regarded as revisionary proved too much for the
veteran Premier, M. Stephanos Dragoumis, who resigned ;
whereupon the King sent for M. Venizelos, who insisted that
the only *raison d'être* of the Assembly was to revise the Constitution. Failing, however, to obtain a vote of confidence he
Venizelos obtains resigned, and the King promptly dissolved the
an overwhelming Assembly. The new elections gave M. Venizelos
majority. such a majority that he could feel that the whole
country was behind him in his efforts to evolve
harmony out of chaos.

The Second Revisionary Assembly sat from January to June 1911, when it issued the Revised Constitution which *The Revisionary Assembly.* included a number of reforms which lapse of time and new conditions had rendered necessary since the original constitution was drawn up. The Crown Council was revived ; the quorum in the Chamber reduced to one third ; officers on the active list were declared ineligible to sit as deputies ; and the civil servants obtained a guarantee of security of tenure. Primary education was made compulsory and gratuitous. A new post of Inspector-General of the Army was created and bestowed on the Crown Prince, who was thus able to return to Athens.

The completion of the work of the Revisionary Assembly brought back its normal life to the state, and at the election, which followed in March 1912, M. Venizelos *The restoration of Constitutional Government.* obtained a majority of five-sixths of the House. The Cretans again elected deputies to the Greek Chamber, but the Premier refused them leave to sit in the House on the ground that no action must be taken which might embroil Greece with foreign countries before she was in a condition to defend her national honour. It is a proof of the position which M. Venizelos had already attained that his orders were obeyed without question, and the Cretan deputies, many of whom had already reached Athens, abstained from making any attempt to enter the House. Meanwhile a French Military Mission and a British Naval Mission were summoned to Athens to reorganize the combatant services and did their work so well and found such willing co-operation in all ranks that the Greek Army and Navy were soon in a condition to give a good account of themselves.

Any one who, like the present writer, visited Greece in the spring of 1912 after several years' absence could not help being *Greece in 1912.* struck by the change which had come over the Greek people and their capital. All classes in a nation formerly notorious for the inconstancy of its political allegiance were obviously inspired with an enthusiasm for their Prime Minister such as it would be difficult to parallel in the history of any country. Wherever M. Venizelos went, he was the object of universal demonstrations of affection and admira-

tion. A change seemed even to have come over the city of
Athens itself, which in place of its former character of a
second-rate and semi-oriental capital seemed suddenly to have
attained to the dignity of a great European city. In the
provinces there was such security of life and property as
had never before been known. Hellenism, which had survived
centuries of slavery and, since its emancipation, had passed
through nine decades of internal and external difficulties, had
for the first time found a statesman capable of uniting the
nation and appealing to all that was best in the Greek
character and leading Greece along the path to national
greatness.

The fruits of M. Venizelos' statesmanship were soon apparent not only in the purification of the administration, the
Relations of reform of the Army and Navy, and the improved
Greece with the lot of the peasants, but also in a new conception
other Balkan of the relations between Greece and her Balkan
States. neighbours. Turkey's policy of ' *Divide et*
impera ' and the exploitation of national
jealousies in her European territories had made co-operation
impossible among the Christian States in the Balkans. But a
favourable moment for ending for ever the curse of Turkish
misrule had at last arrived ; Turkey was embroiled in a war
with Italy in Libya, her fleet dared not leave the Dardanelles,
Albania was in revolt, and the condition of Ottoman finances
was even worse than usual. If only the Balkan States could
bring themselves to lay aside their mutual antagonism and co-
operate together, each of them might solve the pressing problem
of its national unity.

Between Greece and Serbia, whose territories were nowhere
in geographical contact, there were no conflicting claims, and
Greece and indeed no formal agreement was concluded
Serbia. between them until after the close of the First
Balkan War ; but both states had an outstanding feud with Bulgaria. During the summer of 1912,
mainly through the mediation of Russia, Serbia and Bulgaria
Serbia and concluded a secret agreement, whereby the
Bulgaria. ultimate fate of the Uskub district, which was
debatable territory, was to be referred to Russian
arbitration in event of a successful campaign against Turkey.

Between Greece and Bulgaria the conflict of interests was more
acute owing to the inextricable intermingling
of the two nationalities in Macedonia, which
rendered impossible any delimitation of a
frontier between the two countries. M. Venizelos realized that
the only possible course was to agree to postpone the question
of dividing the spoil until victory had been achieved, and with
characteristic skill he succceeded in persuading the Bulgarian
Government to accept his point of view. The Balkan League,
the unrealized dream of so many Balkan patriots, was now an
accomplished fact.

Greece and Bulgaria.

It soon became obvious to observers throughout Europe
that a crisis was at hand in the Near East. Anarchy was again
rife in Macedonia, Albania had practically
thrown off the trammels of Turkish rule, and
serious incidents were occurring on the Turkish
frontiers; at the same time the Ottoman
Government showed no signs of being able to cope with the
situation. In August 1912 a final attempt to preserve peace was
made by Count Berchtold, the Austro-Hungarian Foreign
Minister, who made suggestions for dealing with the Macedonian
question by administrative reforms and decentralization and
advised the Balkan States to adopt an attitude of moderation.
But it was too late; and before the Powers had had time to
ponder over the Austrian proposals, the Greek, Serbian, Bulgarian,
and Turkish Armies were ordered to mobilize (1st October
1912). A few days later the Porte announced its intention of
at last carrying out the Provisions of the Treaty of Berlin by
enforcing the Vilayet Law of 1880; while the Powers issued
notes promising to safeguard the integrity of the Ottoman
Empire and the sovereignty of the Sultan and promising reforms,
but at the same time warning the Balkan States that they would
permit no territorial modification, even if Turkey were defeated.
Thus up to the very last moment the Powers persisted in ' backing the wrong horse ' and adopting an attitude from which the
defeat of Turkey soon obliged them to descend not without
considerable loss of dignity. On 13th October the Balkan
Allies made a demand for reforms in Macedonia and
elsewhere far more radical than Turkey could dream of
granting. The Porte declared war on Serbia and Bulgaria

The Balkan League against Turkey.

on 17th October. The Greek Government had already taken the decisive step of admitting the Cretan deputies to the Chamber, and on the next day, 18th October, declared war on Turkey. The Balkan crisis had come to a head.

CHAPTER VI

THE BALKAN WARS (1912–13)

THOUGH the Turkish Government had been the first to declare war on Serbia and Bulgaria, it was in no condition to justify

The Bulgars advance into Thrace. this step by putting its forces immediately into the field and the initiative rested with the Allies. In Thrace the First Bulgarian Army marched on Mustapha Pasha, which was occupied on 18th October 1912, and thus threatened Adrianople, while the Third Bulgarian Army under General Dimitrief occupied Kirk Kilesse on 14th October. If the Bulgars had not been too exhausted to push on, they might have placed the Turkish forces in Thrace definitely *hors de combat*, but a delay of a few days enabled the latter to rally. The Bulgarian offensive was resumed on the 28th, and a fierce battle raged at Lule Burgas until 1st November, when the Turkish retreat became general ; but again the Bulgars were too exhausted to press home their success,

The Bulgars reach the Tchataldja Lines. and it was 16th November before the two armies were again in touch on the naturally formidable Tchataldja Lines. The Turks meanwhile had taken advantage of the delay to strengthen their positions both with artillery and spade-work and to accumulate stores ; with the result that, when the Bulgarians attacked, they were in a position to resist and by an almost superhuman effort succeeded in holding their own in a four days' battle and beating back the enemy, thus saving for the moment the last remnant of Turkey in Europe and forcing King Ferdinand to invest Adrianople instead of fulfilling his dream of entering Constantinople in triumph.

Meanwhile in North-Western Macedonia the Serbians advanced towards Uskub with the object of forestalling an invasion of Serbia and Bulgaria by the Turkish Army in that region and capturing the capital of the Old Serbian Empire. In the battle of Kumanovo on 23rd to 24th October with

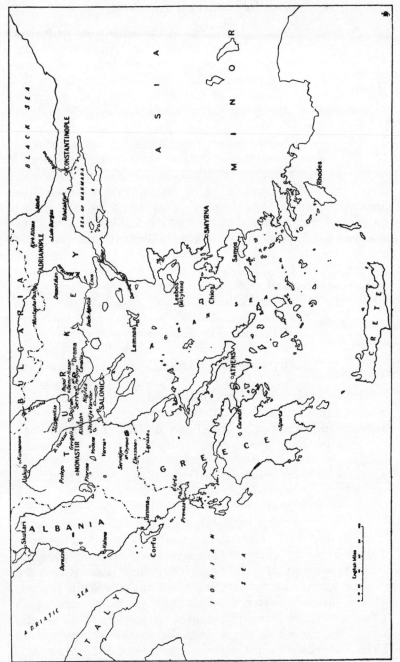

THE BALKAN WARS, 1912–13.

greatly inferior forces they defeated the enemy in what was

The Serbians advance on Uskub. perhaps the most desperate encounter in the whole war, and showed the world what was to be expected from the Serbian infantry. The occupation of Uskub followed, and, while the Second Serbian Army was dispatched to reinforce the Bulgars before Adrianople, the remainder advanced down the Vardar

The capture of Monastir. Valley, where they met with determined opposition at Prilep, but eventually occupied Monastir on 12th November after a battle which lasted for two days and in which the superior strategy of the Serbian Higher Command was ably supported by the supreme qualities of endurance and bravery of the Serbian soldiers. The defeat of the Turkish Army in North-Western Macedonia was thus achieved by Serbia without the promised aid of Bulgaria, and the whole of Old Serbia and most of Albania occupied.

Similar success attended the Greek arms. The Hellenic forces immediately after the declaration of war crossed the frontier, as

The Greek advance into Southern Macedonia. in the Greco-Turkish War, both in Thessaly and in Epirus. The main army under the Crown Prince advanced through the difficult passes of Olympus and occupied Elassona ; then, meeting with resistance at Servidje, they inflicted a defeat upon Hassim Tahsim Pasha and occupied Verria and Vodena, thus cutting the railway communication between Salonica and Monastir. The Turks divided their forces and retreated on these two towns. Another victory at Yenidje Vardar on 1st November opened the road to Salonica, which was in no condition to resist a siege and could only

The Greeks enter Salonica. surrender. On 9th November the Greek Army entered the coveted city in triumph with King George and the Crown Prince at its head, having thus achieved its main objective in little more than three weeks after an unbroken series of successes, which showed how quickly and completely the Greek Army had recovered from the demoralizing effect of the Military League.

The Greeks had reached Salonica only just in time, for within a few hours a Bulgarian Division under General Todorof also arrived on the scene. Ever since the abortive Treaty of San Stefano the Bulgars had regarded the reversion of Macedonia and its capital as theirs by right if ever Turkey in Europe should

The Bulgars also reach Salonica. be partitioned, and the claim of Greece to Salonica in virtue of prior conquest was one which they could not bring themselves to admit. Thus the first seed was sown of a quarrel between hereditary enemies only momentarily reconciled which was to end in the hostilities of the Second Balkan War. For the moment the danger of an open breach was prevented by the dispatch of the greater part of the Bulgar troops from Salonica to Dedeagatch in Greek shipping in order to assist in the siege of Adrianople. A small garrison, however, of about 1500 Bulgarians remained in Salonica.

Meanwhile the small Greek force sent north in pursuit of the Turks after the victory at Servidje had reached Banitsa, between Monastir and Florina, on 1st November. Here it was attacked by a superior Turkish force and driven back to Sorovits, where it entrenched itself and resisted until the temporary crisis was relieved by the Serbian pressure on Monastir. After the completion of the occupation of Salonica a force of four divisions under the command of the Crown Prince set out to the support of this northern Greek force and, after an engagement near Lake Ostrovo, reoccupied Banitsa. Zekki Pasha, however, the Turkish general, succeeded in escaping westward into Epirus, taking with him a force of about one division. Here a small Greek column, after a slow advance through difficult country, had captured Preveza, driving the Turkish Army in retreat to Jannina, which was garrisoned by a force much superior in numbers to the besiegers, especially after the arrival of Zekki's troops.

On 3rd December 1912 Turkey signed an armistice with the Allies except the Greeks, who were engaged in occupying

The Armistice with Turkey. the islands and besieging Jannina. Greek delegates, including M. Venizelos, took part, however, in the Conference which opened in London on 16th December, when the representatives of the Powers met the delegates of the Balkan States and Turkey.

The Conference of London. The Conference ended without any result, largely owing to the attitude of the Bulgarian representatives, who not only refused any compromise with Turkey, but also rejected M. Venizelos' overtures

5

for a friendly settlement of the Greco-Bulgarian differences and intrigued with the Austrians against Serbia.

Accordingly early in February 1913 the truce came to an end and hostilities were resumed. The two chief centres of *The capture of Jannina.* interest were Jannina and Adrianople. The former surrendered on 6th March, four divisions having been sent round from Greece by sea to reinforce the besiegers ; and one of the dreams of Greek nationalism thus at last became a reality.

At Adrianople the period of the armistice was employed by the Turks in strengthening their defences, but it was obvious *The siege of Adrianople.* that the town would be taken unless some effort were made to relieve it from without. A plan was, therefore, conceived of moving troops up from the Gallipoli peninsula, and a large concentration of troops took place there during the armistice. As a countermove the Bulgarian Fourth Army advanced from Demotika to Bulair at the neck of the peninsula, where fighting took place on 4th February and subsequent days, which ended in favour of the Bulgars and destroyed any hopes entertained by the Turks that they would be able to relieve Adrianople. But the siege dragged on amid the severest winter weather, until, after several *Fall of Adrianople.* attempts, the Serbians and Bulgarians both succeeded in entering the town from different sides on the night of 25th–26th March. It is a question which of the two nations had the honour of receiving the submission of the Turkish commander, and here, as at Salonica, the harmony between the Allies was disturbed by an event which should have been an occasion for mutual con- *Bulgarian ingratitude to- wards Serbia.* gratulation. The behaviour of the Bulgarians in refusing to the Serbians any share in the triumphal entry into Adrianople, and the cold and almost hostile reception given to the Serbian troops on their journey home through Bulgaria, was a poor return for the assistance which the Serbians had rendered by sending not only infantry but also their siege guns, particularly in view of the fact that they were under no obligation to send any troops to Thrace, since the Bulgarians had not given the assistance in Macedonia contemplated by the Serbo-Bulgarian Treaty. With the fall of Adrianople the only remaining point of Turkish resistance was Skutari in Northern Albania, which was surrendered to the Montenegrins on 23rd April.

Throughout the campaign on land invaluable, though less spectacular, services were rendered at sea by the Greek Navy *The services of* under Admiral Koundouriotis, which absolutely *the Greek Navy.* controlled the Ægean and prevented any attempt on the part of the Turkish Navy to emerge from the Dardanelles. Its greatest contribution to the Allied success was that it prevented the dispatch of reinforcements by sea from Asia Minor and made the Turks entirely dependent on railway transport, which quickly broke down. The Greek mercantile marine also performed significant services by transferring troops and material both for the Serbs and for *The Greek* the Bulgarians. The Greek Navy was also *occupation of the* usefully employed in taking over from Turkey *Ægean Islands.* the islands of the Ægean, such as Lesbos, Chios, and Samos, which were not only essentially Greek in population and busy centres of industry, but also strategically important as dominating the coasts of Asia Minor.

The fall of Skutari brought the First Balkan War to a close. The result of the resumption of hostilities after the armistice was *The end of the* further to strengthen the position of the victorious *First Balkan War.* Allies, whose successes had justified their most sanguine expectations and had forced European opinion to change its conception of the invincible Turk and the Powers to modify the lofty attitude which they had adopted only a few months before and accept the new condition of affairs.

For the moment the Allies still presented an outward appearance of solidarity, and negotiations were resumed in London *The Treaty of* which terminated on 30th May with the Treaty *London.* of London, whereby the frontier of Turkey was drawn from Enos on the Ægean to Midia on the Black Sea, depriving Turkey of Adrianople ; and all *Crete ceded to* territory beyond this line except Albania was *Greece.* ceded to the Balkan League as a whole. The suzerainty of Crete was definitely renounced by Turkey, but the future ownership of the Turkish Islands of the Ægean was left to the decision of the Powers. The most striking effort of the Powers was the erection of an independent Albania, a step which was destined to have far-reaching effects as barring Serbia from access to the Adriatic.

The emancipation of the Christian populations of Turkey in Europe, which was the object of the Balkan League, had been achieved, but the problem still remained of dividing the spoils. The Bulgars were not only as obsessed as ever by the idea of the 'Great Bulgaria' of the San Stefano Treaty, but also relied on the Treaty with Serbia for the satisfaction of their claims in Northern Macedonia. Serbia, disappointed of her ambition to possess an outlet on the Adriatic and cut off to the north by Austro-Hungary, was forced to look for an exit down the Vardar Valley and was naturally averse to seeing two frontiers erected between herself and the Ægean ; at the same time she could claim that the Treaty with Bulgaria was rendered void by the fact that the Bulgarians had not fulfilled their part by sending assistance to the Serbian armies, whereas Serbia had done more than her share by sending troops to Thrace. Greece was firmly established at Salonica and naturally claimed an extension of her frontier in Southern Macedonia. She could urge with justice, if Macedonia was to be partitioned, that, since the whole of the Ægean littoral was inhabited by a preponderance of Greeks with a minority of Turks and Bulgaria had no ethnological claims to any portion of it, the western section at least as far as the Struma should be regarded as her legitimate share of the spoils. In return for this, M. Venizelos was prepared to give up all claim to the conquered territory east of the Struma, thus carrying conciliation towards Bulgaria to its utmost limit in order to avoid a rupture of the League.

On 18th March King George of Greece, then in the fiftieth year of his reign, was murdered by a half-witted Macedonian *The murder of* while walking, according to his wont, almost *King George of* unattended in a street of Salonica. It was not *Greece.* the least of the services which he rendered to Greece that he refused to leave Salonica as long as his presence could serve to demonstrate to the world in general, and to Bulgaria in particular, that the Greeks were determined to maintain their hold on their legitimate conquests. His martyrdom in the cause of Greek Nationalism could not fail to confirm the determination of his subjects to assert their rights and seemed likely also to strengthen the position of the Glücksberg dynasty on the throne of Greece. But his death also lessened the chance of a peaceful settlement with Bulgaria by the removal of a sovereign of long experience and wide knowledge of foreign political relations, whose personal influence had done much to preserve harmony among the Balkan Allies. His successor, Constantine, a man of headstrong character and little political insight, who was already beginning to regard himself, in virtue of the successes of the Greek Army, as a 'War-Lord' on the model of his Imperial brother-in-law of Germany, soon showed himself less willing than his father to listen to the advice of his Prime Minister.

Owing to the uncompromising attitude of the Bulgarian Government the Greeks and Serbians found it advisable, in *The Greco-* view of possible eventualities, to enter into a *Serbian Treaty.* secret treaty for mutual defence. Already on 5th March the Bulgarians had tried to dislodge the Greeks from their positions at Nigrita on the right bank of the Struma; but in the interest of harmony the Greek Government consented to regard this attack as a 'local incident'. In May, while the Treaty was under discussion, the danger from Bulgaria was made much more obvious by a determined attempt on the part of Bulgarian troops to expel the Greek forces of occupation from the district of Mount Pangaeon to the east of the mouth of the Struma; hostilities here lasted for several days and resulted in a victory for the Greeks.

The Protocol of the Greco-Serbian Treaty was dated 5th May 1913, and the final Treaty of Alliance was signed on 1st June *Its provisions.* and ratified on 21st June. This agreement has acquired such importance, in view of the questions which arose regarding it during the European War of 1914-18, that the more important of its provisions may be stated here. By Article I of the Treaty each Power undertook to come to the assistance of the other if attacked and only to make peace by common consent, while under Article II each undertook not to conclude any separate agreement with Bulgaria. Article III arranged for a common Greco-Serbian frontier west of the Vardar, and Article IV fixed the Greco-Bulgarian and Serbo-Bulgarian frontiers 'on the principle of actual occupation and of the equilibrium between the three States'. By Article V it was arranged that, if negotiations with Bulgaria broke down, all differences should be submitted to the arbitration of the Sovereigns of the Triple Entente or other Heads of States. Article VI provided for a military convention. By Article VII Greece guaranteed commercial facilities to Serbia along the Vardar railway and at Salonica. Article VIII arranged for co-operation between the general staffs of the two countries, while Article IX provided for the discussion in the future of a Customs Union between Greece and Serbia. Under Article X the Treaty became operative immediately after its signature and was to remain in force for ten years.

Under the Military Convention, in case of an attack by Bulgaria, or another third Power, Greece undertook to provide

The Military Convention between Greece and Serbia. a force of 90,000 rifles and to co-operate with her fleet in the Ægean, while Serbia agreed to provide 100,000 rifles. If hostilities were declared by one of the two parties against Bulgaria or another Power without previous agreement with the other party, the latter was to observe an attitude of benevolent neutrality and immediately mobilize its army.

The Greco-Serbian Agreement was concluded none too soon; for by the date of its final ratification the Bulgarian armies had already been concentrated against Greece and Serbia. Towards the end of June the position was such that the Rumanian Government formally declared to Bulgaria that, in event of hostilities, it could not remain neutral, thereby performing a notable service to Greece and Serbia by preventing any intervention in favour of Bulgaria by Austro-Hungary, which would not risk the alienation of Rumania.

At the end of June five Bulgarian armies were ready

The Bulgars attack the Serbians. to attack all along the front from the Danube to the Ægean. Early on the morning of 30th June, without any declaration of hostilities, they treacherously attacked the Serbians with whom they had been fraternizing only a few hours before. They succeeded in advancing at certain points, but the Serbians gradually asserted their superiority and in a little more than a week the invaders were defeated.

Meanwhile, acting in concert with the Northern Bulgarian Army, the Second Bulgarian Army under General Ivanof

The Bulgars attack the Greeks. attacked the Greeks on a wide front. These operations are of particular interest as having taken place over ground which became familiar to the Allied Armies in the Macedonian campaign of 1915–18. The very suddenness of the attack gave the Bulgars a temporary success at the two extremities of the front, enabling them to seize Gevgeli and to drive in the Greek outposts near the mouth of the Struma. The plan of attack adopted by the Greek General Staff was to attack the right wing of the Second Bulgarian Army, and, if possible, isolate it from the Fourth Army on its right, and simultaneously to advance on its own right wing and interrupt the Bulgarian rear communications by cutting the Salonica-Constantinople railway beyond Serres. Accord-

Greek victory at Kilkish. ingly on 2nd July the Greeks attacked vigorously on the line Gevgeli-Kilkish-Likovan, recapturing the first of these places and advancing victoriously on a wide front. The action was fought in blazing heat, and the heavy casualties bore witness to the obstinacy of the Bulgarian resistance and the devotion and dash of the Greek infantry, who were ably supported by batteries of mountain guns. Next day the formidable Bulgar positions at Lahana on the Salonica-Serres road, on the crest of the hills just before they begin to slope down to the Struma plain, were captured by bayonet assault, and the Bulgarian Army was definitely defeated. His communications being by this time threatened, General Ivanof could see no alternative to retreat and ordered his troops to retire in two directions, over the western end of the Belashitsa Range to Strumnitsa and up the Rupel Pass. On 6th July

The capture of Doiran. the town of Doiran, which had been an important depot of stores, was occupied by the Greeks without a struggle. Serres and Demir-Hissar were the scenes of unspeakable horrors perpetrated by the *comitadjis* who accompanied the retreating army.[1] The pursuing Greek Army following the retiring Bulgars up the Struma

The Greeks reach the Kresna Pass. Valley found them on 21st July in a strongly defended position at the narrow Kresna Pass, and the struggle passed from open warfare into a war of positions.

Meanwhile the general situation had been greatly modified

Rumania threatens Sofia. owing to the fulfilment by Rumania of her threat to join in the hostilities; and the Rumanian Army had advanced to within fifty miles of Sofia. At the same time the Turks had taken advantage of the

Recapture of Adrianople denuded condition of the Thracian frontier to recapture Adrianople, and might have extended their operations westwards had not the Greeks taken the precaution of landing troops at Dedeagatch.

Bulgaria then found herself surrounded by enemies on all sides and was forced to agree to a cessation of hostilities on

Bulgaria surrenders. 30th July, which brought to a close the desperate struggle which had been waged for more than a week between the Greeks and Bulgars in the upper valley of the Struma. This armistice brought the Second Balkan War to a close after only a month of warfare, with the result that Bulgaria not only lost much of the Turkish spoil which she might have obtained if she had been willing to come to an amicable settlement, but also alienated the sympathy of public opinion in those countries to which she owed her very existence as a nation.

Before closing this chapter we may revert briefly to the

The Fate of the Bulgar force in Salonica. fate of the Bulgar garrison, which had been left behind in Salonica during the First Balkan War. At the end of June 1913 the strained relations between the Greeks and Bulgars in Salonica had reached breaking-point. Abandoned by their

---

[1] The present writer visited these towns in the winter of 1915–16, when they were still occupied by Greek troops and before the Bulgarian descent into Eastern Macedonia. The Greek quarter of Serres was a mass of ruins; at Demir-Hissar he was introduced by the Commander of the garrison to the sole survivor of a number of Greek inhabitants who were driven to the edge of a deep pit, bayoneted by Bulgars and hurled, still living, into the abyss.

officers the men barricaded themselves in a girls' school near the Church of St. Sophia and for a time maintained a stout resistance. They were eventually forced to surrender by the fire of Greek machine-guns which effectually commanded their place of refuge from the minaret of St. Sophia, where marks of Bulgar bullets are still traceable.

CHAPTER VII

FROM THE TREATY OF BUCHAREST TO THE OUTBREAK OF THE WAR OF 1914–18 (1913–14)

THE Treaty of Bucharest, which was ratified on 10th August 1913, was an attempt on the part of Greece and Serbia to deal

The Treaty of Bucharest.

fairly with Bulgaria in spite of her record of treachery. As has already been shown, the nationalities were so inextricably intermingled in Macedonia that to fix ethnological frontiers was a sheer impossibility. The Greco-Serbian frontier was drawn in accordance with the provisions of the Treaty of Alliance. Bulgaria

The Serbian gains.

had gambled for high stakes and had lost, and so had to pay the penalty. Serbia, therefore, annexed certain districts in Northern and Central Macedonia, of which the inhabitants were Bulgarian rather than Serbian in sentiment, but their annexation was a necessity to secure a satisfactory frontier and to prevent the creation of any semblance of a ' Great Bulgaria ' which would have given her enemy a predominant position in the Balkans. There was, no doubt, less justification for the Rumanian annexation of part of the Bulgarian Dobrudja ; but Rumania could legitimately demand some compensation, and was thus placed in possession of territory which she could use as a pledge of Bulgarian good behaviour.

Greece under the Treaty saw her territory almost doubled and a large Greek population ' redeemed ' after centuries of

The new frontiers of Greece.

slavery ; but at the same time she acquired an enormous Northern Frontier, which would require large forces for its protection.[1] Her treatment of Bulgaria was eminently fair. We have seen how, after the First Balkan War, Greece, in order to secure harmony in the Balkan League, had been willing to

[1] See map on p. 149.

concede to Bulgaria all the Ægean littoral east of the Struma
in spite of the predominance of the Greek
Generous treat- population in that region. It was characteristic
ment of Bulgaria. of the far-seeing statesmanship of M. Venizelos,
who realized that Greece and Bulgaria must try to live peaceably
together, that he decided in favour of granting Bulgaria access
to the Ægean by making the River Mesta the frontier and thus
giving her the ports of Dedeagatch, Makri, and Porto Lago.
The only possible advantage to Greece which can be traced in
this concession is that it placed a tract of buffer territory between
Greece and Turkey. Had it been possible, M. Venizelos would
have gone even further and conceded the Cavalla district, but
he realized that such a sacrifice would have only stimulated the
voracity of Bulgaria and given her a position of vantage for
possible aggression in the future.[1] The real test of the fairness
with which Greece treated Bulgaria is the fact that the Treaty
of Bucharest gave Greece a Bulgarian population smaller than
the Greek population which remained under Bulgarian rule.
There can be little doubt that, had not the European War broken
out so soon, the question of populations might have been to a
large extent solved by the emigration of Greeks from Bulgaria
into Greece and of Bulgarians from Greece into Bulgaria ; a
beginning had already been made by the exchange of Greeks
from the districts of Melenik, Strumnitsa, and Nevrokop with
Bulgarians from the Struma Plain.

To Turkey the Second Balkan War brought nothing but
gain. She recovered almost all that she had lost in Central and
Eastern Thrace and with oriental fatalism
Turkey retains quickly reconciled herself to the loss of the
Adrianople. provinces of Macedonia and Albania, which
had long been thorns in her side ; at the same time the successful
defence of the Tchataldja lines and the recovery of Adrianople,
her European capital before the capture of Constantinople, did

[1] Though from a casual glance at the map the inclusion of the Cavalla-
Drama district in Greece seems to be anomalous in view of the fact that the
country north of it is Bulgarian, it must be remembered that the mountain
ranges absolutely cut off the coastal region from the interior, and that the real
exit from Western Macedonia towards the Ægean is down the Vardar and
Struma valleys to Salonica, the only Macedonian harbour on the Ægean
which is really worth consideration. Geographically Bulgaria faces the Black
Sea and not the Ægean.

much to rehabilitate her in her own estimation. Incidentally the recapture of Adrianople had far-reaching effects in that it restored the credit of Enver and the Committee of Union and Progress, and placed them in a position to dictate Turkish policy in the early part of the European War.

Though the Treaty of Bucharest brought only a partial solution of the Greek National problem and large Hellenic populations still remained under a foreign yoke, yet so great was the extent of new territory won by the successes of her army and navy during the Balkan Wars that Greece required

The Greek problem only partly solved.

a long period of peace in which to organize and consolidate her gains. In the words of M. Venizelos, 'For a whole generation Greece would have to be occupied in the extensive development of her doubled dominion, and during this period of development she must either hope that the Greeks in Turkey would find a tolerable *modus vivendi* under the existing system, or else be certain that, when the time came for the break-up of the Turkish Empire, a leading place would be taken by a strong Greece, strong enough to solve by her own effort the problems which await a national solution'. But external events were destined to allow little time for internal development, though an excellent start was made in the organization of the new territories. In the year which intervened between the signature of the Treaty of Bucharest and the outbreak of the European War difficulties had already arisen with Turkey on the one hand and Italy on the other.

During the First Balkan War the Greeks had taken advantage of their supremacy at sea to occupy a number of Turkish islands inhabited almost exclusively by Greeks. Crete had been formally united to Greece on the declaration of war and the Porte had definitely resigned its suzerainty over it in the Treaty of

The question of the Turkish Islands.

London ; the Dodecanese, which we will consider later, was in the occupation of Italy. The fate of the rest of the Turkish islands of the Ægean was left to the decision of the Powers, who assigned them all to Greece with the exception of Imbros and Tenedos, which command the approach to the Dardanelles. The three most northerly islands, Thasos, Samothrace, and Lemnos, were consequently annexed by Greece ; but the Turks refused to agree to the Greek occupation of Lesbos (Mitylene), Chios, and Samos, opposing the surrender of the first two in particular on the ground that they command the approach to Smyrna and lie too close to compact Greek subject populations on the west coast of Asia Minor. The Porte suggested as a compromise that all three islands should be given a form of autonomy such as Samos had long enjoyed under Turkish suzerainty. The question was still undecided when the European War broke out, and, with the participation of Turkey in that war, the islands passed automatically into the control of Greece and were conspicuous for their enthusiastic adherence to the National Movement in 1916.

The ' unredeemed ' Greeks of Turkish Thrace and the mainland of Asia Minor were far less fortunate than their brethren *The unredeemed* of the islands, and their plight was aggravated *Greeks in Turkey.* rather than alleviated by the result of the Balkan Wars. While Greece doubled its territory and population in Europe, nearly two and a half million Greeks found themselves still in the clutches of their tormentors, who were embittered by the defeat which they had received and were still more set than ever on the policy of ' Ottomanizing ' those Christians who still remained in their power. The conclusion of the Balkan Wars saw the beginning of a new era of martyrdom for the Greek subjects of the Porte, which lasted for six years.

In Thrace, which during the First Balkan War had been the scene of the desperate struggle between Turkey and Bulgaria, *The Greeks in* the large Greek population had inevitably suffered *Thrace.* all the horrors of war. During the Second Balkan War, when the young Turks advanced to the reoccupation of Adrianople, the disorderly hordes of Turkish and Kurdish soldiers were let loose upon the Christian inhabitants. After the pillage and devastation of the armies, the unhappy survivors were left a prey to the Moslem peasants, who seized anything that had been preserved from the general ruin, well knowing that the Turkish courts would grant their victims no redress. A minority of the Greek inhabitants of Thrace managed to escape from the country and found new homes in Greek Macedonia.

In Asia Minor the large Greek population soon found itself

the object of systematic persecution by the Young Turks, who
The Greeks in Asia Minor. adopted this method of avenging the defeat inflicted upon them by the Greeks of Free Hellas. Throughout Asia Minor, wherever the traveller went, he found the learned professions and trade almost entirely in the hands of Greeks, who formed the intellectual *élite* of the population. Along the south coast of the Sea of Marmora and all the west coast of Asia Minor the Greek element was larger than that of any other nationality, and there was a compact mass of Greek population on the south coast of the Black Sea in the district of Trebizond. If Asia Minor had been partitioned on the basis of nationality, the Greeks would have had a good claim to the *vilayets* of Aidin and Brousa and the *sandjak* of Ismid ; while there was ample justification for the desire of the Christian inhabitants of the *vilayet* of Trebizond to form an independent Greek ' Republic of Pontus '.

Upon this Greek population of nearly two millions the Young Turks, re-established in power after the recovery of
Persecution of the Asiatic Greeks. Adrianople, began to vent their rage as soon as peace was signed. They found a ready excuse for expropriating Greeks by urging the necessity of providing for the Moslem refugees from the lost provinces. Expulsion was the easiest and least conspicuous means of reducing the Greek population. The pretexts for this were various, the favourite excuse being that Greeks had taken part in anti-Moslem demonstrations during the war. The number of Greeks denounced by professional informers and expelled from Turkey was very large and included some of the most influential members of the Greek communities. Another
The boycott. method adopted for the ruin of the Greeks was a boycott of all Greek commerce. Moslems were forbidden to frequent Greek shops or to have any commercial transactions with Greeks, while it was solemnly announced in the mosques that the payment of debts due from the Faithful to Christian creditors was an unpardonable sin. The Turks failed to realize that, if the results achieved had come up to their expectations, they would have destroyed any prosperity which the country enjoyed ; but the Greeks, in spite of heavy losses both in numbers and wealth, continued to hold their own with the characteristic vitality of their race. A large number of in-

dividual firms were, however, forced to suspend operations and many of the richer Greeks left the country.

The commercial boycott affected the towns only. In the rural districts robbery and expropriation were still easier. The Christian peasants, being unarmed, were an easy prey to armed bands who instituted a reign of terror. Forbidden to leave their villages in order to till their fields, they were forced to sell all they possessed to save themselves from starvation and left the country in large numbers, thus enabling the Turkish Government to settle Moslems on their property.

This systematic persecution of the Greek element in Turkey could not fail to arouse a strong protest in Greece, and *Venizelos pro-* M. Venizelos found himself obliged to address *tests against the* an ultimatum to the Porte, making it clear *treatment of the* that if the persecutions did not cease Greece *Asiatic Greeks.* would go to war. This firm language, which was followed by reprisals on the property of Turkish subjects in Greece, had its effect, and, when the European War broke out, M. Venizelos was actually on his way to meet the Grand Vizier in order to negotiate a better understanding between the two nations.

Two other questions arose during this period in which Greek interests were involved, those of the Dodecanese and of *The question of* Northern Epirus. The Dodecanese is a group *the Dodecanese.* of islands lying off the southern part of the west coast of Asia Minor, the most important of which are Rhodes, Cos, Patmos, and Carpathos. These islands were seized by the Italian fleet during the war with Turkey in Tripoli in 1912–13, and were condemned by the Treaty of Lausanne to remain in Italian occupation until all the Turkish troops were withdrawn from the Tripolitana. They still remain under the Italian yoke, which the unfortunate inhabitants, who are almost exclusively Greeks, have found more grievous than that of Turkey, under whose rule they enjoyed virtual independence and self-government in return for the payment of a small tribute. On the arrival of the Italians the islanders welcomed them with enthusiasm as liberators ; but it soon became evident that the Italians contemplated something more than a temporary occupation. On 1st July 1912 a General Assembly drew up a declaration addressed to

the ' Sister-nation Italy ', expressing the desire of the islanders
to be united to Greece but their willingness to form for the
moment an independent state to be known as the ' Ægean
Commonwealth '. The only result was a more stringent policy
on the part of the Italians, who not only forbade all public
gatherings and the display of the Greek flag, but also did much
to ruin the trade of the islands and force the inhabitants to leave
their homes. The condition of the unhappy Greeks of the
Dodecanese under Italian rule cannot be better illustrated than
by the fact that since 1912 the population of some of the islands
has fallen by as much as 50 per cent. owing to emigration and
expulsions.

In Epirus also Greek interests came into collision with Italian
imperialistic aims. The capture of Jannina in the First Balkan
War had put Greece in possession of an ancient
seat of Greek culture, whose schools had done
much to keep alight the flame of Hellenism
during the dark centuries of Turkish oppression, and added a
large tract of essentially Greek territory to the kingdom of
Greece. The justice of the claims of Greece to annex Southern
and Central Epirus was so obvious that they could not be dis-
puted, but in Northern Epirus, or as the Italians called the
district ' Southern Albania ', Greek claims came into collision
with Italian ambitions which aimed at making Italian influence
predominant along the coasts of the Adriatic. Northern Epirus
may be roughly described as the triangular tract of country of
which the base is the stretch of coast between a point a few
miles south of Valona and a point on the mainland opposite
the town of Corfu, while the apex of the triangle is the southern
extremity of Lake Ochrida. It was inhabited by Greeks and
Albanians, partly Christians and partly converted Moslems in
about equal proportions, the Christians being probably slightly
more numerous ; Northern Epirus, however, must not be
considered by itself, but as an integral part of Epirus to which
historically it has always belonged. Its Greek character is
indicated by the fact that under Ali Pasha of Tepelini, who
ruled Epirus early in the nineteenth century and was practically
independent of the control of the Sultan, Greek was the official
language of the Government ; and the district has remained
predominantly Greek in spite of the influx of Albanians from

The question of Epirus.

the north and the emigration of Greeks to other countries. The intensely national spirit of the Northern Epirotes cannot be better illustrated than by recalling the numerous and costly benefactions made to Greece by natives of this district, such as the brothers Zappa, who built the Exhibition Hall at Athens which bears their name, and Arsakis, who provided the Normal School at Athens. There were, moreover, 238 Greek schools in Northern Epirus besides numerous other public institutions.

During the Balkan Wars M. Venizelos, anxious to avoid any friction with Italy, came to a private understanding with
Northern Epirus annexed to Albania. the Italian Government that the Greek Army should not occupy Valona or Berat, the Italians in return verbally agreeing not to oppose the Greek annexation of Northern Epirus. As a proof of good faith the Greeks evacuated the small but strategically important island of Sasseno at the entrance of the Gulf of Valona, which had been ceded by Great Britain to Greece with the Ionian Islands in 1864. At the conclusion of the Balkan Wars the Powers created an independent Albania ; whereupon Italy and Austria demanded the evacuation by Greece of Northern Epirus. The Greek Government naturally appealed to the Powers, urging that the question should be decided on the basis of self-determination by the inhabitants, and won the support of the Triple Entente. The importunities, however, of Italy and Austria led to a compromise by which a commissioner was dispatched to the district to ascertain the language of the inhabitants—notoriously a false criterion of national sentiment —instead of the more natural course of taking a plebiscite as to whether they wished to belong to Greece or Albania. The result was that in November 1913 the Commission by the Protocol of Florence decided that Northern Epirus should form part of the Albanian State.

The Greek Government acquiesced in this decision and withdrew its garrisons from Northern Epirus ; but the inhabitants
The Powers recognize the autonomy of Northern Epirus. showed their true inclinations by proclaiming a Provisional Government and flying to arms. Reinforced by volunteers from all parts of Greece they resisted the attacks of the Albanian Moslems from the north, with whom were a number of Italian officers, until the Powers found themselves

obliged to come to terms with the Provisional Government; and at a conference held at Corfu, Northern Epirus was recognized as autonomous under nominal Albanian suzerainty, a clear recognition of the special interest of Greece in that region. The subsequent story of the question of Northern Epirus belongs to the history of the European War.

Bulgaria, having been forced to sign the Treaty of Bucharest, was soon deep in her old game of intrigue. It was not long *Bulgarian intrigues.* before she had become reconciled, through the mediation of the German Ambassador at Constantinople, with her former enemy Turkey, whose recovery of Adrianople she seems deliberately to have forgotten. The sinister influence of the Central Powers was thus exerted to keep alive for their future advantage the racial antipathies of the Balkan States and to employ their common hatred of Greece and Serbia as a bond of union between Bulgaria and Turkey. While Bulgaria was encouraged to look forward to possessing herself of all Macedonia, Turkey was promised the recovery of the whole of Thrace and the Turkish Islands in the occupation of Greece and was even offered the Cyclades as an additional bait. It was not long before *comitadji* bands in the pay of the Bulgarian Government were active in Albania and Macedonia, especially on the Greek and Serbian frontiers adjoining the Strumnitsa district, whence they descended upon the railway line leading down the Vardar Valley from Serbia to Salonica. The Bulgarian Government could always plead that the action of the *comitadjis* was beyond its control, but several ' incidents ' were so serious as almost to lead to a renewal of open hostilities.

The history of the Austro-German intrigues in the Balkans between August 1913 and July 1914 is somewhat obscure ; but it is difficult to realize how the diplomatists of the Entente failed to conclude from the behaviour of Bulgaria that she was already a willing tool in the hands of the Central Powers—just as the Mpret [1] of the newly-created state of Albania was their puppet—to thwart the ambitions of Serbia and Greece.

Of their attitude towards Greece during this period, the

[1] This title, which is a corruption of *imperator*, was revived for the Prince of Wied when he was appointed ruler of Albania.

Central Powers made no secret.   In April 1914, when the crisis
between Greece and Turkey was at its height,
The attitude of the Kaiser accompanied by Bethmann-Hollweg
Germany towards was paying his annual visit to Corfu, where he
Greece. had purchased the Achilleion, formerly the
estate of the Empress Elizabeth of Austria.   Great Britain having
promised her support to enforce the decision of the Conference
of London regarding the islands, M. Venizelos took the opportunity of asking the German Chancellor to define the attitude
of Germany on this question.   Bethmann-Hollweg replied that
Greece could not under any circumstances count on German
support against Turkey.   The attitude of Germany was formulated even more positively in a secret communication, which
subsequently came to light, from the Kaiser to King Constantine
in reply to a question put to him by the Greek representative
who had proceeded to Berlin to announce the succession of
Constantine to the throne, as to whether Greece could count
on the lasting friendship of Germany.   The reply ran as follows :

> ' The Imperial Government finds itself unable to adopt
> the Greek point of view.   The alliance which unites Germany
> to Austria-Hungary and Italy prevents her from entering into
> negotiations on subjects which touch the interests of her
> Allies.   Germany regards it as her duty to second these
> interests without any evasion, and this duty hinders her
> from taking any initiative in a question which lies within
> the sphere of influence of her Allies.   *Unfortunately Germany
> can do nothing for Greece.   All the interests of the Empire push
> her towards those states whose views do not accord with those
> of Hellenism.*'

It was thus clear that Greece must look for support solely to
her natural protectors, the Guaranteeing Powers ; and it was a
serious obligation on the statesmen and diplomatists of the
Entente to devise how best they could serve her interests.

The drama enacted at Serajevo at the end of June 1914
set in motion a train of events destined to involve
The murder of all the Great Powers of Europe in hostilities
the Archduke and eventually to force the Balkan States to
Franz Ferdinand. range themselves with one or other group of
combatants.

PART II

GREECE DURING THE WAR OF 1914-18

CHAPTER VIII

GREECE AT THE OUTBREAK OF THE WAR OF 1914-18

IN July 1914 the Greek nation was united as it never had been before in the course of its history. Victory had recently crowned

The political unity of Greece in 1914.

its arms and doubled the territory of the kingdom. There were problems, internal and external, still to be solved, but the nation was of one mind in the conviction that its destinies were in the hands of a statesman who would find the right solution ; there can hardly be said to have been any real political opposition to the Liberal Party which supported M. Venizelos. The Greek Chamber had become a sedate and businesslike body ; the most flagrant abuses which had characterized the administration had been swept away ; the national finances were on a sounder footing than they had ever been before ; industry was developing, and the flag of the Greek merchant marine was conspicuous in every part of the world. The reigning dynasty had every outward appearance of stability, since the occupant of the throne had but lately led the national arms to victory and was the son of a sovereign who, after fifty years of constitutional rule, had fallen a victim to his devotion to the cause of Greek nationalism.

In her external relations it seemed obvious that the interests of Greece were bound up with those of the Entente Powers, to

Greece and the Entente Powers.

whom she owed her existence as an independent nation and who had on the whole supported her cause. If at times Greece had been disappointed by the attitude adopted by the Protecting Powers, she was generous enough to think of the Philhellenism of Byron, Cochrane and Fabrier and the championship of Gladstone and Dilke rather than of those occasions when the conflict of interests

73

in the Concert of Europe had led to the neglect of what she regarded as her due rights. It was to France and Great Britain that Greece had turned for the reorganization of the army and navy which had won the victories of the Balkan Wars. Owing to her geographical position, too, Greece, with her large seaboard, would clearly be consulting her interests in siding with the group of Powers whose fleets were predominant in the Mediterranean. At the same time the attitude adopted by the Central Powers during and since the Balkan Wars had made it clear that they would support Bulgaria and Turkey rather than Greece and Serbia.

The monarchy in Greece being essentially constitutional, it would have seemed obvious that the Crown could have but little influence in shaping the policy of Greece. *The position of the Crown.* If King George I had been still living in 1914, there can be no doubt that Greece would have devoted herself whole-heartedly from the first to the support of the Entente Powers. Not only the evident interests of the country but also the close family ties of the dynasty under King George I attached Greece to Great Britain [1] and Russia, while his constant visits to France, where he enjoyed great personal popularity, showed his sympathy with the other Entente Power. With the accession of King Constantine a new set of family relationships came into play. Not *King Constantine and Germany.* only had Constantine received his military education at the *Kriegsakademie* in Berlin, but also, by his marriage with Princess Sophia of Prussia, he was brother-in-law of Kaiser Wilhelm II, whose personality appears to have had an overpowering influence over him. There can be little doubt that the Kaiser deliberately set himself to mould the impressionable Constantine to his own views of the function of a sovereign as the All-Highest and sole controller of the destiny of his people rather than the constitu- *King Constantine as a ' War- Lord'.* tional ruler and interpreter of the people's will. The successes of the Balkan Wars, which were popularly attributed to Constantine's leadership, convinced him that he too was a ' Supreme War-Lord' and superior to any democratic form of government.

---

[1] English was the language invariably spoken by the Royal Family in private life.

When he visited Germany after the Balkan Wars, the flattering reception with which he met and the baton of Field-Marshal conferred upon him by the Kaiser led him into the stupid mistake of publicly attributing to his German military education successes which had been won by the irresistible *élan* of the Greek soldiery trained by a French Military Mission and armed with French guns and rifles. Even before he succeeded to the throne his wife, the favourite sister of the Kaiser, had begun to exercise a powerful influence in favour of Germany not only upon her husband but upon Court and military circles at Athens.[1]   With the accession of Constantine the Germanophil tendencies of the royal couple were given a larger and freer scope ; it seemed, however, hardly possible that pro-Germanism, either in the Royal Family or elsewhere, could set itself in 1914 against the obvious desire of the people to support the pro-Entente policy of the Prime Minister.

M. Venizelos, like so many others, was, as we have seen, abroad when the Austro-Hungarian ultimatum was presented

Venizelos promises Greek support to Serbia.

to Serbia on 25th July 1914. He was at Munich on his way to Brussels to confer with the Grand Vizier on the questions outstanding between Greece and Turkey. It was here that he received a question from the Serbian Premier, M. Pashitch, as to the attitude which Greece intended to adopt. M. Venizelos without hesitation gave the only possible reply, that, with regard to war with Austria, fuller information would be necessary before the government would reply, but that in case of a Bulgarian attack the place of Greece would be at the side of her Serbian ally. It was an anxious moment for the Greek Premier, who saw that the fruits of two victorious campaigns were endangered, especially in view of a possible understanding between the Bulgarians and Turks, who might take advantage of the European situation to fall upon Greece and partition her rich possessions while her Serbian ally was engaged elsewhere. Not only was the Greek attitude clearly stated to the Serbian Government, but it was also made clear to the German government that in

[1] No one, who, like the present writer, attended the Oriental Congress at Athens in 1912, could fail to notice the marked preference shown by the then Crown Prince, who was President of the Congress, for the very numerous German delegates.

the interests of self-preservation Greece could not tolerate an attack by Bulgaria upon Serbia. On 2nd August it was pointed out to the Serbian government that Greece could best serve the interests both of herself and of Serbia by observing a benevolent neutrality and keeping her forces intact in view of possible aggression by Bulgaria, which would only be precipitated by a general mobilization of the Greek Army.

Meanwhile Constantine behind the back of his ministers was in communication with the Kaiser. While the Prime Minister, *Constantine's communications with the Kaiser.* with his sovereign's knowledge, was promising Serbia the assistance which she owed her under the Treaty of Alliance, Constantine telegraphed as follows to his brother-in-law : [This telegram [1] was found annotated by the Kaiser with the remarks which are placed in brackets.]

' Athens, 2nd August 1914.—Sincerest thanks for your telegram. We have never thought of helping the Serbians. But it seems to me impossible to join their enemies and fall upon them, seeing that they were once our allies.' [*You ought to march against Russia.*] ' It seems to me that the interests of Greece require an absolute neutrality and the maintenance of the *status quo* in the Balkans as established by the Treaty of Bucharest.' [*Impossible ; there can be no more talk of this. The Balkans are marching.*] ' If we depart from this standpoint, Bulgaria will be enlarged by the annexation of the part of Macedonia recently conquered by Serbia and will envelope our whole northern frontier and become enormously dangerous to us. I have no guarantee against this. These considerations compel us to observe neutrality, and for that end to avoid, with Rumania, anything which may give Bulgaria ground for interference.' [*Twaddle. If Greece will not join us, she will lose her position as a Balkan Power and will be no more supported in her wishes by us, but will be treated as an enemy.*]

This telegram was answered by the Kaiser on 4th August through M. Theotokis, Greek Minister at Berlin and an ardent Germanophil. In this reply the Kaiser informed King Con-

[1] Published in *Die Deutschen Dokumente zum Kriegansbruch* (4 vols., Charlottenburg, 1919).

stantine that an alliance had been concluded that day between
The Kaiser's Germany and Turkey, and that Bulgaria and
reply. Rumania were also ranging themselves on the
side of Germany, while German men-of-war
were joining the Turkish fleet; thus all the Balkan States were
with Germany in its struggle against Slavism. He, therefore,
appeals to Constantine ' as a comrade, as a German Field-Marshal,
of whom the German Army was proud when the title was
conferred upon him, and as a brother-in-law, to order the
mobilization of the Greek Army and march hand in hand with
the Germans against the common foe. . . . If Greece does not
side with Germany, a break between the two countries is inevitable. . . . In short,' writes the Minister, ' His Majesty says that
he requires you to carry out *all that he and Your Majesty have so
often discussed.*' (This last phrase seems to show that Constantine
had long been in the Kaiser's confidence.) A further telegram
from M. Theotokis of the same date states his belief that it has
been arranged between Vienna and Sofia that, if the Central
Powers are victorious, Bulgaria will receive compensation in
' those territories over which she has historical and ethnological
rights' (i.e. Greek and Serbian Macedonia); if, on the other
hand, Greece listens to the Kaiser's appeal, she should inquire
precisely what Germany will promise her, if the Central Powers
are victorious : ' I have the impression,' he adds, ' that no objection will be made to our aggrandisement at the expense of Serbia'.

On 7th August Constantine replied that while his personal
sympathies and political opinions draw him to the German
side, he cannot see how the mobilization of the Greek Army
will benefit Germany; the Entente fleet controls the Mediterranean, and Greece might easily be wiped off the map without
being able in the least degree to serve German interests. In
reply the Greek Minister at Berlin states (9th August 1914) that
Herr von Jagow has informed him that he believes the Kaiser
will understand the necessity stated by Constantine of observing
neutrality for the moment.

This exchange of telegrams makes it clear that King Constantine, though a constitutional monarch, was induced to
follow his own personal wishes without any regard to the will
of the Greek people, and that, while seeming to accede to the
wishes of his brother-in-law, he desired to remain neutral, so as

to avoid any collision with the Allied Powers. This policy of trying to run with the hare and hunt with the hounds could only end in disaster for himself and his people.

But in spite of his personal wishes Constantine was unable to influence the course of events, and M. Venizelos, with the country behind him, proceeded to protect the interests of Greece. His frank statement of the position of Greece and the determination of the government to observe a benevolent neutrality towards Serbia and to intervene if Bulgaria attacked her, had the effect of keeping Bulgaria for the moment out of the war— possibly because it gave the crafty Ferdinand a plausible excuse for not yet fulfilling his promises to the Central Powers.

The nation supports M. Venizelos.

In the middle of August M. Venizelos took a further step, which may be described in his own words : ' I asked for and obtained authorization to declare that Greece, not merely in the consciousness of her indebtedness to the Protecting Powers but from a clear perception of her vital interests as a nation, understood that her place was at the side of the Entente Powers ; and that, whereas in the war that was being waged it was not possible for her to take a military part, since she could not, owing to the danger from Bulgaria, reinforce the Serbians . . . nevertheless, she thought it her duty to declare to the Powers of the Entente that, if Turkey went to war against them, she placed all her military and naval forces at their disposal for war against Turkey, provided that Greece was guaranteed against the Bulgarian danger '. This declaration was made to the governments of Great Britain, France, and Russia in the Entente's darkest hour, when the outcome of the Battle of the Marne still hung in the balance.

Greece declares her sympathy with the Entente.

The result was all that M. Venizelos could desire. The British Government informed the Greek Government that the British fleet would not allow the Turkish fleet to leave the Dardanelles, even if Turkey proposed to attack Greece only—a promise which relieved Greece from all fear of a sudden naval attack. But this was not all : in December the three Protecting Powers and Italy consented to the provisional occupation of Northern Epirus on the same conditions

The British Government promises Greece protection against Turkey.

as those under which Italy occupied Valona, leaving the question of Epirus and Albania to be settled at the Peace Conference.

Beside the official intimation of the British Government that the British fleet would close the exit from the Dardanelles,

Suggested Greek co-operation against the Dardanelles.

King George V addressed a personal telegram to Constantine expressing his gratification that Greece had not hesitated to take her stand by the side of Great Britain. Admiral Kerr, chief of the British Naval Mission in Greece, was also instructed to come to an understanding with the Greek General Staff and study the subject of an attack on the Gallipoli Peninsula. In this connexion a strange incident occurred which illustrates

Vacillation of King Constantine.

the inconsistencies of Constantine's attitude. After assenting to the dispatch of the friendly message to the Entente Powers, when he gave an audience to Admiral Kerr, he confronted him with the statement that he had no intention of making war on Turkey, but that, if Turkey declared war on Greece and the Allies wished to help Greece, he would accept their help. He requested Admiral Kerr to communicate this statement to the British Government after consulting M. Venizelos. The latter could not allow the despatch of a communication which conflicted with the policy already proposed by the Greek Government to the Entente. Essentially a weak man, Constantine could always be won over by the arguments of his latest visitor, especially if they happened to accord with his own wishes. When M. Venizelos was with him, his personal force and the consciousness that he was the mouthpiece of the people's will prevailed with him ; but then other advisers would be summoned and overpersuade him. Pro-German influence was already making itself felt through highly-placed personages in Greece, particularly General Dousmanis and Dr. Streit, the Minister of Foreign Affairs, who found King Constantine a ready listener.

M. Venizelos, after informing Admiral Kerr that the King's new proposal to the British Government could not be sent,

Venizelos' letter to the King.

addressed a letter to the King pointing out that, in view of the declaration already sent to the Entente Powers, it was impossible now to say that Greece refused to fight against Turkey so long as Turkey was not the aggressor, since such a policy was manifestly opposed to the interests of Greece ; but she could not reject the possibility of waging war on Turkey with the help of numerous and powerful Allies. ' What confuses the issue ', wrote M. Venizelos, ' and produces in the mind of Your Majesty and M. Streit an opposition to the policy which I recommend, is a desire not to offend Germany . . . who proposes, if her ascendancy in the war is complete, to create a Greater Bulgaria extending to the Adriatic as a bulwark against Slavism, the Germans having recently discovered that the Bulgars are not Slavs but Tartars. Why should we have so much regard for a Power whose aim is to strengthen by every possible means the two chief foes of Hellenism, Turkey and Bulgaria ? Why should we show ourselves indifferent to the very Powers who revived the Greek State, who have defended Greece in every emergency, and to-day again are prepared, if Turkey falls upon us, to stand at our side ? '

M. Venizelos concluded his letter by saying that, in the circumstances, he could only resign. His resignation was naturally not accepted ; the telegram to the British Government was never sent ; and arrangements were made for Admiral Kerr to confer with the Greek General Staff.

The effect of M. Venizelos' firm attitude was, as we have seen, to prevent Bulgaria for the time being from openly entering the war. Probably the German General Staff was opposed to action in the Balkans in the autumn of 1914, and the second offensive against Serbia was undertaken by Austro-Hungary on her own initiative. Bulgaria, however, carried *comitadji* warfare into Serbian territory and harassed the Serbian communications. The Austro-Hungarian offensive completely miscarried, and the Serbians, against tremendous odds, fought one of the most successful campaigns in the whole war. They were materially assisted by the benevolent neutrality of Greece, which enabled them to obtain munitions and supplies of all kinds by way of Salonica and the Vardar railway.

Venizelos' attitude secures the neutrality of Bulgaria.

CHAPTER IX

POLITICAL EVENTS IN GREECE FROM JANUARY TO OCTOBER 1915

EARLY in 1915 fresh negotiations were opened between the Allies and Greece on the understanding that Greece had definitely

Greece is offered territory in Asia Minor if she joins the Entente Powers.

ranged herself on the side of the Allies. On 24th January Sir Edward Grey proposed to the Greek Government that Greece should join in concerted action in the Balkans in return for very important concessions in Asia Minor. This was the first official acknowledgement by the Protecting Powers of the claims of Greece to extensive territories in the Turkish Empire inhabited by a large Greek population. The proposal raised a serious problem, with which

M. Venizelos' memorandum to the King.

M. Venizelos immediately dealt in a memorandum addressed to the King. 'Greece', he wrote, ' is again confronted with a crisis in the history of the nation. Hitherto our policy has consisted in the preservation of neutrality, as far as the treaty obligation with Serbia does not oblige us to depart therefrom. We are now called on to participate in the war, no longer only to fulfil moral obligations, but in view of compensations, which, if realized, will create a great and powerful Greece, such as the boldest optimist could not have imagined a few years ago. To obtain these compensations great dangers will have to be faced. . . . Above

He urges concessions to Bulgaria.

all we must seek the co-operation of Rumania and, if possible, of Bulgaria. . . . In order to bring this about, I think we should make adequate concessions to Bulgaria. . . . I would not hesitate, however painful the severance, to recommend the sacrifice of Cavalla ' (the port and district in S. Thrace, which would give Bulgaria an exit to the Mediterranean) ' in order to save the Greeks in Turkey and create a Great Greece which would include nearly all the provinces where Hellenism flourished through the long periods of its history.' In a further memorandum written when it had become clear that Rumania would not co-operate, M. Venizelos pointed out to the King that the cession of the Cavalla district involved a Greek population of only 30,000, whereas there were 800,000 Greeks in the proposed new territory in Asia Minor. He appealed to Constantine to create by the sword a Greater Hellas and achieve the reunion of the Greek nation, ' a task such as few kings had even had the opportunity of undertaking.'

This appeal seems to have been successful, and the proposed concessions to Bulgaria were agreed upon by the Council of

King Constantine consents.

Ministers. Clearly Constantine could not yet bring himself to yield to his personal inclinations and place himself in direct conflict with the will of the nation. The negotiations, however, fell through, and Bulgaria preferred to accept the offer of a large loan from the Central Powers and throw in her lot against the Allies. The willingness of M. Venizelos to make concessions to Bulgaria, though in doing so he had been supported by the King and the Government, was afterwards used as a basis of attacks on him.

In February 1915 the first attack on the Dardanelles was made by the Allied fleets only, with results which are well

The first attack on the Dardanelles.

known and which showed that the Straits could be forced only by a joint naval and military attack. M. Venizelos, understanding that the Allies required a landing-force to co-operate with the Allied fleet, proposed to the Crown that this should be supplied by Greece and suggested that an Army Corps

Venizelos suggests Greek co-operation against the Dardanelles.

should be mobilized for this purpose. This gave Greece an opportunity of doing a real service to the Allies, who had no landing-force ready near at hand, and at the same time it pledged Greece to only a limited amount of assistance. The suggestion met with strong opposition from the Greek General Staff, which, under Colonel Metaxas, was already beginning to oppose any action which might offend Germany. They urged that it was inexpedient on military grounds and that the proposed extension of Greek power to Asia Minor would raise international problems of difficulty.

The King at first opposed the enterprise, but afterwards

appeared to be convinced by the arguments of the Prime
Minister and gave a reluctant assent. As he
Constantine left the palace, however, M. Venizelos was
reluctantly confronted by Colonel Metaxas, who handed
consents. him an envelope containing a letter of resignation. To make this step irrevocable he had already sent
the news of his resignation to the Press. This action implied
that, in the opinion of the responsible head of
The attitude of the military executive, Greece could not send
Col. Metaxas. an Army Corps abroad without endangering
her position at home. M. Venizelos, therefore, demanded that
the Crown Council should be summoned. At this he obtained
support for his policy, but, in order to obtain
The Crown absolute unanimity, he reduced his demand to
Council assents to an Expeditionary Force of one division only.
the dispatch of There was a general impression in the Council
one division. that the King could not do otherwise than
accept this proposal, and the objection that Russia might look
unfavourably upon Greek co-operation against the Dardanelles
was effectively answered by the announcement that the French
Government had obtained Russia's unconditional assent.

On the following day, however, King Constantine suddenly
announced his absolute refusal to the enterprise,
Constantine and M. Venizelos had no alternative but to
changes his mind submit his resignation, which was accepted.
and Venizelos There is no doubt that he resigned under the
resigns. idea that the King, as a constitutional monarch,
regarded the matter of such importance that an appeal to the
country was necessary, especially as three years
Gounaris became had passed since the last election. The King,
Prime Minister. however, showed that he had no intention of
following this course ; for he summoned M. Gounaris, a personal
opponent of M. Venizelos, and asked him to form a Cabinet.

If a Greek Army Corps had been landed on Gallipoli at that
time, it seems likely that it would have found a very small
Turkish force defending the peninsula, which
An opportunity was still practically unfortified. It is also clear
lost. that the first naval attack was within an ace of
success and produced a condition bordering on panic in Constantinople. If it had been followed up immediately by a second

attack from the sea combined with a landing, the course of the campaign against Turkey might have been very different. As it was, owing to the impossibility of bringing troops up in time for an immediate landing after the attack by sea, a period was allowed to elapse during which the peninsula was converted into a veritable fortress. Meanwhile the behaviour of the Greek General Staff and its fraternization with the German and Bulgarian military attachés at Athens made it clear that the Greek military authorities could not be trusted not to divulge any information which they might receive from the Allies, with the result that, when the joint military and naval attack was made, the Greeks were not invited to co-operate.

The Gounaris Government, through M. Zographos, the new Foreign Minister, took an early opportunity of formally acknow-

The Gounaris Cabinet admits the obligations of Greece to Serbia.
ledging the treaty obligations of Greece toward Serbia. They instructed the Greek representatives in London, Paris, and Petrograd to inform the Entente Governments that the new Cabinet would pursue the policy announced at the beginning of the war, which was dictated by the traditional sentiments of the nation and the close bonds which united Greece to the Protecting Powers. There seems no doubt that M. Zographos and certain other members of the Cabinet honestly wished to carry out as far as possible the programme of the Liberal Party. As regards M. Gounaris himself, it is possible that he had not yet allowed himself to become a tool of Germany, and his chief motive in taking office may have been his personal rivalry with M. Venizelos. Meanwhile the diplomatists of the Allied Powers were still obsessed with the idea that Bulgaria could be won over, and wished to have the option still open of offering her the bribe of Eastern Macedonia. Thus a deadlock ensued, which gave the German propaganda an opportunity of which it readily availed itself.

At the outbreak of the war there seemed little reason to fear that German influence could counteract the general sentiment of

The beginnings of German propaganda in Greece.
Greece in favour of the Entente. A certain number of officers, some of whom had received their training in Germany, realized that a Germanophil attitude was an easy road to royal favour and promotion, while others were genuinely persuaded that the German Army was invincible.

Only one of the many daily journals in Athens was definitely pro-German, the rest openly pro-Entente. But before long an elaborate system of German propaganda had been established under the direction of Baron Schenck, nominally the representative of the Wolff Agency. With ample resources at their command, Schenck and his minions began to buy up newspaper-editors, deputies and private persons, and inaugurated the systematic poisoning of public opinion. The pro-German Press propaganda was the first in the field and aimed at creating rather than following public opinion, until by dint of repetition it succeeded in persuading many of its readers that Germany was invincible and King Constantine a heaven-sent political genius. The Protecting Powers were attacked, and the personal hostility against M. Venizelos of other would-be political leaders, who were jealous of his popularity, was exploited. He was represented as a traitor who wished to abandon national territory to the enemies of Greece, while the King was portrayed as the defender of national rights. So successful was this campaign that M. Venizelos, returning from a well-earned holiday after five years of office, was prevented by a police order from landing at the Peiræus and later besieged in his own house.

On 13th June the elections, which could no longer be postponed, were held in circumstances very unfavourable to the *The elections* Liberal Party. In the new provinces, where *favour the* the elections were being held for the first time, *Liberal Party.* flagrant corruption was practiced and only four out of seventy-three constituencies returned Liberal members. In the old provinces anti-Venizelist agents represented the issue as being one of King Constantine and peace against M. Venizelos and war, but in spite of this the Liberals gained 123 seats out of a total of 184.

But, though the Liberal cause had triumphed, the Gounaris Cabinet refused to resign until seventy days had passed, alleging *M. Venizelos* that the King was too ill to take the necessary *resumes office.* steps towards summoning a new Cabinet. At last, on 10th August, M. Venizelos again took office, but apparently only because the pro-German propaganda had not yet sufficiently prepared public opinion to enable the opposition to act openly.

On assuming office M. Venizelos made it clear that Greece

must continue to follow the policy laid down at the beginning of the war and, in particular, must do everything possible to prevent Bulgaria from crushing Serbia. The Cabinet, therefore, informed both the Entente Powers and the Central Governments that this was the policy which Greece would follow. It is clear, however, that the King was determined that Greece should follow a different course. Already, on 17th July, the Greek Minister at Bucharest had telegraphed as follows to Athens : ' My British colleague informs me that, according to positive information, Germany has given the Sofia Government a formal assurance that the neutrality of Greece is definitely secured even in the event of a Bulgarian attack on Serbia'. It appears, therefore, certain that the King had agreed with the Kaiser that in no circumstances would Greece carry out her treaty obligations towards Serbia. The Kaiser had doubtless informed his brother-in-law of the impending attack on Serbia, in which Bulgaria had agreed to join, and was assured of Greece's neutrality. The King's conduct was in this matter unconstitutional and at the same time an act of treachery towards Serbia, since he had allowed the Cabinet to inform Serbia that it could rely on the support of Greece. The desertion of Serbia by her ally made her destruction a matter of certainty, since Germany had decided to crush her in order to open the road to Constantinople.

The attitude of King Constantine.

Meanwhile the Allies were bringing further pressure to bear on M. Venizelos and on M. Pashitch, the Serbian Premier, to offer definite concession to Bulgaria. On 14th September the Serbians unwillingly yielded and were prepared to sacrifice the Monastir district. But it was too late. On 22nd September a general mobilization was proclaimed in Bulgaria. King Ferdinand, like Mussolini in 1940, seems to have decided that the moment for action had come and that he must throw in his lot with the side which he was convinced must win and obtain his share of the spoils. He saw that the Russian advance had been stopped, that the Allies were held up at the Dardanelles, and that their diplomacy in the Balkans was meeting with no success ; Germany and Austria, on the

The Greek and Serbian Governments consent to concessions to Bulgaria.

Bulgaria mobilizes.

other hand, had at last resolved to concentrate overwhelming forces on the Danube and wipe Serbia off the map of Europe.

M. Venizelos recognized what the Bulgarian mobilization meant. Receiving the news in the early morning he telephoned

Venizelos insists on Greek mobilization ; the King resists.

to the King, who was at his country house, asking to be received in order to submit an order for the Greek mobilization. The King fixed 5 p.m. for the audience, and, while not denying the obvious obligations of Greece, feebly protested that he did not want to help Serbia, because Germany would certainly win. M. Venizelos replied that his Government, whose policy had been approved at the recent elections, represented the sovereign will of the people and that the King could only refuse to endorse that policy by abrogating the constitution by Royal Decree and assuming full responsibility. In his reply, the King showed himself an apt pupil of his Imperial brother-in-law. While recognizing that he was bound to obey the popular will on questions of internal policy, he claimed that, in questions of foreign affairs and international problems, if he believed that a thing was right or not right, he must insist on its being done or not being done, because he was responsible before God. This was defying the Constitution and claiming the

Venizelos threatens resignation.

Divine Right of Kings, and M. Venizelos could only request the King to accept his resignation. Presented with this ultimatum, Constantine persuaded the Prime Minister to retain office and consented to the Decree of Mobilization ; but the anti-Venizelist press, inspired by the General Staff, stated that the

The King gives way.

King and the Prime Minister were in disagreement as to the object of the mobilization, the former regarding it as a measure of defence, the latter of war ; and the General Staff took no steps to send help to Serbia. They raised the objection that Serbia was not in a position to supply the 150,000 men to fight against Bulgaria, as was stipulated in the treaty. M. Venizelos, therefore,

Venizelos asks the Entente to send troops.

suggested that the British and French Governments should be asked if they were willing to take upon themselves the obligation of Serbia and supply this force. This request was made, and within two days a reply was received that the required force of 150,000 men would be sent by Britain and France. The King raised objections to this course, and at his desire the British and French Ministers were informed that, as long as Bulgaria did not attack Serbia, these troops should not be sent, since their landing on Greek soil would involve a breach of Greek neutrality. But it was too late, and the Greek Government was informed that the troops were already on their way and that the Entente Powers assumed full responsibility for their action.

On 28th September in the House of Commons, Sir Edward Grey made it clear that the British Government had at last renounced as hopeless the policy of trying to win Bulgaria over and declared—when it was already too late to give any effective help to Serbia—that the Allies were resolved to give every support to their friends in the Balkans without reserve or qualification.

The British Govt. abandons policy of concessions to Bulgaria.

On the next day the Greek Chamber met for the first time since the elections. The Prime Minister painted the situation in gloomy colours and insisted that, though Bulgaria pretended that she had mobilized only in defence of her neutrality, the Greek Government was determined to fulfil her obligations to Serbia should the *casus fœderis* arise. The opposition, under M. Gounaris, maintained that the Greek mobilization should be utilized only for the defence of the vital interests of Greece without any regard for the obligations of the Serbian Treaty.

The debate on the object of the mobilization.

On 2nd October M. Venizelos, yielding to the King's insistence, issued a protest against the proposed landing of Entente troops at Salonica, but at the same time made it clear that the protest was merely formal.

Protest of Greek Govt. against landing at Salonica.

On 3rd October Russia, at last aroused, addressed an ultimatum to the Bulgarian Government, calling upon it openly to break within twenty-four hours with the enemies of the Slav cause. When Bulgaria refused, a state of war between Russia and Bulgaria came into existence.

Russia at war with Bulgaria.

On 4th October a stormy meeting of the Greek Chamber

took place, at which all the forces of the Opposition, under the
leadership of four ex-Premiers, were arrayed
The debate of against the Prime Minister. M. Venizelos declared
4th October. categorically that he had official assurances from
the Entente that all offers to Bulgaria of concessions of Greek
and Serbian territory were null and void, and stated his opinion
that the Bulgarian mobilization would never have been ordered
if Bulgaria had not been misled by the declaration of the late
Government. He concluded by reiterating the
The Chamber determination of the Government to fulfil to
supports the letter the Treaty with Serbia. This policy
Venizelos. was approved by 147 votes to 110. If we take
into account the circumstances under which the elections had
been held and the fact that it was notorious that the King was
supporting the opposition, it is obvious that public opinion was
strongly in favour of the Liberal Party's policy.

Thus a clear breach was at last opened between the Government and the King, who had before him the alternative of either
yielding to the expressed will of the people, or
The King refuses following his own desires and violating the
to support the Constitution. He chose the latter course, and
Liberal policy. on 5th October sent for the Prime Minister
and informed him that he was in disagreement with his policy.
M. Venizelos, thereupon, submitted his resigna-
Venizelos' tion rather than raise the Constitutional ques-
second tion at such a moment. Four hours later the
resignation. first detachments of the Allied troops landed at
Karaburun near Salonica.

CHAPTER X

GREECE AND HER OBLIGATIONS TOWARDS SERBIA

M. VENIZELOS resigned because he foresaw that, if he resisted the Crown at so critical a moment, civil war would be the only
The motives of Venizelos' resignation.
result. The army being mobilized, a National and a Royalist camp would have been formed, and, while Greece was torn by internecine war, Bulgaria would have occupied Eastern Macedonia and then turned on Serbia without let or hindrance. M. Venizelos therefore preferred to resign and to bide his time.

Another factor in the situation was that M. Venizelos had had no encouragement to suppose that, if he opposed the King,
The diplomacy of the Allies.
his action would be supported by the Protecting Powers. The record of Allied diplomacy in the Balkans since the outbreak of war had not been a brilliant one. The obvious course at the beginning of the war would have been to give every possible support to Serbia, already an ally, and Greece, a potential ally; but, instead of this, attempts were made to win over Turkey—where the task was soon seen to be hopeless—and afterwards Bulgaria, which was to be induced to join the Allies by the promise of receiving as a bribe the spoils so hardly won by Greece and Serbia in the Balkan Wars. By trading on the readiness of M. Venizelos to submit to every possible sacrifice in order to demonstrate the sympathies of Greece, the Entente offered a ready handle to his enemies, who vilified him as the betrayer of Greek national interests. When in September 1915 the British and French Governments at last recognized the hopelessness of trying to
The failure to support Venizelos.
win over Bulgaria, the least they should have done was to show themselves willing to give M. Venizelos their whole-hearted support; and their failure to do so turned the scale against him. At the very moment when they were landing troops in

Greece to hasten at last to the succour of Serbia, they witnessed the expulsion from office of the Minister at whose suggestion these troops had been sent. It may be urged in excuse for the earlier mistakes of Entente diplomacy that during the first year of the war the situation in France was so critical that it absorbed all the energies of the Allied Governments and little thought could be spared for Balkan affairs ; but, when once they had made up their minds to send troops to Salonica, it was a matter of elementary precaution to take measures to ensure a safe base of operations. This could only have been secured by supporting M. Venizelos and thus obtaining, if not the military aid, at any rate the political sympathy of Greece.

The British public did what it could to make amends to M. Venizelos by giving him on his visit to England in 1917 a welcome such as it has seldom accorded to any foreign ruler or statesman ; but in 1915 public opinion in this country, always notoriously indifferent to foreign affairs, had not before it the necessary data for forming an impartial opinion on the Balkan situation. Further the sense of fair-play, which is admittedly a British characteristic, unfortunately often errs in the direction of a willingness to listen to pleading in favour of the weaker cause, and in this case the Bulgarian point of view had the advantage of being advocated by the leading organ of the British press through its able representative at Sofia and the small but active 'Balkan Committee', which was at pains to represent the Bulgars as nature's gentlemen, living simple and blameless lives under an ideal democracy.

The British public and the Balkans.

The excuse, which was urged at the time, that Britain, France, and Russia had no right to interfere in the internal affairs of Greece is one which cannot be maintained for a moment. On the contrary, as Protecting Powers, they were bound to uphold the Constitution which they had themselves established and guaranteed, and which Constantine had violated by dismissing a Prime Minister of whose policy the elected representatives of the people had expressly approved.

The duty of the Protecting Powers.

That Great Britain and France were the Protecting Powers

of Greece was also one of the justifications of the landing of

Justification of the Salonica landing.

troops at Salonica. It was expressly laid down in the Treaty of 1864 that any one of the three Powers might send troops to Greek territory with the consent of the other two signatories, that is, that, if the three Powers were agreed, the consent of Greece was not necessary. In this case, however, the Greek Government had invited the dispatch of troops in order to help Serbia in the fulfilment of her treaty obligations to Greece.

After the dismissal of M. Venizelos, M. Alexander Zaïmis was summoned to form a Cabinet, in which as many as four

M. Zaïmis becomes Premier.

other ex-Premiers took office—MM. Theotokis, Rallis, Dragoumis, and Gounaris. On 8th October M. Zaïmis issued a circular telegram to all the Greek Legations in which he stated that his policy would 'rest on the same essential bases as that followed by Greece since the beginning of the European War'. In these conditions M. Venizelos promised his provisional support. On 11th October, however, the new Premier found himself directly confronted with the question of the application of the Serbian Treaty. An inquiry was received from the Serbian Government as to whether, in view of the fact that the impending attack by Bulgaria upon Serbia realized the *casus fœderis* provided for by the Treaty, the Greek Government would issue orders to the Greek General Staff to co-operate with the Serbian military authorities in order to settle the details of the joint action of

The Zaïmis Government repudiates the obligations of Greece to Serbia.

the two armies. To this M. Zaïmis replied that the Greek Government regretted its inability to accede to the request of the Serbian Government owing to the fact that the Treaty had in view only the case of an attack by Bulgaria alone, and, since Germany and Austro-Hungary were also taking part in the invasion of Serbia, the terms of the Treaty did not come into operation. This interpretation of the Treaty is one which cannot for a moment be maintained. As we have seen, at the express demand of the Serbian Government the Treaty had been so drafted that its application was not merely Balkanic but had a wider scope.

It is difficult to understand the part played by M. Zaïmis on this occasion. 'Of M. Zaïmis,' said M. Venizelos in his great

The responsi-
bility of M.
Zaïmis.

speech in the Chamber on 13th August 1917, 'I have always spoken with great respect, and even to-day I do not wish to depreciate his great gifts and attainments in a country which unfortunately, if I may say so without offence, is suffering from a temporary lack of leading men. But his responsibility, in accepting office at that moment in order to repudiate the Treaty with Serbia, was tremendous. . . . The greatest dishonesty which a State can commit is to repudiate a promise to help another State after using that promise to obtain a corresponding pledge of mutual assistance.'

Meanwhile the Entente Powers seem to have made up their minds to try and win over Constantine, just as they had attempted

The Entente tries
to win over King
Constantine.

to gain Bulgaria, by the offer of concessions. In October they offered to cede the island of Cyprus as the price for his aid to Serbia. The possession of this island with its population of more than 250,000 Greeks had long been an ideal of Greek Nationalism, and it was expected that its cession to Greece would be welcomed with enthusiasm. The gift, however, was refused, and its refusal was tantamount to an admission that Constantine had received promises from the opposite camp of a still more alluring kind in the event of the victory which he was persuaded would crown the German arms. This refusal must certainly be ascribed to the influence of the pro-German group of advisers who were daily exercising more and more pressure on the King, and not to M. Zaïmis. The latter's policy was certainly one of genuine neutrality, and during his term of office he maintained friendly relations with the Entente, who even supplied him with a loan.

On 3rd November the Minister for War, General Yannakitsas, insulted the Chamber in so flagrant a manner that M. Venizelos

The debate in
the Chamber on
3rd and 4th Nov.

provoked a political debate during which he delivered one of his most powerful speeches in support of his national policy. The Minister for War having refused to apologize and receiving the support of the majority of the Cabinet, M. Venizelos gave utterance to an indictment of the unconstitutional nature of the

The Chamber supports Venizelos. existing régime and challenged a vote of confidence in the Government. By 147 votes against 114 the Chamber declared its adherence to the policy of the Liberal Party and censured the conduct of the Minister for War. Constantine replied by appointing General Yannakitsas his aide-de-camp and, having

M. Zaïmis resigns. accepted the resignation of M. Zaïmis, summoned M. Skouloudis to form a new Cabinet (6th November). Here we will leave for the moment the internal affairs of Greece and briefly examine the military situation in the Balkans during the late autumn of 1915.

The great Austro-German Army, which had concentrated on the northern frontier of Serbia, crossed the Danube on

The Invasion of Serbia. 7th October and entered Belgrade on the 9th. During the following weeks so overwhelming an army poured into this country that the unhappy Serbians, in spite of a brave resistance, could do nothing to save themselves. Meanwhile the Entente Powers had determined to help Serbia—but only when it was too late. We have already seen how, acting on the suggestion of M. Venizelos, they had promised to send troops to replace the 150,000 men whom Serbia was obliged, under the terms of her Treaty with Greece, to supply against Bulgaria. By 9th October there were

The Allies at Salonica. some 15,000 French and 5000 British troops at and near Salonica. On 11th October General Sarrail (who as Commander of the French Third Army had materially contributed to General Joffre's success on the Marne) took over the command of the Allied Armée de l'Orient, which by the end of October numbered rather over 30,000 men, including the Tenth British Division from Gallipoli.

On 11th October the Bulgarians, seeing that the position of Serbia was hopeless, crossed the frontier and attacked the Serbian

The Allied Force fails to rescue Serbia. Army on the flank, in order to cut off the retreat of the Second Serbian Army down the Vardar Valley. General Sarrail attempted to effect a junction with the Serbians by advancing up the Vardar Valley to Demir Kapu,[1] but it was too late, and when

[1] See map on p. 133.

the Serbians had been driven back and retreated before superior forces towards Prilep, the French retreated down the Vardar Valley, fighting rearguard actions against heavy odds. On 9th December they reached the line of the Boyemia River, which they held for a time to cover the disembarkation of British and French troops who were now reaching Salonica in considerable numbers ; but it soon became clear that the small Franco-British force could not remain so far from its base in the depth of winter and without proper communications. Meanwhile Serbia, which they had come to rescue, had ceased to exist, and a remnant of the Serbian Army was retreating towards Corfu and suffering indescribable hardships in the mountains of Albania. The French and British, therefore, withdrew to Salonica.

M. Skouloudis, who was summoned to form a ministry after the resignation of M. Zaïmis, was an octogenarian banker,

The Cabinet of M. Skouloudis. who, having become a millionaire, aspired to become Prime Minister—a position which he would never have achieved even in Greece under normal conditions. He was a man absolutely devoid of any qualifications for such a position, and in fact merely served as a screen for the operations of the ' shadow ' Government which had its headquarters at the Palace and really exercised political power. His Cabinet included such well-known anti-Venizelists as Gounaris, Micheladakis, and Yannakitsas. At the same time the Chamber was dissolved—an illegal act, because the object of this second dissolution was to impose the same policy as had been the motive of the first dissolution, which had failed in its object because the voice of the people condemned that policy.

Meanwhile the Entente forces were reaching Salonica in formidable numbers, and it was necessary to throw dust in their

Skouloudis declares his friendship for the Allies. eyes. On 9th November, therefore, M. Skouloudis addressed to the Greek Legations, for communication to the governments in London, Paris, and Petrograd, a declaration of the ardent affection felt by the Greek Government towards the Entente Powers. ' Be good enough ', he wrote, ' to give the most categorical assurance of our fixed determination to maintain our neutrality in the form of the most sincere benevolence towards the Powers of the Entente. Kindly add that the new Cabinet adopts the repeated declarations of M. Zaïmis as regards the friendly attitude of the Royal Government towards the Allied forces at Salonica and that it is sufficiently conscious of its true interests and of its debt to the Protecting Powers not to deviate in the slightest degree from this line of conduct ; and that it hopes that the sentiments of friendship felt by these Powers towards Greece will never for a moment be prejudiced by the malicious and tendencious reports which are being deliberately circulated in the vain attempt to damage the cordial relations between the Entente and Greece '. The effect of this declaration was somewhat marred by a threat which he uttered, on the inspiration of the German Minister at Athens, that he would intern the Serbians if they retreated into Greek territory. This utterance, which revealed his real wishes, took a good deal of explaining away.

As the Greek Government had allowed the Entente troops to land at Salonica, it was difficult to deny them the right to *The position of the Allies at Salonica.* remain there. On the other hand, the fact that, owing to the Greek mobilization, large Greek forces were present in Macedonia provided the elements of an awkward situation if the Central Powers should decide to push on against Salonica. On 23rd November, therefore, the French and British Governments, showing unusual energy, presented the Skouloudis Government with a note stating that, in view of the attitude of the Greek Government on certain questions affecting the security and freedom of action of the Allied troops, they considered it necessary to suspend the economic and commercial facilities which Greece had hitherto enjoyed at their hands. About the same time Lord Kitchener and M. Denys Cochin both visited Greece and had audiences of King Constantine, but only obtained vague promises that the Greeks would not attack the Allied troops. The partial blockade was, therefore, continued until 12th December, when the Greek Government accepted the Entente demands and *The Entente decides to retain Salonica as a base for future operations.* withdrew all its forces from Salonica, except a single division. At the same time the Paris Conference of the British and French Governments came to the momentous decision, the wisdom of which was so often questioned by those who failed to realize the importance of Salonica, that, although the salvation of Serbia, which had been the original object of the landing, had not been achieved, Salonica should nevertheless be held as a base for future operations.

At this time it was still confidently anticipated that the Austro-German and Bulgarian forces would attempt to drive *The Germano-* General Sarrail and his army into the sea ; and *Bulgarian threat* indeed there is strong evidence that the Bul- *to Salonica.* garian Government and Supreme Command was strongly in favour of an immediate attack. It seems probable that it was the German Higher Command which decided against acceding to this demand. It was perhaps hoped that by energetic propaganda in Greece the position of the Allied troops at Salonica might be made untenable, or else that pressure elsewhere and, in particular, the attempted invasion of Egypt, might cause their withdrawal. Moreover, if the attack was to be made, it would have necessarily been carried out by Bulgarian troops, who, if successful, would have claimed Salonica as their reward ; and Austria, who had so long had her eyes fixed upon Salonica, would never have been induced to tolerate this.

By the middle of December the Allied Army at Salonica consisted of eight French Divisions and five British (the 10th, *The Allies* 22nd, 26th, 27th, and 28th). With these troops *construct the* at his disposal General Sarrail was faced with *Fortified Camp* the problem of devising the most suitable line *of Salonica.* of defence. His force was inadequate to hold the great mountain barrier which follows more or less exactly the Serbo-Greek and Greco-Bulgarian frontiers, but there was a shorter line, some fifty miles in length, which could easily be made defensible, running from the mouth of the Vardar along the hills north of Salonica to the Gulf of Orphano at Stavros.[1] The ground round the mouth of the Vardar is marshy and difficult of approach, while farther east the hills which form a chain cutting off Salonica and Chalcidice could easily be turned into a strong line of defence and are partly protected by the lakes of Langaza and Beshik. The nearness of this line to Salonica along several miles of its extent, where it comes within about seven miles from the city, was a possible source of weakness, but the danger could be largely neutralized

[1] See map on p. 133.

by the guns of a powerful fleet. The western part of the line was entrusted to the French, the eastern to the British ; and within a very few weeks the entrenched camp of Salonica was in a condition to resist any attack that the enemy was likely to be able to attempt.

CHAPTER XI

THE ELECTIONS OF DECEMBER 1915 AND THE BETRAYAL OF THE RUPEL FORT

ON 19th December 1915 elections to the Greek Chamber were held, though there was no real justification for them, since there was a clear Liberal majority. However, the *The Elections of* pro-German clique hoped that, if an election *19th Dec. 1915.* took place while the mobilization was in force, they might obtain a majority and so avoid applying the Treaty with Serbia and prejudicing the interests which they had pledged themselves to further. In these conditions M. Venizelos decided *The Liberal* that the only dignified course to pursue was to *Party holds aloof.* advise his supporters to abstain from any participation in the elections. He, therefore, addressed a manifesto to the Liberal Party stating that their abstention would throw upon the Government, which had brought about the situation, full and entire responsibility for the degradation of Greek political life and for the disasters which their policy was bringing upon the nation ; at the same time he hoped that this action would prevent the occurrence of internal strife at a time of external crisis.

During the election every device of intimidation and compulsion was employed. Editors of newspapers were threatened, *Intimidation of* and the right of assembly was denied in a most *the electorate.* arbitrary manner ; but the Liberal Party could not be seduced from its loyalty to M. Venizelos and held aloof. The result was that, whereas in June 750,000 electors went to the poll, in December only 200,000 voted— less than one-fifth of the electorate. All the members of the late Cabinet were re-elected—except M. Skouloudis, who, however, remained in office—and were pledged to support the pro-German clique, who under the leadership of General Dousmanis were working hand in hand with the chiefs of the German propaganda. From this time dates the deliberate attempt to strangle the soul of the Greek nation by a system of organized terrorism. Athens became the headquarters of an army of spies and informers recruited from the lowest of the people. All freedom of opinion was suppressed, and no one dared to express himself freely on questions of the day for fear of being dragged before the courts.

Among the many nefarious methods adopted, none was more reprehensible than the use of the Army as an agency of *The use of the* propaganda. Pro-German pamphlets were in- *Army for political* dustriously distributed to all ranks, who were *purposes.* at the same time forbidden to read the Liberal papers. There was no justification for the prolongation of the mobilization, and indeed during the elections it had been urged that by voting against M. Venizelos, who was the cause of the mobilization, the electors would obtain the release of themselves and their relatives from military service. As the result of the elections had been the triumph of the policy of neutrality, there was no further need for the Army to remain under arms, especially as the finances of the nation were in no condition to bear the enormous expense of maintaining the Army and the injury to the economic life of the country caused by the withdrawal of so many men from agriculture and industry.

Salonica was likewise a hot-bed of *espionnage* and intrigue, and every movement of the Allied Armies was reported to the *The expulsion of* enemy. In order to mitigate this evil General *the enemy* Sarrail arrested the Consuls of Germany, *Consuls from* Austria, Bulgaria, and Turkey, whose consulates *Salonica.* had become the headquarters of such activities, and transported them to France, whence they were returned to their own countries. It was obviously an act of elementary precaution and was fully justified by the evidence provided by their archives ; but the Greek Government protested on the ground that the sovereign rights of Greece were violated. On 12th January 1916 General Sarrail took a farther step to *The Struma* insure the safety of his army by sending up a *railway bridge* small force to blow up the large iron bridge on *blown up.* the Salonica-Constantinople railway over the Struma at the entrance of the Rupel Gorge, near Demir-Hissar. This act caused a great sensation at the time,

but its wisdom was amply justified by subsequent events. Further,
The occupation of on 28th January a French force took over the
the fort of fort of Karaburun, which dominates the
Karaburun. entrance to the inner Gulf of Salonica, the
Greek Commander surrendering it without
offering any resistance. Otherwise there was little military
incident during the first few months of 1916 beyond skirmishes
between the advanced patrols of the opposing forces and a
certain amount of aerial activity. The Anglo-French positions
The difficulties round Salonica were too strong to invite an
of an Allied attack, and reinforcements were continually
advance. arriving; but an Allied advance could only be
possible after a vast amount of preliminary
road-making. It was to this and to training in new methods of
fighting that the Allies devoted their energies, while the enemy
was busy rendering almost impregnable the positions which he
had taken up along the northern Greek frontier.

Meanwhile, though the fact did not come to light till a
much later date, the Greek General Staff had already come to a
The Greek definite agreement with the Central Powers,
General Staff and on 8th February a secret memorandum was
intrigues with the issued to the Corps and Divisional Commanders
Central Powers. ordering them to allow the Bulgars to advance
into Greek territory without offering any resistance. This act does away with any possible excuse that the
mobilization was being prolonged in order to protect the
neutrality of Greece; it was obviously being continued simply
to serve the interests of the Central Powers.

But a clearer proof of the real nature of the 'sincerely benevolent neutrality' of the Skouloudis Govern-
Skouloudis pro- ment was provided by the protest which it issued
tests against the on 10th January against the landing of Allied
landing of the detachments at Corfu to make preparations to
Serbians at Corfu. receive the unhappy remnant of the heroic
Serbian Army. It was adding insult to injury that those who
had repudiated the Treaty between Greece and
Refuses the Ser- Serbia should refuse hospitality to the wreck of
bian Army passage the army of their allies whom they had so basely
through Greece. deserted in their hour of need. Moreover, in
April, when the Serbian Army had been re-equipped and

8

CARL A. RUDISILL LIBRARY
LENOIR RHYNE COLLEGE

was ready to join the Allies at Salonica, the Skouloudis Government categorically refused it permission to travel over Greek territory or even through the Corinthian Canal—another proof that the secret government had pledged itself to do nothing which could possibly forward the interests of the enemies of Germany.

But these manifestations of ill-will were nothing in comparison with the act of treachery towards Greece and the Allies

The importance of the Rupel fort. which soon followed. M. Venizelos, during the negotiations which preceded the Treaty of Bucharest, had demanded and secured for Greece the frontier fort of Rupel,[1] which commands the exit from the Struma defile into the Struma plain near Demir-Hissar, the possession of which he rightly regarded as absolutely essential to the safety of Eastern Macedonia. Since the Balkan Wars large sums of money had been spent on bringing this fortress up to date, the details of its defences being kept a profound secret from all except those who actually formed part of its garrison.

This key-position the Skouloudis Cabinet, in co-operation with the Secret Government, betrayed to the hereditary enemies

Its betrayal by the Greek Government. of Greece. The fact that the Allies had blown up the railway bridge at the entrance of the Struma defile had made it clear that they had no intention of advancing in this direction, and they obviously regarded the presence of two Greek Army Corps in Eastern Macedonia as a guarantee that the Bulgarians would not be allowed to invade Greek territory for which so much blood had been shed in the Second Balkan War. The surrender of Rupel was thus both a direct challenge to the Allies and a base betrayal of Greek national interests.

On 10th May the General commanding the Sixth Division at Serres telephoned to the Greek War Office that one of his officers had been informed by an officer of the Bulgarian frontier guard that, in accordance with an agreement between Marshal Mackensen and the Greek Government, the Germans and Bulgarians had received permission to occupy points within two kilometres of the frontier, and so had occupied the hills overlooking Lehovo. This arrangement was in accordance

[1] See map on p. 133.

with a secret understanding into which the Greek Government had entered in the previous February. M. Skouloudis, to cover his treachery, made a formal protest, which was not taken seriously. In reply he received similar notes from the German and Bulgarian Ministers in Athens, stating that Germany and her Allies found themselves under the necessity of entering Greek territory to secure the free passage of the Rupel Gorge in view of the offensive measures recently taken by the troops of the Allies, but it was a merely defensive measure and the territorial integrity of Greece would be respected. The Greek Premier replied by simply acknowledging the note and making no protest whatever.

On 23rd May a large force of Bulgarians, accompanied by German officers, appeared before the Rupel Fort and demanded *The surrender of the Fort to the Bulgars.* its surrender. The garrison offered resistance and informed the Divisional Commander, who, on telegraphing to Athens for instructions, received orders to put into force secret orders which were in his possession and which, he found, contained instructions that no resistance was to be offered. Orders were, therefore, sent to evacuate the Fort, and the garrison was withdrawn after a resistance of twenty-four hours, during which casualties had been inflicted on the invaders. A large quantity of material fell into the enemies' hands.

The surrender of the Rupel Fort created a painful impression both in Greece and abroad. It was felt that the Greek Govern- *Impression created abroad.* ment, by its passive attitude in the face of an invasion which prejudiced the military situation of the Entente, had abandoned its policy of neutrality, and that the only course open to the Entente was to assume the necessary liberty of action to assure the safety of her armies in Macedonia.

On 5th June, at a meeting of the Chamber, M. Skouloudis attempted to justify the policy of the Government on the *Skouloudis attempts to justify himself.* ground that further resistance would have involved Greece in a conflict which would have necessitated the violation of her neutrality. Such pretexts might suffice for the servile majority in the Greek Chamber, but they could satisfy no one who was not infected by the poison of German propaganda. The duplicity of the Government was proved by the subsequent publication of documents, which showed that the Prime Minister had been, through the Greek Minister in Berlin, in constant communication with the German authorities regarding the measures to be taken by Greece to hamper the movements of the Entente armies in Macedonia.

CHAPTER XII

THE BEGINNINGS OF THE NATIONAL MOVEMENT

THE betrayal of Rupel, as no doubt its perpetrators intended, seriously affected the military position of the Allied Armies in

The effect of the betrayal of Rupel on the military situation.

Macedonia. Instead of relying on the Greek Army to hold the Greek territory of Eastern Macedonia, they were henceforward obliged to hold at least the line of the Struma and to detach for this purpose considerable forces which might have been usefully employed elsewhere. It also showed the necessity of taking measures to assure the security of the base at Salonica and of the area of operations. General Sarrail, therefore, having lately received wider powers of action, on 3rd June 1916, the King's Name-day, proclaimed martial law in Salonica and all the districts occupied by the Allied Armies, and assumed control of the police and the postal and telegraphic services. The Greek Government protested against the *fait accompli* as a violation of Greek sovereignty and used the incident to foment popular feeling against the Allies and M. Venizelos.

But not only was Greek sovereignty temporarily revoked in Macedonia, but Greece was also deprived, as a result of the

The loss of Northern Epirus.

treachery of her Government, of the control of Northern Epirus, which had been occupied by her with the consent of the Allied Powers at the beginning of the war. The Italians were only too ready to believe that the Greeks would betray Northern Epirus, just as they had abandoned Eastern Macedonia to the Bulgars. The Italian Government, therefore, with considerable show of justice pointed out to the other Powers that it was essential that this region should be taken over by Italian troops, with the result that the Italian occupation, which was based on Valona, was eventually extended until an Albanian front was created which joined hands with the Macedonian front. Thus the distrust of Greece engendered by the Skouloudis Government gave Italy the opportunity of gaining a hold, which she would not willingly let go, upon territory which she had long coveted.

The results of the Skouloudis administration may be summed up as the abolition of Greek sovereignty in Macedonia, the revocation of the Greek occupation of Northern Epirus, and the suppression throughout Greece of every form of civil liberty and every expression of political opinion except through a corrupt and servile Press in the pay of the Government and of Germany. But the days of his term of office were numbered, and the patience of the Protecting Powers was becoming exhausted.

After the surrender of Rupel the Military Party in Athens began to show its hand. Towards the end of May, the Minister of War, General Yannakitsas, took it upon himself to warn the troops that they might be called upon to fight; while Constantine himself, addressing his soldiers on manœuvres, pointedly insisted on the duty of a soldier to obey whatever orders he might receive and ' not to give way to sentiment '. Such remarks could only be interpreted as preparatory to possible military action against the Allies. On 12th June bands of hired partisans assembled outside the British and French Legations and demonstrated against the Protecting Powers.

The Military Party in Greece defies the Entente.

The obvious hostility of the King and Government of Greece could not fail to awaken the Allied Powers to the fact that their apathy in the past was leading to a really dangerous condition of affairs. They appear to have resolved to take effective measures, and a landing force under General Moreau was organized and transported to Salamis. There is reason to suppose that it had been determined to settle the Greek question by a bold stroke and to re-establish a Constitutional régime. Unhappily, at the last moment this intention seems to have been suddenly modified, owing either to some diplomatic intervention or to a pretended submission on the part of the King ; and the Allied representatives contented themselves with sending an ultimatum to M. Skouloudis on 21st June. After calling attention to the evident collusion of the Cabinet with the enemies of the Entente and the hostile activities of foreigners in Greece,

The ultimatum of 21st June 1916.

they demanded without delay the execution of the following measures :

1. The total demobilization of the Greek Army.

2. The replacement of the Skouloudis Cabinet by a ' Service Government without political colour', which should guarantee the loyal fulfilment of the benevolent neutrality which Greece had undertaken to observe.

3. The immediate dissolution of the Chamber to be followed by fresh elections.

The King yielded, though many of his advisers urged him to resist. On 23rd June M. Skouloudis resigned, and M. Zaïmis

The King yields and summons M. Zaïmis.
was again summoned to form a Government charged with the duty of carrying out the terms of the Allied Note. On 29th June a Decree of General Demobilization was issued ; but the Chamber was not dissolved, on the pretext that it was impossible at the moment to fix the date of the new elections. Moreover, as quickly as the troops were dismissed from the

The 'Reservists'.
ranks, they were formed into ' Leagues of Reservists ', pledged to support the King, who openly placed himself at their head and appeared in the political arena as leader of the anti-Venizelist Party. The Liberal Party, however, in spite of actual threats to the life of M. Venizelos,

The approach of the elections.
actively pursued its campaign and with such success that it seemed likely to obtain a substantial majority at the coming elections. But, before these could take place, the Bulgarian invasion of Eastern Macedonia entirely changed the situation and made it clear that the Liberal Party could no longer co-operate in the Government of the country and that revolution was the only alternative. But we are anticipating events and must return for a moment to the military situation in Macedonia after the betrayal of the Rupel Fort.

The Allied Army in the Balkans, already reinforced by the arrival of the Serbians, was strengthened in July by a Russian

The Allied Army in Macedonia moves forward.
and in August by an Italian contingent. It was determined, therefore, to move up country and occupy a wider front in closer touch with the enemy, whose line roughly followed the Greco-Serbian and part of the Greco-Bulgarian frontiers. The sector

assigned to the British Army extended from a point south-west of Lake Doiran to Lake Butkovo in the Struma Plain and thence to the mouth of the Struma River. The French occupied the centre of the line from Lake Doiran to a point west of the Vardar River with the Serbians on their left.

Meanwhile political events, and in particular the approaching abandonment of her neutrality by Rumania, demanded operations on a wider scale, and on 10th August an Allied offensive was opened in the region of Doiran which met with some success. But on 17th August the situation suddenly changed. The enemy, persuaded that the arrival of Allied reinforcements meant that the Macedonian campaign was beginning in earnest, themselves attacked all along the front. Their object was partly to dissuade Rumania from joining the Entente and partly to induce the Allies to send more troops to the Balkans and so relieve the pressure elsewhere, particularly in view of the offensive on the Somme. The attacks on the Doiran-Vardar line met with little success, the object being to hold the Allied troops rather than attempt to break through. More result was to be hoped for on the flanks of the Allied line, where it adjoined the areas nominally held by the Greeks, who could be counted on to offer no serious resistance. On the west the First Bulgarian Army pressed forward and occupied Florina, a small Greek town some seventeen miles south of Monastir. On the other flank, east of the Struma, units of the Second Bulgarian Army crossed the River Nestos and invaded the extreme corner of Eastern Macedonia, and at the same time poured down the Rupel Pass into the Struma Plain and advanced from Demir-Hissar toward Serres. This district being occupied by considerable Greek forces, the French and British forces east of the Struma were withdrawn to the west of that river and the task of defending Greek soil was left to the Greeks.

Military operations in the summer of 1916.

The Bulgarian Army overruns Eastern Macedonia.

If the Athens Government did not actually invite the hereditary enemies of Greece to invade Greek Macedonia, their guilty complicity is proved by the fact that, when they surrendered the Rupel Fort, they made no stipulation that Eastern Macedonia should not be invaded. It was only after the invasion had begun and atrocities were being committed against the helpless inhabitants that the Government was forced by public opinion to make a protest to Berlin, whence came the assurance—which was promptly proved by events to be worthless—that Serres, Drama, and Cavalla would not be occupied.

In their advance through the Struma Plain the Bulgarians met with unexpected resistance from the Greek Sixth Division, *The gallantry of the Greek 6th Division.* which was temporarily under the command of Colonel Christodoulou, whose personal bravery had made him one of the heroes of the Balkan Wars. After inflicting heavy casualties on the enemy, he managed to extricate his force and to reach Salonica, where his men afterwards formed the nucleus of the famous Serres Division of the National Army.

On the other hand, Colonel Hadjopoulos, Officer Commanding the Fourth Greek Army Corps, proved himself a willing *The Germans intern the Greek 4th Corps.* tool of the Athens Government by surrendering with 8000 men without striking a blow. When this force was sent to Germany and interned in Silesia, the Greek Government acquiesced almost without protest in this deliberate insult to Greece. The capture of Cavalla involved the loss of a large quantity of military stores as well as of immense quantities of tobacco, which had not been removed in consequence of assurances that the invaders would respect private Greek property. The whole of Eastern Macedonia was abandoned to the invaders, who set up a reign of terror, reducing the inhabitants by systematic starvation, deporting able-bodied citizens to work in Bulgarian mines, and denuding the whole country of agricultural produce and animals.

The sacrifice of a rich province which had been won by the sacrifice of so much Greek blood only three years before produced a most painful impression in Athens. *Protest of the Liberal Party at Athens.* On 27th August a mass meeting of Liberals was held and marched through the principal streets to M. Venizelos' house. The Liberal leader, amid demonstrations of enthusiasm and devotion, addressed the people from a balcony. He pointed out the deplorable result of the pro-German policy and contrasted it with what might have happened if a different course had been taken. Greece, he said, had fallen from the height to which she had ascended, and, instead of being respected or feared, was pitied by her friends and despised and insulted by her enemies. Addressing the King, he begged him to give up the rôle of party-leader to which intriguers sought to degrade him and take counsel how he might revive the temper of the people which had been depressed by the long mobilization, by barrack-room election-eering, and by the poison of foreign propaganda, so that Greece might again have an army and be in a position to defend her vital interests in co-operation with powerful Allies, who were her traditional defenders and benefactors. ' The Liberal Party ', he concluded, ' is no enemy of the Crown, the Dynasty, or Your Person ; it is the respectful guardian of our free Con-stitution ; only those who are exploiting the Crown, and who are, in fact, your worst enemies, can seek to persuade you otherwise.' A deputation was chosen to wait upon the King, who refused to grant an audience ; moreover, on the plea that he was ill, he delayed the signature of a decree dissolving the Chamber. However, alarmed by the violence of popular feeling, he authorized M. Zaïmis to inform M. Venizelos that he had decided to abandon neutrality and to authorize negotiations with the Entente. Soon afterwards, however, he decided that the popular excitement had evaporated and did nothing, except that, as a sop to the Entente, General Dousmanis was dismissed from his post as Chief of the General Staff.

On 28th August Rumania abandoned her neutrality in favour of the Entente ; but, although it had always been under-

Rumania joins the Entente. stood that, if Rumania decided to enter the war, Greece would do likewise, the Rumanian declaration made no difference to the attitude of Greece, whose Government had determined not to enter the war against Germany on any terms whatever.

During the King's illness German propaganda became so rampant in Athens and so many hostile acts were committed

The Allied Fleet sails to Salamis. against the Allies, that, early in September, a strong Allied fleet under Admiral du Fournet was sent to Salamis, and the French and British Ministers demanded the control of postal and telegraphic com-munications and the expulsion of enemy agents and spies. Though these concessions were granted, disorders, due chiefly to the Reservist Leagues, tended to increase and culminated in hostile demonstrations against the French Legation, for which an apology had to be made.

Meanwhile in the freer air of Salonica the patriotic impulse of those who could no longer tolerate the humiliating position of Greece led to the somewhat premature formation of a League of National Defence, which by a curious coincidence met in the building which had been the headquarters of the Young Turk Movement some nine years before.

The beginnings of the National Movement at Salonica.

On 30th August a proclamation was issued at Salonica calling on the citizens to cease to obey those who had betrayed the national honour. A large proportion of the Greek garrison proceeded to the French G.H.Q. and offered their services to the Allies. Those who refused to join the movement were dispatched to Athens, where they were solemnly received by the King, who complimented them on their loyalty in fulsome terms. ' With such an army,' he said, ' and at the head of men like you, possessing your moral, your sentiments, and your faith, I am ready to face no matter what enemy.' These words were probably inspired by a telegram which King Constantine is known to have received about this time from his Imperial brother-in-law, assuring him that within a month he would have conquered Rumania and driven General Sarrail's army into the sea.

Be this as it may, the King's return to the old policy of neutrality was too much for M. Zaïmis, who resigned the premiership on 11th September and was succeeded by M. Kalogeropoulos, a prominent Germanophil, who got together a ministry of such notorious partisans that the Ministers of the Entente refused to carry out the usual diplomatic formality of visiting the new Premier.

M. Zaïmis resigns the Premiership.

On 20th September the King, in a speech delivered at the ceremony of swearing in the new conscripts, insisted on the unquestioning devotion which the Army owed to the will of the King. On 22nd September the Prime Minister declared that the Government intended to institute proceedings against all officers and men who joined the revolutionary movement.

The position in which M. Venizelos found himself was an exceedingly difficult one. On the one hand, he could argue *The difficult* that he had done all that was humanly possible *position of* to save the State without violating the law of *M. Venizelos.* the land ; on the other hand, he could not but realize that, since he had a powerful following in the nation which looked to him for guidance, his acquiescence in a thoroughly unsatisfactory state of affairs might be interpreted as implying that the situation was beyond all remedy. He decided, therefore, that it was his duty again, as in former days in Crete, to become a rebel and, by setting up a rival Government, to try, if it were not too late, to save Greece from the fate which was threatening her, knowing that in doing so he was interpreting the desires of the soundest elements in the nation. The islands, including his own motherland, Crete, were ready for revolution ; at Salonica, a detachment of the National Army had already left for the front to fight by the side of the Allies.

Accordingly early in the morning of 25th September, M. Venizelos embarked at Phaleron for Crete, accompanied by *M. Venizelos* Admiral Koundouriotis, the Commander-in-*embarks for* Chief of the Greek Navy, and a large following *Crete.* of friends and supporters. Reaching Canea, he was received with every demonstration of devotion and inaugurated the National Movement by a proclamation calling on the Greek people to return to the policy, *The Revolution* which the national conscience demanded, of *proclaimed at* co-operation with the Protecting Powers and *Canea.* Serbia and of fighting to free Greek territory from the invader—a policy which would at the same time help to deliver Europe from German hegemony and the Balkans from Bulgarian pretensions to supremacy. 'Since the Government', said M. Venizelos, 'has betrayed its obligations, it is incumbent on the nation to attempt the task. We invoke the support of every Greek citizen who feels that any further toleration of the disasters and humiliations, which the policy hitherto followed has caused, would be equivalent to the death of the nation.' The movement met with immediate success, and all the islands through which M. Venizelos made a triumphal tour adhered to it and deposed the Royalist authorities, establishing Venizelists in their place. On 9th October M.

The Provisional Government is set up at Salonica.

Venizelos, amid scenes of great enthusiasm, landed at Salonica, which became the seat of the Provisional Government. A Triumvirate was appointed, consisting of M. Venizelos, Admiral Koundouriotis, and General Danglis, with a Cabinet composed of prominent Venizelists of tried administrative or commercial experience, such as M. Nicholas Politis, formerly Director of the Ministry of Foreign Affairs at Athens, who became Foreign Secretary, and M. Embeirikos, the well-known shipowner, who received the portfolio of supplies. Adherents to the national cause arrived in increasing numbers from old Greece, including numerous officers and Government functionaries, whose co-operation was invaluable in the organization of the army and civil administration.

Thus was launched a movement which was destined to deliver Greece from absolutism and tyranny, to recreate the National Army, and to enable her to range herself by the side of her natural allies and take a glorious part in vindicating the cause of freedom.

CHAPTER XIII

THE EVENTS OF 1ST AND 2ND DECEMBER 1916 IN ATHENS

BEFORE continuing the story of political events at Athens, it is necessary briefly to review the military position on the Balkan front in the latter part of 1916. The Rumanian campaign having begun, General Sarrail had before him the double task of keeping the Bulgarians as busy as possible, so that they should not be able to attack Rumania, and of trying himself to achieve some success to justify the presence of the Allied Army in Macedonia. As the ground was not promising for an advance up the Struma or the Vardar Valley, the most desirable objective which offered a good prospect of success was Monastir, the capture of which from the Serbians had fulfilled one of the chief objects of Bulgaria's entry into the war, while its recapture would constitute a small instalment of the obligation which the Allies owed to Serbia.

The military situation in the autumn of 1916.

While the British were active on the front from the Vardar to the mouth of the Struma, a force consisting of the French, the Serbians, and the Russians began, on 7th September, to attack on the western portion of the front. The Serbians, starting from the line Ostrovo–Vodena, on 20th September, stormed and captured the formidable summit of Mount Kajmakchalan, ten miles north of Ostrovo.[1] Farther west the French and Russians retook Florina and thus held the southern approach to the Plain of Monastir. Crossing the River Tcherna on 5th October, the Serbians gradually forced back the enemy northward through the Tcherna Loop. Then, while the French and Russians broke through the Kenali lines and forced the enemy back to their last line of defence within four miles of Monastir, the Serbians worked their way round to the north-east of the city and were threatening their line of retreat on the road from Monastir to Prilep. The Germans

The capture of Monastir.

[1] For these operations see map on p. 133.

and Bulgarians had thus no alternative but to evacuate Monastir, which was entered on 19th November by French cavalry, closely followed by the Serbians, who thus reoccupied the town exactly four years after they captured it from the Turks in the Balkan Wars. This success restored a corner of Serbian territory to the much-tried Serbian Army and proved that it was still capable of maintaining and even enhancing its reputation as a fighting force.

Meanwhile the position of M. Venizelos after the establishment of the Provisional Government at Salonica was still an

Difficult position of M. Venizelos. extremely difficult one. He had definitely broken with the Athens Government and thrown in his lot with the Allies ; but, while they tolerated his presence at Salonica, they found themselves unable to define exactly the attitude which they intended to adopt towards him. In proclaiming the National Movement in Crete, M. Venizelos had stated clearly that, if the Crown would subordinate itself to the national will, the Liberal Party was willing to co-operate. When, however, the King showed no disposition to change his attitude, the natural course for M. Venizelos to take would have been to throw off his allegiance and give the revolution a definitely anti-dynastic character

The attitude of the Allies. which would have greatly strengthened his hand. The Allied Powers, however, were unwilling to allow this and made it a condition of any form of recognition of the Provisional Government that it should abstain from any declaration of opposition to the King. Moreover, at the Allied Conference held at Boulogne on 30th October, it was decided not to recognize the Provisional Government officially and not to accredit to it any diplomatic representatives. France and Great Britain, nevertheless, undertook to bear the expense of the Nationalist Army which was being formed and granted a loan. While the impetus of the National Movement was undoubtedly lessened by the refusal of recognition, it must be admitted that the Entente Powers were in a difficult position. The acknowledgement of the Provisional Government as a lawful authority and the severance of relations with Athens might have precipitated civil war in Greece, which would probably have involved the dispatch of Allied troops into Old Greece and so weakened the hand of the

Allies on the Macedonian front. So the Allies played the usual game of waiting to see what would happen. It is possible that, if Great Britain and France had been acting alone, events would have taken a different turn ; but they had to co-operate with Italy and Russia. Italy, with her own imperialistic aims in the Balkans and Asia Minor, refused to support M. Venizelos, the success of whose policy of a Greater Greece might injure her own pretensions ; while Russia was naturally opposed to the creation of any anti-monarchial precedents and to the overthrow of a dynasty so closely allied to the House of Romanoff.

Attitude of Italy and Russia.

M. Venizelos, with characteristic patience, accepted the position and worked quietly for the consolidation of his Government and the formation of an army which might in due time give valuable assistance to the Allies. He probably realized that the Athens Government would, sooner or later, proceed to acts which would exhaust the patience even of the Allied Powers.

At Athens M. Kalogeropoulos finally abandoned the attempt to obtain the recognition of his Government by the Allied representatives and resigned, being succeeded on 10th October by M. Lambros. A less suitable choice could hardly have been possible. M. Lambros was a university professor who had achieved a high repute as a palæographer, but he had never been a deputy and had had no experience of public affairs.[1] The other portfolios were distributed among a miscellaneous collection of civil servants and professors whose only recommendation for office was their willingness to accept it.

M. Lambros becomes Premier.

On 10th October, in view of the facts that troops and artillery were being sent to Thessaly and new recruits being called to the colours and that the Greek Navy was being ' purged ' of any officers who were suspected of Venizelist leanings, Admiral du Fournet commanding the Allied fleet off Salamis presented a note to the Greek Government demanding the control of the Larissa railway, the surrender of certain vessels of war, and the disarmament of the land-batteries at Salamis and the

The Allied note of 10th Oct. 1916.

---

[1] He is said once to have remarked that, if he had not been a professor, he would like to have been a monk at Mt. Athos ; he would certainly have been better suited for monastic life than for the post of Prime Minister.

Peiræus. On 17th October a further demand was made that civilians should be forbidden to carry arms. All these conditions were accepted, but it afterwards became known that about this time secret orders were issued to provide the reservists in the provinces with arms and that troops and material were being collected in Thessaly and Epirus. Moreover, King Constantine, addressing the crews of the surrendered vessels, used language which could only be interpreted as threatening the Allies. His defiance was no doubt due to assurances which he had received from Germany, which seemed to him all the more invincible now that the Central Powers had begun to overrun Rumania.

The note is accepted but the conditions not carried out.

On 21st October a fresh turn was given to events by the visit to Athens on a special mission of M. Benazet, a French deputy, who obtained an audience of the King. It appears that King Constantine was able to persuade his visitor of his friendly attitude towards the Allies, and that M. Benazet demanded that he should give some solid proof of his benevolent neutrality. The King then himself suggested the surrender of a large quantity of guns and other equipment, only stipulating that the Entente press should not make capital out of his concessions. This seemed reasonable, and M. Benazet left the Royal presence under the impression that he had arranged for the solution of a difficult situation. A few days later Admiral du Fournet, persuaded that the King genuinely wished to come to a satisfactory arrangement, ordered the withdrawal of two of the French companies which had been stationed at the Zappeion, near the Royal Palace.

M. Benazet at Athens.

King Constantine suggests the surrender of material of war.

Early in November, owing to a slight collision at Ekaterini in Southern Macedonia between Royalist troops and those of the Provisional Government, the Allied authorities established a neutral zone between the territories of the Athens and the Salonica Governments. This was in effect a concession to Athens, since it prevented the extension of the National Movement to Epirus and Thessaly, where M. Venizelos had many adherents. Further, on 13th November, the Entente allowed without protest the

Establishment of the Neutral Zone.

9

summoning of the Chamber on the dissolution of which they had insisted in vain in the previous June.

On 17th November the Allied authorities showed further complaisance in a note sent on by the Admiral demanding the *Allied Note of 17th November.* surrender of a smaller quantity of arms than the King had suggested, namely, 18 field batteries, 16 mountain batteries, and a number of machine-guns and rifles. About the same time the departure of the personnel of the enemy Legations at Athens was demanded and effected without incident.

During the last days of November, the effort was redoubled to stir up public opinion against the Allies. Systematic pro-*Anti-Entente propaganda.* paganda was carried out among the troops, to whom the demand for the cession of military material was represented as an insult to the Greek Army. Every reservist was warned to be ready for any emergency which might presently arise. Open threats and even acts of violence were used against the supporters of M. Venizelos. Excitement in Athens was stimulated to fever-heat by fabricated news of outbreaks in the provinces and massacres of Royalists in Southern Macedonia ; the Government actually decreed a solemn memorial service for the supposed victims. The adherents of the Government were worked up to *The Government refuses to surrender war material.* such a pitch of excitement that they were ready to go to all lengths to prevent any con-cessions to the Allies. On the 27th the Govern-ment added fuel to the fire by issuing a protest against the Allied control and blockade and against the expulsion of the enemy diplomats, and by refusing point-blank to surrender any arms.

The French Admiral, however, still believed that an amicable settlement was possible, and on 29th November returned from *Admiral du Fournet prepares to land a force.* an interview with the King convinced that the arms would be surrendered if the Allies made such a manifestation of force as would save the King's face and make it appear that the Government, in giving way, was yielding to *force majeure*. It is even categorically stated that an assurance was given that the troops who were to land to take over the arms would meet with no opposition. The landing force, which included British as well as French units without artillery, was to set out on 1st December to march to certain fixed points to take over the material, unprepared for resistance which they did not expect and unsuspicious of the trap which was being set for them. They were destined to be speedily disillusioned.

On 29th November the Greek Government issued a decree permitting voluntary enlistments, which added many thousands

The Greek Government orders resistance.

to the garrison of the city, and secret orders were given to the troops to take up positions in front of the city and offer resistance to any attempt on the part of the Allies to carry out the purpose for which they were landing. Important buildings were occupied by troops and trenches prepared.

The Allied force of 2000 men disembarked without incident, but came into collision with Greek troops as soon as it advanced

The landing-party is treacherously attacked.

towards the city. Attacks were simultaneously made upon the detachments left behind at the Zappeion and on the headquarters of the Allied police. As the main Greek position was just in front of the Acropolis, it would have been impossible for the guns of the fleet to support the landing-force, even if any proper *liaison* between the troops and the navy had been arranged, which apparently had not been done. It is easy to picture the outcry which would have been raised if one stone of the Acropolis had been injured. The landing-force advanced in the face of opposition, with the result that six Allied officers and 126 men were killed and some 250 wounded; but, although they were unprepared for hostilities, they inflicted over 200 casualties upon the Greeks. The fighting continued until communication was established with the fleet and some shells were fired which fell not far from the Royal Palace.

On orders being given to cease fire, the French Admiral, who was at the Zappeion, had no alternative but to consent to

Withdrawal of the Allied detachments.

the opening of negotiations between the Allied naval and diplomatic authorities and the Greek Government. Eventually the humiliating compromise was arranged that the Greeks should hand over only six batteries and that the Allies should make no further demands for material. The survivors of the landing-force accompanied by the Control Officers and the detachments from Athens were escorted back to the quays by Greek troops, leaving behind their dead unburied and their wounded untended. It is difficult to find any excuse for Admiral du Fournet's failure to estimate the position of affairs in Athens and make preparations, if he was determined on a display of force, for any emergencies which might conceivably arise.

Not only were the Allies grievously humiliated but Athens was immediately delivered up to a reign of terror. The *Attack on the* houses of all those who were known to entertain *Venizelists in* Venizelist opinions had been marked down *Athens.* beforehand, and on the 2nd of December there began a systematic hunting down of all those Venizelists who had not already fled. The offices of the Liberal papers were wrecked and their machinery destroyed. Many Venizelists were killed in cold blood and others thrown without trial into prison. The details of these atrocities had obviously been arranged beforehand, and it was announced by way of justification that an anti-Royalist plot had been discovered. The Royalist press burst into hymns of triumph for the victory of the Greek Army over its oppressors and the delivery of Greece from the yoke of foreign tyranny. The Minister for War, voicing the sentiments of the King, in an order of the day congratulated the troops on their exemplary conduct and self-sacrifice, which had saved Greece from enemies who hoped to overthrow the dynasty. 'Our enemies', he added, 'must realize that such troops are invincible.' The Government decreed a solemn Te Deum in honour of the victory of the Greek arms and a service of *anathema* against M. Venizelos.

It is interesting to read Queen Sophia's account of these *The Queen's* days in a telegram to the Kaiser, afterwards *telegram to the* discovered and deciphered : *Kaiser.* 'By a miracle we are safe after a bombardment of the Palace for three hours by the French fleet, which fired without warning. The shells burst quite near, and we took refuge in the cellars. Violent encounters took place the following day in the streets. The revolutionaries fired from the houses. The army and the people fought magnificently and remained faithful. The tables are now turned. It was a great victory over the four Great Powers, whose troops fled before the Greeks and afterwards withdrew under the escort of Greek troops. . . . The panic has now subsided. . . . What will be the demands of the Entente ? We are prepared for anything. . . . Please let me know when the Macedonian Army will be sufficiently enforced to begin a definite offensive.'

The effect produced by the events at Athens in the countries of the Entente was one of indignation against the muddling and

Effect of the events of 1st to 2nd Dec. in the Entente countries.

incapacity which had made such a state of affairs possible, and encouragement was given to the opinion which regarded any form of intervention in the Balkans as a useless dissipation of energy, since it had brought no military advantage and was merely lowering the prestige of the Entente in the Near East. At Salonica the events of 1st and 2nd December

The Revolution assumes an anti-dynastic character.

led to a substantial change in the direction of the Revolution. It was no longer possible to recognize a king who had aspired to become a party leader. A definitely anti-dynastic character was therefore given to the Revolution by the official declaration of the Provisional Government that every bond with the King of the Hellenes was henceforward severed. Before the end of December the British and French Governments, by the appointments of Lord Granville and M. de Billy as their diplomatic representatives at Salonica, had given a definitely official recognition to the Government of M. Venizelos.

CHAPTER XIV

GREECE IN DISUNION

IN spite of his ' victory ' over the Entente, the position of King
Constantine was a difficult one. He must have been aware that

*The position of
King Constantine
after the events of
1st and 2nd Dec.*

the events of 1st and 2nd December would
bring their own retribution and that there was
a limit to the patience even of the Allied Powers.
His sole hope of salvation was to play for time
and try to keep his throne until the Central
Powers could begin the hoped-for offensive on the Macedonian
front which was to drive General Sarrail and his army into
the sea.

The compromise between the French Admiral and the
Greek Government had been made without consultation with

*Want of agree-
ment among the
Allies.*

the Entente Governments and obviously did
not bind them. The French Government
immediately made a proposal to the other
Allies, the nature of which has not been
disclosed, but which apparently failed to obtain the consent of
all of them. Its suggestions were probably regarded as too
radical by Italy and Russia. By 7th December, however,

*The blockade of
Old Greece.*

sufficient agreement had been reached to enable
a blockade of Old Greece to be declared.
Meanwhile the persecution of Venizelists
continued, and the pro-German press did not cease to
celebrate the ' victory ' of the Greek Government and to
vilify Great Britain and France. On 14th December a

*Entente Note of
14th Dec.*

new Note was delivered to the Athens
Government demanding reparation for the
outrages of 1st and 2nd December and the
transfer of the Greek Army under Allied control to the
Peloponnese. The Government promised to carry out these
demands but asked that the decision to blockade Greece should
be reconsidered, at the same time assuring the Allies of the sincere

desire of the Greek Government and people for the restoration
of the traditional friendship and good relations between Greece
and the Protecting Powers.

As no real attempt was being made to comply with the
requirements of the Allies, a further Note was delivered on
Entente Note of 31st Dec. 31st December demanding the reduction of the
Greek Army to the bare number necessary for
the maintenance of public order, the transfer of
all war-material to the Peloponnese, the prohibition of meetings
of ' Reservists ', the re-establishment of Allied controls, the
release of political prisoners and the indemnification of the
victims of the outrages, the permission for the Allies to use Itea
on the Corinthian Gulf as a base and the Larissa-Salonica railway
for the conveyance of troops, and, lastly, the holding of a public
ceremony at which the Allied flags should be saluted in apology
for the incidents of 1st and 2nd December. These measures, if they
had been carried out in their entirety, would have done much to
remedy a difficult situation ; but the Allies at the same time
made a concession to the King which encouraged him to believe
that they would never take extreme measures against him and
his Government. They undertook not to permit the armed forces
of the Provisional Government at Salonica to profit by the withdrawal of troops from Epirus and Thessaly and cross the Neutral
Zone. This showed that they could not make up their mind
even yet definitely to throw Constantine over and give M.
Venizelos their whole-hearted support.

On 8th January 1917 a Conference of the Allies at Rome
discussed the Greek Question and reaffirmed the Note of 31st
Conference at Rome, 8th Jan. 1917. December, fixing a time limit of fifteen days
for its execution. They again spoilt the effect
of any pretence of severity by reiterating their
intention not to allow any extension of the
sphere of the Provisional Government. On 16th January the
Greek Government accepted the conditions of the Note and
formally apologized for the ' regrettable incidents ' of 1st and
2nd December.

On 29th January 1917 a solemn parade was held, at which
detachments of the Greek Navy and Army, which included
Prince Andrew, the King's brother, saluted the colours of the
Allies.

The Athens Government had thus nominally given in to the demands of the Allies ; but actually the position was little changed. Some show was made of transferring troops and material to the Peloponnese, but large quantities of arms were being secreted instead of transferred, and the soldiers soon began to return from the Peloponnese, either one by one as civilians, or, still in uniform, on the pretence of leave. The movements of the ' Reservists ' were less conspicuous in Athens, but their activities had been merely transferred to the provinces. The anti-Venizelist outrages abated somewhat, chiefly from lack of victims. The Government employed every possible subterfuge to prevent the meeting of the Mixed Tribunal which was to deal with the indemnification of persecuted Venizelists, many of whom remained in prison. The Press continued to use un-measured language against the Allies, in particular alleging that the blockade, which was already entailing some hardship, was being continued in spite of the fact that the conditions imposed had been carried out by Greece. Meanwhile the Allied Ministers, who had taken refuge on men-of-war, were still unable to return to the Legations in Athens.

Evasion of the terms of the Entente Note.

Though the King was loud in his protestations that his sole object was to observe an attitude of strict neutrality, intrigues against the Allies were as active as ever ; in particular, irregular bands were formed in Epirus and Thessaly to harass the rear of the Allied Army in Macedonia. The extent of intrigues with Germany at this period was not fully recognized at the time, but have been made clear by subsequent revelations. Whether the Kaiser and the German Higher Command ever really intended to make an attempt to effect a junction between the German and Bulgarian forces and the Greek Army is doubt-ful ; but it appears certain that the King at one time believed in his brother-in-law's promises. The telegraphic correspondence in code between the Greek Court and Berlin at the end of 1916 and the beginning of 1917 has been published and gives a vivid picture of the hopes and fears and final disillusionment of the King and his Consort.

Royalist intrigues with Germany.

Meanwhile the patience of the public in the Entente countries was becoming exhausted, and protests against the policy of inactivity in Greece began to find voice in the British and

Effect of political changes in the Entente countries. French press. In March 1917 two events occurred which affected the attitude of the Entente towards the Greek problem—the fall of the Briand cabinet, which had supported King Constantine, and the Russian Revolution involving the deposition of Nicholas II, who, closely related to the Greek Royal house, had been a powerful prop of the Royalist Party in Greece. The attitude of Italy was also modified after the Conference of St. Jean de Maurienne on 29th April, which gave Italy a wider liberty of action on the Adriatic sea-board and made her more ready to consent to drastic measures in Greece.

During the spring of 1917 the National Movement at Salonica, in spite of obstacles placed in the way of its expansion

Growth of the National Movement at Salonica. by the Allies, continued to grow, Corfu, Cephalonia, Zante, Cythera, and Sciathos all declaring for M. Venizelos. Further, almost all the diplomatic and consular representatives of Greece in foreign countries proclaimed their adherence to the Provisional Government. The Hellenic communities, too, outside Greece had almost without exception supported M. Venizelos from the first, and their representatives, meeting in a Congress at Paris on 1st May, officially repudiated their allegiance to King Constantine. The National Army at Salonica was continually strengthened by the arrival of officers and men from the Islands, from Old Greece and from foreign countries, until by the end of May 60,000 men had been enrolled to fight with the Allies in Macedonia. Even in Athens the Liberal Party was beginning to raise its head, and by the end of March two of their daily papers had begun to appear again, to be followed by two more in April.

On 6th May a great demonstration was held at the White Tower in Salonica, at which resolutions were passed repudiating King Constantine and his dynasty and calling on the Allied Powers to cease to recognize the Athens Government.

In the second half of April considerable anxiety began to be displayed in the Royalist press at Athens, especially when it became clear that the result of the Conference of St. Jean de Maurienne would be a severer attitude towards Greece. The Lambros Government had now had three full months to carry out the terms of the Allied Note but had resorted to so many

*Growing appre-
hension in
Athens.*

evasions that the Entente had been unable to put an end to the blockade. On 22nd April M. Lambros resigned, and the King accepted his resignation, hoping by a change of Ministers to avert or postpone the crisis which was threatening. At the end of April a rumour was spread abroad that King Constantine intended to abdicate in favour of the Crown Prince, but the suggestion recommended itself neither to the Allied Powers nor to the Liberal Party.

After much hesitation, the inevitable M. Zaïmis was induced again to form a Cabinet, the composition of which was announced

*M. Zaïmis be-
comes Premier.*

on 3rd May. He himself assumed the portfolio of Foreign Affairs. His return to power failed to excite any enthusiasm in Great Britain and France, where the Press continued to attack the régime and demanded that definite measures should be taken. M. Zaïmis' statement on assuming office that he took full liberty of action and responsibility for his policy was widely commented on as a confession that the Lambros Cabinet had not enjoyed freedom of action and was merely a tool in the hands of the pro-German

*Attempts of
M. Zaïmis to
improve the
situation.*

clique. He publicly announced that the task before his Government was to overcome the difficulties existing between Greece and the Entente and that he and his colleagues undertook, as successors to the Lambros Government, to fulfil the obligations imposed by the Allied Note. The effect of this declaration was somewhat marred by the discovery a few days later of large quantities of hidden arms. However, a decree was published removing from the Army several officers who had made themselves conspicuous for their violent pro-German opinions ; and the new Minister of War issued an order to the troops urging them to devote themselves to their military duties and to leave politics alone. At the same time General Moskopoulos, who had gained credit for his correct attitude towards the Allies as Commander of the Salonica Army Corps in 1915 and who was now Chief of the General Staff, was commissioned to carry out an inquiry into the alleged presence of irregular bands on the Neutral Zone, the Government undertaking to punish severely any persons involved in such activities. M. Zaïmis, in reply to a protest from the Allied Ministers, also promised to take stern measures against any newspapers which used insulting language towards the Allies.

By the beginning of June, in spite of the assurances of the Press that the position was improving and that the Government *M. Zaïmis meets* was making every effort to establish better *with no success.* relations with the Entente, M. Zaïmis after a month of office had failed to bring about any improvement in the situation. The Entente Powers maintained an attitude of reserve and instructed their representatives at Athens to avoid the discussion of any questions of policy with the Government. The position of affairs was not improved by the attempted murder of two British naval officers at Phaleron. The truth seems to be that there were secret forces at work which were too strong for M. Zaïmis and which thwarted his attempts to satisfy the Allies. The activities of the pro-German clique were in fact so notorious as to excite the indignation even of a section of the Royalist press, particularly the *Athenai*, which published on 2nd June an article accusing M. Gounaris of attempting to force a rupture of diplomatic relations between Greece and the Allies. Meanwhile the Press in the Entente countries continued to urge that strong measures should be taken in Greece and, in particular, that the Thessalian crops should be seized to feed the Allied Army ; in its desire to conciliate the Entente, *The Entente* the Government let it be known that Greece *decides to take* was willing to concede half the crop to the *action.* Allies. But by this time decisions had already been taken by the British and French Governments which were destined at last to bring about a radical solution of the Greek question.

CHAPTER XV

THE TRIUMPH OF M. VENIZELOS AND THE ALLIED VICTORY IN MACEDONIA

ON 6th June 1917 it was noticed that a powerful Allied fleet had arrived and was anchored off Keratsini. On board one of

The arrival of M. Jonnart.

the vessels was M. Charles Jonnart, formerly Governor-General of Algeria, who had arrived as High Commissioner of the Protecting Powers and who immediately left for Salonica to confer with M. Venizelos and General Sarrail.

On 10th June M. Jonnart returned to Athens and, at an interview with M. Zaïmis, announced that the Protecting Powers

The deposition of King Constantine.

demanded the abdication of King Constantine, on the ground that he had violated his oath to rule as a constitutional monarch. The King accepted the situation, and on the next day the High Commissioner was informed that, ' solicitous as ever of the interests of Greece ', King Constantine had decided to quit the country, accompanied by the Crown Prince, and had designated Prince Alexander as his successor. The King then withdrew to his country house at Tatoi. It is noteworthy that he did not officially abdicate, no doubt in the hope that in event of a German victory, for which he still hoped, he would return in triumph to Athens.

Prince Alexander, Constantine's second son, who thus ascended the throne, was in his twenty-fourth year. He held

The Accession of King Alexander.

a commission as Captain of Artillery, and little was known of him outside Court and military circles. He immediately took the customary oath in the presence of the Ministers and the members of the Holy Synod. His first public utterance, in which, after expressing his grief at his separation from his beloved father, he stated his determination to ' follow the lines of his brilliant reign ' created a somewhat unfavourable impression, until it was explained that these words referred to the successes of the Balkan Wars rather than to the recent activities of King Constantine. A few days later the King addressed a letter to M. Zaïmis stating that he was watching with interest the steps which were being taken to re-unite Greece, that it was his intention faithfully to observe the Constitution, and that he was persuaded of the benevolent intentions of the Entente.

On 13th June Constantine quitted Greek soil without returning to Athens, embarking on the Royal Yacht on the east coast of Attica. He is said to have refused to travel on an Allied warship, remarking, ' I am not King Otho'. According to an account in the paper *Nea Imera*, at the moment of the departure of the yacht an eagle—we are not told whether it was of the Byzantine or Prussian variety—appeared on the horizon and flew towards the vessel, which it accompanied on its journey ! Convoyed by an Allied destroyer the yacht set sail for Italy by way of the Corinth Canal, and Constantine betook himself to Switzerland.

The departure of King Constantine.

On 16th June M. Jonnart issued a proclamation to the Greek people, in which he stated that the Protecting Powers would labour for the independence, the greatness, and the prosperity of Greece and her deliverance from her hereditary enemies ; they would re-establish Constitutional Government and the unity of the nation. At the same time an Allied force crossed the Neutral Zone and occupied Thessaly, thus securing the Thessalian crops and putting an end to the activities of the Royalist *comitadjis*.[1]

Proclamation of M. Jonnart.

In Athens, though there were rumours of intended action by the ' Reservists ', there was no serious disturbance of the peace, and the general attitude was one of relief at the ending of the blockade. The tame surrender of Constantine could not but discourage his active supporters, who realized that their wisest policy was to make themselves as inconspicuous as possible. In a very short time life at Athens had become normal, but there remained an undercurrent of discontent—which was destined to break out in the

The attitude of the Greek people.

[1] The comment of the German wireless is worth quoting : ' For the first time the Entente has carried through with complete success a joint military action. This success has been won at the expense of an army which had previously been disarmed and a people who had been starved.'

years to come—chiefly among the dispossessed civil servants and cashiered officers of the old régime, who refused to accept the new order of things, and whose sense of grievance was exploited by propaganda from the exile in Switzerland.

The Allies now turned to M. Venizelos as the only man able to deal with the situation. On 19th June a committee was

The Allies turn to M. Venizelos. formed, consisting of two members each of the Provisional and the Athens Governments to confer with him on the measures to be taken to unite Greece. M. Venizelos made it clear from the first that he would insist on the recall of the Chamber elected in June 1915, which had been unconstitutionally dissolved, and the recognition as valid of the Acts of the Provisional Government. On 25th June M. Zaïmis resigned, and two days later M. Venizelos reached Athens and became Prime Minister.

On 27th June the new ministry, which was substantially the same as the Provisional Government, proceeded to the

The New Cabinet. Palace and were sworn in. On the same day the new Prime Minister was the object of an enthusiastic demonstration by a vast crowd. The next day two Cretan regiments, which had been fighting on the Macedonian front with the Allies, arrived in Athens and halted in front of M. Venizelos' hotel and were addressed by him from the balcony.

The new Cabinet now set itself to reconstruct completely the political life of the country. The chief members of the

The task before the new Government. pro-German clique, Dousmanis, Metaxas, Streit, and others, were already on their way to exile in Corsica ; the ministers who had been their puppets, such as Skouloudis and Lambros, were placed under supervision. The Ministries of War and the Navy took in hand the reorganization of the army and fleet. The Treasury was found to contain only 300,000 drachmas and funds had to be hurriedly fetched from Salonica to carry on the administration.

On 5th July General Sarrail arrived, and the French National

King Alexander takes the oath. Fête was celebrated by a review of detachments by the Allied and National armies. On 4th August the King took the oath before the Chamber. On 8th August the Minister of Finance revealed the fact that the previous Cabinets had received loans from Germany amounting to 120,000,000 drachmas and that the second instalment was paid at the time of the surrender of the Rupel Fort.

Two days later the Chamber met to discuss the reply to the King's speech, and M. Venizelos uttered an eloquent defence of his policy from 1912 to 1917 and a vigorous

M. Venizelos addresses the Chamber.

indictment of his opponents in a speech which lasted, with the interval of an hour, from 5.30 p.m. to 3 a.m. on the following day. He said that the worst fears which he felt when he left office in 1915 had been realized ; Greece's ally Serbia had been overwhelmed, the national economic system of Greece was in ruins, and the army in a state of dissolution, but he was optimistic for the future, since the nation, he was convinced, still possessed sufficient vitality to achieve its own salvation. 'In taking part', he said, ' in the world-wide war at the side of the democratic nations, who have been brought together in a common cause, in a truly Holy Alliance, to combat the claims to the empire of the world made by Germany assisted by our two hereditary enemies, we shall re-establish our honour as a nation. We shall not only effectively defend our national interests at the Peace Conference and secure our national future, but we shall also win a place among the family of free nations which that Congress will organize, and hand down to our children a Greece such as generations past have dreamed of, a Greece such as we ourselves foreshadowed in our recent victories of 1912 and 1913.'

The President of the Chamber then put a resolution which constituted a plenary vote of confidence in the

Vote of confidence in the Government.

Government. Out of the 198 deputies present 188 voted in favour of the resolution, the ten ministers abstaining from voting. Thus the final seal was set on the reunion of Greece.

In November M. Venizelos visited Paris and London, where he received an enthusiastic welcome and was

M. Venizelos in Paris and London.

entertained by the Lord Mayor. He secured the re-provisionment of Greece both in foodstuffs and in equipment and munitions of war for the Greek Army.

From a military point of view the year 1917 was the least fruitful of the three years during which the Allied Army operated in Macedonia. An offensive in April against formidable enemy positions in the Doiran sector, after meeting with initial success, achieved no result.

The military situation in Macedonia in 1917.

In June the Allies, as we have already seen, advanced southwards and occupied Thessaly. A move was also made by the Italians, who had previously established a continuous line from the left of the French at Koritza to the Albanian port of Valona on the Adriatic. On 3rd June Italy proclaimed the independence of Albania under her protectorate, and advancing into Greek Epirus occupied Jannina, on the pretext that the Greeks of that region were hostile to the Entente, and deposed the Greek authorities. This action produced considerable tension between Greece and Italy ; but with the accession of M. Venizelos to power the situation improved, and the Allied Conference held in Paris in July arranged that Italy should evacuate Greek Epirus but continue to occupy Northern Epirus for military reasons.

Italy proclaims the independence of Albania.

Tension between Greece and Italy.

In the autumn of 1918 the long-delayed offensive on the Macedonian Front began under General Franchet d'Espérey, who now commanded the Armée de l'Orient. The critical situation on the Western Front had prevented the dispatch of reinforcements ; in fact, troops had even been withdrawn from Macedonia and sent to France. But Greece was now in a position to supply the necessary effectives. Three divisions, mostly of volunteers, had been formed under the Provisional Government before the reunion of Greece ; by the middle of 1918 ten divisions were ready in Macedonia, amounting to at least 250,000 men with ample reserves.

The Greeks reinforce the Allies.

On 30th May Greek forces had gone into action for the first time and had won a notable success by the capture of Srka di Legen on the Vardar, where they took 1500 prisoners. For the general offensive the Greek Divisions were posted to various points on the front ; one at Florina, one on the River Tcherna, five with the British in the Doiran sector, and the rest holding the line of the Struma.

Greek victory at Srka di Legen.

The offensive opened on 15th September 1918. The spear-head of the attack was formed by the Serbian Army and a

The general offensive on the Macedonian Front.

French Division, who assaulted an almost impregnable position at Dobropolji. The attack met with immediate success and resulted in a complete break-through, and in a few days a lightning advance separated the enemy forces in the Vardar Valley from those in the Monastir area. On

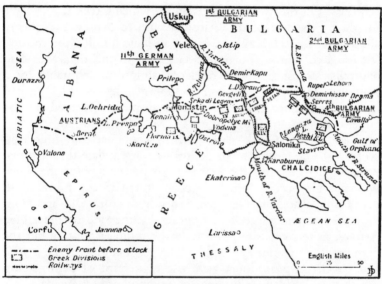

POSITIONS OF THE GREEK DIVISIONS BEFORE THE FINAL
OFFENSIVE ON THE MACEDONIAN FRONT (SEPT. 1918).

18th September the British and Greek divisions began an offensive on the Doiran front and, after stubborn fighting, captured the strongly fortified lines which had defied attack for so long.

On 21st September the French, Greek, and Italian troops in the Monastir region began their advance, and on the following

Allied victory.

day the German and Bulgarian Army was in full retreat and continued to retire until, on 26th September, the enemy asked for a suspension of hostilities, which were brought to an end on 30th September after only a fortnight's fighting.

Thus the first knock-out blow was delivered against the

Central Powers, and the much-maligned Salonica Army—it
had even been described as ' an Anglo-French
The Greek   Internment Camp '—had at last justified its
contribution to   existence and made the first breach in the
the victory.   encircling ring of enemy fronts. It was the
presence of the Greek Army that made this victory possible,
and their fellow-allies were not slow to acknowledge the help
which they had received. General Milne, in an Order of the
Day addressed to the Greek Divisions under his command,
wrote : ' On this the first occasion on which Greek troops have
fought by the side of the British, I wish to express to you my
admiration for the way in which you have fulfilled the mission
entrusted to you. You have attacked with incomparable dash
naturally strong positions rendered almost impregnable by a
stubborn enemy.' The French Commander-in-Chief picked
out for special praise ' the brilliant aptitude displayed by the
Greeks for mountain warfare'. M. Venizelos addressed a
message to the Greek Army which contained the following
words : ' The Government desires to congratulate the National
Army and to express the gratitude of the nation for the work
which it has accomplished. Reconstituted in the midst of so
many difficulties, the National Army both from Old and from
New Greece has succeeded, fighting by the side of the Allied
Armies, in re-establishing not only the military prestige but the
honour of the country as well.' The co-operation of the British
and Greeks in Macedonia gave rise to a spirit of comradeship
which was destined to be renewed on another battlefield.

The military consequences of the victory were decisive.
Turkey was cut off from the Central Powers, and the Austro-
Hungarians, threatened with attack from the
Military conse-   south-east, faced Italy with growing appre-
quences of the   hension on the Piave. Von Hindenburg ad-
victory.   mitted that the collapse in Macedonia was one
of the causes that excluded all hope of forcing the Entente to make
peace. It was not long before an armistice was concluded with
Turkey (30th October) and on the Western Front (11th November). Greek men-of-war and troops took part in the entry of
the Allied fleet and army into Constantinople.

PART III

GREECE FROM 1918 TO 1957

CHAPTER XVI

THE PEACE CONFERENCE (1919–21)

IN January 1919 the Peace Conference opened in Paris. The Greek delegation was headed by M. Venizelos, who soon

M. Venizelos at the Peace Conference.

became a prominent figure and impressed all those whom he met with his statesmanlike qualities and his skill in presenting the case for his country. The claims of Greece were extensive, Thrace, Northern Epirus, Smyrna and the adjoining coast of Asia Minor, and the Dodecanese. But there were claims prior to those of Greece to be considered and the future of Greece remained for the time undecided. Meanwhile Greek troops had taken part in the ill-starred expedition to South Russia against the Bolsheviks, where heavy losses were suffered.

In May 1919, however, the Greek Government was granted permission to occupy Smyrna. Unfortunately disturbances

Greek occupation of Smyrna.

occurred at the landing of the Greek troops, and severe sentences were passed on those who had been responsible, Greeks as well as Turks and Armenians. A Greek administration was before long established under a High Commissioner, and by the end of the year British residents in Smyrna were able to report that the Greek authorities were carrying out their difficult task with strict justice towards the different elements in the population.

Meanwhile divergences had arisen between the British and French about the policy to be pursued regarding Turkey. The

The Treaty of Sèvres.

Greek cause, however, found an ardent supporter in Mr. Lloyd George, and at the Conference at Spa (11th May 1920) Greece was granted a mandate to occupy both Thrace and the north-western area of

Asia Minor as well as the Smyrna district. The successful execution of this mandate by the Greeks created so favourable an impression that, by the Treaty of Sèvres [1] (10th August 1920), the whole of Thrace including Gallipoli, the Ægean Islands already in Greek hands, and the Smyrna district were assigned to Greece. The occupation of Smyrna was, however, limited by the proviso that the sovereignty remained nominally Turkish, but a local assembly was set up, which might apply for the definite incorporation of the district in the Greek kingdom at the end of five years. The Islands of the Dodecanese were assigned to Italy, but a convention, signed at the same time by Italy and Greece, but never put into operation, transferred them to the latter country.

In undertaking the occupation of the Smyrna district M. Venizelos was facing a hazardous enterprise, particularly in view of the growing power of the Nationalist Movement in Turkey under Mustapha Kemal Pasha. But the Greek statesman saw that, if he was to rescue the large Greek population in Asia Minor, now or never was the moment to act before Hellenism in the Turkish Empire was extinguished. If the Smyrna district could be secured by Greece, it would constitute a place of refuge where the Asiatic Greeks might find a home.

Hellenism in Asia Minor.

On 12th August 1920, when M. Venizelos was on the point of leaving Paris for Greece, an attempt was made on his life by two Royalist ex-officers of the Greek Navy. His wounds were not serious and he was able shortly to return to Greece.

Attempted assassination of M. Venizelos.

During his absence all had not been going well with the Government. Absorbed in the task of securing the rights of his country, he had been unable to keep a controlling hand on home affairs. His deputy, M. Repoulis, lacked the necessary firmness and decision, and he was unfortunate in some of his subordinates, who used their authority in an arbitrary manner. The discontented elements in the state profited by the absence of the Prime Minister, and Royalist propaganda was active.

M. Venizelos on his return brought before the Chamber the Treaties with Bulgaria, Turkey, and Italy, and received the

[1] Though this Treaty was signed, it was never ratified by the Allies, and so never became operative.

thanks of the House.   He had indeed deserved well of his
country.   By the decisions of the Peace Con-
M. Venizelos ference Greece had obtained territories which she
returns to Athens. had long coveted.   She had become the predominant Power in the Ægean, and her domains extended
from the Adriatic to the Black Sea.   The ideal of a Great Greece
seemed at last to have become a reality.

At the same meeting of the Chamber it was announced that
a dissolution would take place and elections would be held in
the autumn, and that all restrictions on civil liberty would be
abolished.

On 25th October a new factor was introduced into the
situation by the death of King Alexander, who died of blood-
poisoning as a result of the bite of a pet monkey.
Death of King The difficult question of the succession to the
Alexander. throne was thus raised, and in the interim
Admiral Koundouriotis was chosen to act as Regent.   The
Crown was offered to Prince Paul, Constantine's third son, but
refused on the ground that his father and eldest brother had
never renounced their rights to the throne.   It thus became clear
that the main issue of the coming elections would be the question
of King Constantine's return—'Constantine *versus* Venizelos'.

The elections took place on 14th November 1920.   To the
surprise even of the Royalists, out of 370 members only 120
The Elections of Liberals were returned, and, though they still
Nov. 1920. constituted the largest single party, they had
to acknowledge defeat.   M. Venizelos resigned
and left the country.

It is difficult to account for the rejection of one who had
been the saviour of his country and had so greatly enlarged
the bounds of the kingdom.   He had no doubt
Defeat of lost authority by his long absence fighting his
M. Venizelos. country's battles at the Conference table.   The
compulsory retirement of officers and officials and the suppression
of administrative abuses had caused discontent, which was
fostered by Royalist propaganda.   Perhaps also, as the Greeks of
old grew tired of hearing Aristides called 'the Just', so the
ordinary Greek citizen had grown weary of the praises of which
M. Venizelos was the continual object in the European press.
But the chief cause of his defeat was doubtless the war-weariness

of the country whose army had been mobilized almost continuously since the outbreak of the Balkan Wars ; it was hoped that a change of régime might result in a cessation of hostilities and the return of the soldiers to their homes. An arrangement by which soldiers on active service in Asia Minor and Thrace were enabled to record their votes gave the Army an opportunity to express its sentiments and was no doubt prejudicial to the Venizelist cause.

On 5th December a plebiscite was held, which overwhelmingly decided in favour of the recall of King Constantine. The

Recall of King Constantine.

Supreme Allied Council had, on 2nd December, warned Greece in vain of the consequences which the return of King Constantine would entail and refused him recognition and withdrew the financial assistance which Greece was receiving. On 19th December, however, he returned to Athens and was received with every demonstration of enthusiasm by the fickle populace. A new Cabinet was formed with M. Rallis as Prime Minister.

The restoration of King Constantine failed to fulfil the hopes of those who had voted in its favour and bring peace to

The attitude of the Entente Powers.

Greece. The establishment of Greek sovereignty in Asia Minor was only possible if Greece had the support of the Entente Powers. The unanimity of these Powers waned when once the Versailles Treaty had been signed, and their individual interests began to emerge ; and nowhere did they diverge more than on the question of the Near East. Great Britain was averse to giving open support to the Greeks against Turkey, whose ruler was Caliph of Islam, for fear of reactions upon her Musulman subjects in India and elsewhere ; France, in her anxiety about Cilicia, was desirous of keeping on good terms with Turkey ; Italy, who had been promised the reversion of territory in Asia Minor, had always been opposed to the growth of Greek influence in the Levant.

Meanwhile the power of Mustapha Kemal was continually increasing and had enabled him to establish a ' Nationalist '

Growing strength of Turkey.

Parliament at Ankara independent of the Constantinople Government and to challenge the provisions of the Treaty of Sèvres. Greece would obviously need a powerful army to hold the frontier of the territory allotted to her in Asia Minor ; on the other hand, to withdraw was difficult and would expose the large Greek population in Asia Minor to the vengeance of the Turks, besides involving the abandonment of the idea of a ' Greater Greece.'

In February 1921 a Conference was held in London, which was attended by a delegation from Greece, headed by M. Kalo-

The Conference on the Near East in London. geropoulos, who had recently succeeded M. Rallis as Premier, and two Turkish delegations, one from Constantinople and one from Ankara. This recognition of Mustapha Kemal's Government added enormously to his prestige, especially as the Constantinople delegates left the presentation of the Turkish case entirely in his hands. The French and Italian representatives made no secret of their pro-Turkish leanings. A proposal to send out an Inter-Allied Commission to examine the problems of Thrace and Smyrna on the spot was rejected by the Greeks ; and an elaborate compromise, by which Turkey was to retain the sovereignty over the Vilayet of Smyrna, while the city was to be garrisoned by Greek troops and a Christian Governor was to be appointed by the League of Nations, failed to recommend itself to either of the rival claimants. The representative, however, of the Greek General Staff expressed the opinion that the Greeks would be able to establish themselves in Asia Minor within three months and persuaded Mr. Lloyd George as well as the Greek delegation to take his view. But the encouragement of the British Prime Minister was not destined to be implemented in the form of active assistance, and the Greeks were unwise in taking it to mean more than it was ever meant to imply.

The new Chamber, which held its first meetings in February 1921, consisted chiefly of members of various parties who were

Meeting of the Greek Chamber, Feb. 1921. united only in their hatred for M. Venizelos. It declared itself a National Constitutional Assembly and spent its time discussing a variety of questions connected with changes in the administration and in passing measures for the indemnification of those who claimed to have suffered for their political views under the Venizelist régime. They voted large increases in the King's Civil List and passed a measure substituting the ' popular ' language in the schools for the more ' classical ' form of Greek which had been favoured by M. Venizelos. The Greek Treasury was in no condition to support the expense of a war, and the depreciation of the drachma and the consequent rise in the cost of living was beginning to cause distress and discontent. How-

The Centenary of Greek Independence.

ever, the celebration of the Centenary of the Declaration of Greek Independence on 7th April reminded the Greeks of their success against the Turks a hundred years before, and no doubt had a cheering effect. More men were continually called up until there were over 300,000 men serving under the colours.

CHAPTER XVII

THE GREEK CAMPAIGN IN ASIA MINOR AND ITS CONSEQUENCES (1921-2)

OPERATIONS in Asia Minor began at the end of March 1921. The Greek General Staff (who seem to have had no idea of the
The opening of growing strength of the Turkish National Move-
hostilities in ment and the support which it was receiving
Asia Minor. from other countries) were convinced that
victory was certain and that Greece would receive a vast extension of territory. The dream of Constantinople again in Greek hands was at last to come true, and Constantine was hailed in the Royalist press as destined to be crowned Emperor in Santa Sophia.

But the enterprise was doomed from the first. The army was ill-equipped[1] and lacking in munitions, and there were no
Condition of the funds in the Treasury to remedy these defici-
Greek Army. encies. The Corps of officers was rent by
political differences ; many of those who had led the Greek divisions to victory on the Macedonian front had been superseded by the appointment of Royalist sympathizers, who had taken no part in the operations of 1918 and had had no training in the latest developments of warfare. So many adherents of the Government in power had received promotion that there were more generals and colonels than posts for them to fill. In these conditions the Army required an experienced Commander-in-Chief who could enforce an iron discipline and stand up against the pressure exerted by the politicians. General Papoulas, who received the appointment, was singularly lacking in these qualifications, his chief claim to command being that he had suffered for his loyalty to King Constantine in his exile. He proved incompetent and was continually at loggerheads with the General Staff.

[1] For example, the Twelfth Division, commanded by Prince Andrew of Greece, possessed no engineering material, no wireless outfit, and only two batteries of 6·5 guns.

At first the Greek Army made appreciable progress in its advance into Asia Minor. There was as yet no considerable

The advance into Asia Minor. Turkish force to oppose it but merely bands of irregulars who carried on guerrilla warfare, in which every little success gained by the Greeks was hailed as a brilliant victory. The important railway-junctions, however, of Afium Karahissar and Eski Shehr were captured, but the Greeks sustained a serious reverse to the north-west of the latter town on 2nd April and were compelled to retreat.

On 11th June King Constantine left Athens for Smyrna with M. Gounaris, who had become Prime Minister in April, M.

King Constantine leaves for the seat of war. Theotokis, Minister of War, and General Dousmanis representing the General Staff. The last-named urged that the King should assume the supreme command of the Army, but this was opposed by the politicians, with the result that the King held aloof from the direction of affairs.

In June the Greek Army was concentrated in two groups, a smaller body at Brousa and the main body near Ushak. Not

Attitude of the Entente Powers. only were these two groups widely separated from one another but the main body was served by a single railway-line from Smyrna which passed through enemy country and required a large detachment of troops to guard it. During the same month the British, French, and Italian Governments, who in May had proclaimed a state of neutrality towards both the Greeks and the Turks in the zone which they occupied in the area adjoining the Dardanelles and the Sea of Marmara, volunteered their services to negotiate peace between the belligerents, but the Greeks rejected their offer.

A fresh offensive opened on 15th June and resulted in the recapture of Afium Karahissar and Eski Shehr and an advance

The offensive of June 1921. first to Katahia and then to Sivri Hissar, which lies some sixty miles from Ankara, the seat of the Turkish Nationalist Government. The Greek G.H.Q. seems to have thought that the Turkish withdrawal was a rout, but, in fact, the retirement had been made in perfect order. The Greek Commander-in-Chief is said to have wished to halt at the point which he had reached and avoid further risk, but the Prime Minister and Minister for War urged that Ankara must be captured and the enemy defeated.

The country over which the Greeks had now to advance was a more or less desert and waterless land mostly devoid of *Difficulties of the ground.* inhabitants—a formidable obstacle to an army almost entirely lacking in the means of communication and transport. It involved indescribable hardships and privations for the Greek Army. On the plateau of Central Asia Minor the rainy season sets in early

THE GREEK CAMPAIGN IN ASIA MINOR.

in the autumn and the roads, which are mere cart-tracks, soon become morasses almost impassable to heavy wheeled traffic.

The enemy allowed the Greeks to advance until they reached a battle-ground of Mustapha Kemal's own choosing—the line of the Sakharia River, where the heights on the farther bank formed an ideal position for an effective defence.

On 7th August the Greek Commander-in-Chief issued orders, in which he said : ' The whole army will attack so as to annihilate the principal enemy force, will pursue them until they are dispersed, and will then advance to Ankara and destroy the enemy's stores there and the railway line'.

But fate had decided otherwise. The Greek Army was

exhausted by its long march through the desert; it was short
of every kind of food, except meat, which could
Defeat of the   not be cooked for lack of fuel; petrol had run
Greeks on the   short, and the horses were weak through lack
Sakharia River.   of barley and forage; the ammunition was
almost at an end and could not be replaced. The Turkish Army,
on the other hand, was entrenched in a strong position not far
from its base, was fighting in defence of its newly-chosen
capital and was inspired with enthusiasm for the Nationalist
Movement; above all its leader, Mustapha Kemal, was a born
military genius. The result was a foregone conclusion—
a disastrous defeat, though the Greek soldiery fought with
characteristic stubbornness. The casualties were enormous, and
would have been even greater if the enemy had done more to
press home their advantage.

September was occupied with the retreat to the line Eski
Shehr—Afium Karahissar, and at the end of the month King
Retreat of the   Constantine returned to Athens broken in
Greeks.   health. It remained for Greece to find a solu-
tion for an impossible situation, the gravity of
which was hidden as far as possible from the Greeks at home.
The only possible course seemed to be to appeal to the Powers
Greece appeals   to help Greece out of the *impasse*, and the Prime
to the Powers.   Minister accompanied by M. Baltatzis, his
Minister for Foreign Affairs, set out for the
European capitals. In Paris there was nothing to be done, since
the French had been supporting the Turks, with whom on
20th October they concluded the so-called 'Franklin-Bouillon
Agreement', under which Mustapha Kemal received an ample
supply of arms, munitions, and equipment. Italy was, as usual,
unfriendly, and all the hopes of the Greek envoys centred on
Great Britain, whose Prime Minister had given a formal blessing
to their war effort. In an interview at the Foreign Office the
situation was laid before Lord Curzon, and the Greek Ministers
agreed to place the interests of their country in the hands of the
Powers. They were told that, until a new Conference could
be held, they must hold on in their present position, although
winter was approaching. As the British Government could only
act in concert with France, further delays ensued and new
negotiations had to be begun when M. Poincaré succeeded

M. Briand as Premier. In March 1922 the Paris Conference proposed an armistice, which Greece accepted, but Turkey insisted that this should be preceded by the evacuation of Asia Minor, and to this the Powers refused their assent.

On 12th May M. Gounaris resigned and, after M. Stratos had failed to form a government, a Coalition Cabinet was

M. Gounaris resigns.

arranged, which included these two ministers, under the premiership of M. Protopapadakis, who as Minister of Finance had raised a forced loan by cutting all the banknotes in half. The first act of this government was to dismiss General Papoulas and appoint in his place the perhaps even more incompetent General Hadjanestis. In July the Greek High Commissioner in Smyrna proclaimed the independence of the Smyrna Vilayet, a move which had no effect on the situation.

At the end of August 1922 the Turks at last attacked and quickly occupied Afium Karahissar and, breaking through the

Defeat of the Greeks and destruction of Smyrna.

line of defence, drove the Greeks before them and reached Smyrna on 9th September. Amid scenes of indescribable horror the greater part of the town was sacked and burnt. Only a poor remnant of the Greek population managed to escape. It was a sorry end to an adventure which should never have been undertaken and which Great Britain should either have discouraged or else supported with adequate aid.

The Greek Government, after decreeing the demobilization of the routed Greek Army, resigned on 8th September.

Meanwhile a large body of officers, headed by Colonel Plastiras, had taken refuge in the Island of Chios off the coast of

The Revolution in Chios.

Asia Minor, where they collected a considerable number of men and some units of the navy. Having matured their plans, they sent aeroplanes over to Athens, where they dropped copies of a proclamation demanding the abdication of King Constantine in favour of the Crown Prince and threatening to come to Athens

Abdication and death of King Constantine.

with an army of 15,000 men. Though there were troops still loyal to the Crown and ready to fight, King Constantine, realizing that it was no moment for a fratricidal struggle when Greece was defeated and humiliated, took what was no doubt the only possible course in the interests of the country and abdicated, leaving Greece from the same little port of Oropos as on his previous departure. He settled at Palermo in Sicily, where he died in the following January, and the Crown Prince ascended the throne as King George II. It is difficult to avoid the conclusion that on this occasion King Constantine, who had had no part in the decision to make war on Turkey or in its military direction, was made a scapegoat for disasters for which he was in no degree responsible.

One of the first acts of the Revolutionary Committee was to invite M. Venizelos to return to Athens, but on 1st November *M. Venizelos* he declared that he had definitely retired from *decides to remain* public life, a decision which was confirmed by *abroad.* a letter of 19th November ; but he consented to remain at Lausanne and plead the cause of Greece at the negotiations which were in progress there to settle the differences between Greece and Turkey.

Meanwhile the Revolutionary Committee had appointed a Commission of Inquiry which was to fix the blame for the *Trial of the* disasters in Asia Minor. The Commission *ex-Ministers.* decided that three ex-Premiers, two ex-Ministers, and the late Commander-in-Chief (MM. Gounaris, Protopapadakis, Stratos, Baltatzis, Theotokis, and General Hadjanestis) should be brought to trial before a military Court Martial. On 29th October the British and Italian Ministers at Athens issued a warning that to try politicians for their acts while in office would produce a painful impression abroad. On 12th November the Revolutionary leaders called on M. Zaïmis and invited him to assume office, but he refused to do so unless the Revolutionary Committee was first dissolved. Thereupon the Committee formed a Cabinet from among their own adherents. On 23rd November the British Minister at Athens informed M. Politis, the Foreign Minister, that, unless the Government gave a favourable reply to the British representations, he had orders to break off diplomatic relations. Meanwhile at Lausanne Lord Curzon begged M. Venizelos to use his influence to stop the proceedings of the Court Martial and dispatched Commander Talbot, formerly naval attaché at Athens, to intercede with the Government.

The trial, which had dragged on for a fortnight, was brought

to an end on 28th November, when all the accused were sentenced
to immediate execution. M. Gounaris, who was
Verdict and seriously ill and had never appeared in court to
execution of the plead his own cause, was dragged from his
ex-Ministers. bed, and all the unfortunate victims were taken
in lorries outside the city and shot. They refused to have their
eyes bandaged and remained cool and collected to the end.
When Commander Talbot arrived in Athens, all was over ; but
he was able to save Prince Andrew of Greece, who was to have
been brought to trial on the charge of disobeying orders while
in command of the right wing of the army in Asia Minor, and
was allowed to escort him out of the country.

The awful tragedy of the executions caused a painful impression throughout the civilized world, and Great Britain
Effect of the broke off diplomatic relations with Greece.
executions on There was a general feeling that, if the battle
foreign opinion. on the Sakharia River had resulted in a Greek
victory, the murdered Ministers and the Commander-in-chief would have been hailed as national heroes.

It has been urged by his critics that M. Venizelos might have
exerted his influence to prevent the executions. He certainly
Attitude of refused to take any steps while the trial was in
M. Venizelos progress, but on 28th November, when the
towards the trial. verdict was made public, he telegraphed from
Lausanne laying stress on the fatal effect which
the execution of the sentences would have in Government
circles in England and on public opinion everywhere. He
stated that, though he was averse to interfering in home affairs,
he felt it his duty to point out that the executions would render
his position as spokesman of Greece at the Lausanne negotiations
extremely difficult. If M. Venizelos had felt in a position to
make an earlier and a more vigorous protest, he might perhaps
have prevented a pitiful tragedy.[1]

[1] It may be pointed out that of the members of the Court Martial only
two out of nine belonged to the Venizelist party.

CHAPTER XVIII

THE TREATY OF LAUSANNE; AND THE FOUNDATION
OF THE REPUBLIC (1923-5)

THE Lausanne Conference dragged on until February 1923, when the Turkish delegation presented fresh demands, upon

The Lausanne Conference.

which Lord Curzon decided to return to England. The Greeks profited by this lull in the negotiations to send a well-organized force to Thrace under General Pangalos, which threatened Turkey on the European side of her territory and placed a valuable counter for bargaining in the hands of the Greek representatives when the negotiations were resumed on 23rd April. The agreement was at last signed on 24th July 1923.

Under the Treaty of Lausanne Greece renounced all claims to territory in Asia Minor, and the River Maritza was fixed as

Terms of the Treaty.

the boundary between Greece and Turkey in Thrace instead of the Tchataldja Line, which had been laid down in the abortive Treaty of Sèvres. Thus Adrianople and the Gallipoli peninsula remained in Turkish hands and the Sea of Marmara again became a Turkish lake. Turkey, therefore, thanks to her revival under Mustapha Kemal, managed to save the greater part of her European territory, although she had been on the losing side in the war, while the Greeks added the small area round Xanthe and Dedeagatch to the territory which they had gained after the Balkan Wars. The Dodecanese, which, under an agreement made between Greece and Italy at the time of the Treaty of Sèvres, was to pass to Greece, was retained by Italy owing to the non-ratification of that Treaty and was soon converted into a powerful outpost of Italian influence in the Levant.

A pressing problem which faced the Government was the settlement of Greek refugees who had poured into the country from Asia Minor. It was rendered more difficult by the fact that most of those who had come were women and children or

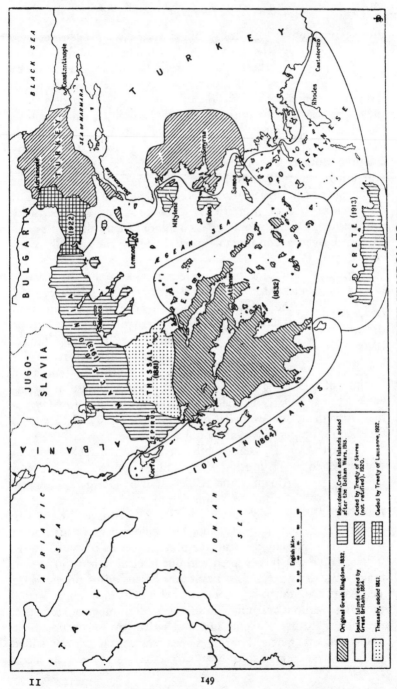

Original Greek Kingdom, 1832.

Ionian Islands ceded by Great Britain, 1864.

Thessaly, added 1881.

Macedonia, Crete and Islands added after the Balkan Wars, 1913.

Ceded by Treaty of Sèvres (not ratified), 1920.

Ceded by Treaty of Lausanne, 1922.

THE GROWTH OF THE GREEK KINGDOM TO 1922.

men above military age, the younger men having been detained
by the Turks. At first the task of finding homes
for these victims of the war was undertaken by
the Greek Government with the generous aid of
American charity, and considerable progress was made ; later
the work was, on the initiative of Dr. Nansen, taken over by a
Commission appointed by the League of Nations. The principle
of the emigration of minorities had already been established by
a Turco-Bulgarian Agreement in 1913 and a Greco-Bulgarian
Agreement in 1919. In January 1923 a Convention for the
Exchange of Minorities was signed by Greece and Turkey. The
resulting process of migration, which provided a noteworthy
solution of an acute problem, encountered many difficulties and
extended over a considerable period, being only finally concluded in 1930.

The refugee problem.

Amongst other measures passed in Greece in 1923 was a
Decree of Amnesty for all political offences (22nd January) and
the reform of the Calendar by the adoption
(1st March) of the system of Western Europe
in place of the old style of the Orthodox Church,
which was fourteen days in arrears. This
change had the effect of putting an end to a
method of reckoning time which was a fruitful cause of incon-
venience, particularly in the business world. On 10th May the
first agreement was signed for the concession by Greece of a
Free Zone for Jugoslavia at Salonica.

Decree of Amnesty and reform of the Calendar.

On 27th August 1923, while an International Commission
was engaged in delimiting the frontier between Greece and
Albania, the Chief Italian Delegate, General
Tellini, was murdered with four members of
his staff just inside Greek territory. The Greek
Government took the matter up, but, before it had had time to
report, Italy presented an ultimatum, the terms of which were
such as could not be accepted without discussion by a Sovereign
State. But Italy refused to grant any extension of time and on
31st August an Italian fleet appeared before Corfu and bombarded
the town without warning, causing a small number of casualties,
most of them in an orphanage, and Italian troops occupied the
island and other neighbouring Greek islands. It was explained
that it was not an act of war but a temporary and peaceful

The Italians bombard Corfu.

measure ! Italy, as we have seen, had always taken every opportunity to oppose the interests of Greece, but this was her first act of aggression—and was not destined to be the last.

Settlement of the incident by the League of Nations. The Greek Government took the correct course of an appeal to the League of Nations, which was fortunately at that moment in session and thus gave an opportunity for the expression of European opinion. The protests raised were so vehement that Italy was obliged to give way, and Corfu was evacuated on 27th September. A Conference of Ambassadors, however, which met in Paris, awarded an indemnity to Italy on the ground that there had been negligence on the part of the Greek authorities. The peaceful settlement of a difficult international incident was a distinct feather in the cap of the League of Nations which has not acquired many such ornaments, and Greece won credit for her moderate and conciliatory attitude.

During the course of the year 1923 it grew more and more obvious that there was an imperative necessity for the re-establishment of a constitutional régime in place of the rule of the nominees of the Revolutionary Committee.[1] An attempt was made in September again to persuade M. Zaïmis to form a Government which should include both Royalists and Venizelists, and, though he found himself unable to accede to this, there was a prospect that some arrangement of this kind might be achieved. Unfortunately, however, the leader• of the ultra-Royalists, General Metaxas, determined to make profit out of the prevailing discontent by organizing a counter-revolution. He was unsuccessful, but the suppression of this movement had the effect of strengthening the hands of the party which favoured the establishment of a Republic as a cure for internal strife.

The Constitutional Question.

On 16th December fresh elections were held, at which, though the Venizelists obtained two hundred seats and the Republicans only a hundred and twenty, it was obvious that the army headed by General Pangalos and the navy headed by Captain Hadjikyriakos were in favour of a republican régime and that disorders were likely to occur. Colonel Gonatas, therefore,

Elections of 16th Dec. 1923.

[1] The principal of these were Colonels Gonatas and Plastiras, with M. Alexandris as Minister of Foreign Affairs.

representing the Government, sought an audience of the King and suggested that, in order that the people might be free to

King George II leaves Greece. decide their future form of government, he should quit Greece for three months while the question was submitted to the National Assembly. On 18th December, therefore, the King and the Queen, who was a daughter of King Ferdinand of Rumania, left Athens for Bucharest. Admiral Koundouriotis was appointed Regent.

The result of the elections had been the clear call for the return to Greece of M. Venizelos, who in his absence had been

M. Venizelos returns and be- comes Premier. nominated and returned for a number of con- stituencies. On an invitation supported by all parties, he consented to return temporarily and attempt to reunite the nation, and arrived in Athens on 4th January 1924. Assuming the office of Premier he proposed that after two months a plebiscite should be held to decide the question of Republic or Monarchy, and that after this elections should again be held. The discussion of these measures gave rise to long and heated debates in the Chamber, where the Prime Minister had to face a powerful opposition led by M. Papanastasiou, an extreme Republican, who favoured the immediate deposition of the dynasty by a vote of the Chamber

M. Venizelos resigns. and the establishment of a Republic. On 4th February after a violent altercation on the floor of the House, M. Venizelos, weary of strife, resigned, and was succeeded as Premier by M. Kaphantaris, who supported the policy of setting up a Republican régime if it were approved by a plebiscite.

M. Kaphantaris remained in office for little more than a month, and was succeeded as Premier by M. Papanastasiou, who

Establishment of the Republic. proposed to abolish the monarchy by a resolu- tion of the House, to be ratified afterwards by a plebiscite. His proposal was carried, and on 25th March 1924 the Republic was proclaimed, the Regent, Admiral Koundouriotis, becoming President. In the following month the plebiscite was held, at which more than two-thirds of the votes were cast in favour of the Republic. All the members of the Royal Family were deprived of their Greek nationality and their property in Greece confiscated. The British Government, which had resumed diplomatic relations in January, recognized the Greek Republic and was officially represented at the Centenary of the death of Lord Byron, which was held on 19th April.

There was little continuity in the government of Greece during the remainder of 1924. The Cabinet of M. Papanastasiou, in which General Pangalos, the future dictator, was Minister of War, resigned in July and a Government was formed by M. Sophoulis, a Venizelist deputy, who was himself succeeded as Premier in September by M. Michalakopoulos. The constant change of government was not conducive to the settlement of the question of a new constitution, especially as several problems of external relations arose, the solution of which occupied the attention of the Government.

We have seen that in 1923 a Convention was signed for the exchange of Greek and Turkish minorities. By October 1924 *Greece and* 370,000 Moslems had left Greek territory, while *Turkey.* practically all the Asiatic Greeks had been transferred to Greece. Under the Convention the Greek inhabitants of Constantinople who had been ' established ' before 30th October 1918 were exempted, but considerable difficulty arose about the meaning of the term ' established '. The Greeks maintained that it meant merely resident, the Turks that it implied the fulfilment of certain legal formalities. On 9th May 1924 the Mixed Commission appointed to carry out the exchange of population decided that certain categories of Greeks were to leave Constantinople on 10th October, and passports were issued to them. When the time came, however, many of them remained, and on 18th October the Turkish police began to round them up, and 3500 of them were placed in a concentration camp in the prison of the Severn Towers. The Greeks appealed to the League of Nations, which decided that the interpretation of the term ' established ' should be settled by the Mixed Commission, who were recommended to apply to the Permanent Court at the Hague for its opinion. This Court decided in favour of the Greek point of view. At the meeting of the Council of the League of Nations in October 1924, M. Politis, the Greek representative, brought forward the case of the Greeks who had been expelled from Constantinople and not allowed to return and the question of the Greek banks in that city, while the Turkish delegate pointed out that 50,000 Turks in Western Thrace were without means of subsistence because the Greeks had confiscated their lands. Finally, however, by direct negotiation an agreement was reached, which was signed in June 1925, and normal diplomatic relations were resumed between Greece and Turkey.

Another and kindred cause of controversy between Greece and Turkey was the question of the Patriarchate. Under the *The Question of* Turkish rule the Patriarch of Constantinople *the Patriarchate.* was, as we have already seen, not only the religious head of the Greek Orthodox Church but also exercised civil functions in connexion with marriage, wardship, and inheritance ; but, when the Christian peoples gained their independence, the office became more and more an anachronism and was an object of suspicion in the eyes of the Turks as a focus for political agitation. At the Lausanne Conference the Turks had demanded its abolition, but a compromise was reached by which the Patriarchate was to continue, but to concern itself entirely with religious matters.

In 1921 Mgr. Meletios, Venizelist Metropolitan of Athens, but at the time an exile in America, was appointed Patriarch. *Meletios IV.* After taking up office he concerned himself with politics and, becoming the object of hostile demonstrations, fled to Salonica and afterwards abdicated and retired to Mt. Athos.

His successor, Mgr. Gregorios VII, was enthroned in December 1923. He was violently attacked, in particular by Papa Eftim, *Gregorios VII.* head of the so-called Turkish Orthodox Church of Anatolia (a sect which held the curious view that the Greeks of Asia Minor were Christianized Turks), who succeeded in seizing the Phanar, the official residence of the Patriarch, and called upon Mgr. Gregorios to resign ; but the Turkish Government adopted a correct attitude and drove Papa Eftim out. He was subsequently unfrocked by the Holy Synod. Since, however, Turkey was at the time taking steps to abolish the Caliph, the head of their own religion, there was a demand that a similar measure should be adopted for the abolition of the Patriarchate. Mgr. Gregorios, nevertheless, succeeded in remaining in office and died a natural death in the Phanar—a feat rarely achieved by any of his predecessors.

The election of his successor, Mgr. Constantine VI, in December 1924 raised the question of the status of the new *Constantine VI.* Patriarch, who, according to the Turks, was not an 'established' resident in Constantinople and therefore 'exchangeable'. On 30th January 1925 he was expelled by the Turkish police and fled to Salonica. The incident caused a very painful impression not only in Greece and the other Orthodox countries but also among members of the Anglican High Church, which has always felt a close sympathy with the Orthodox community. The Turkish Government urged that the easiest solution was to appoint a Patriarch who was not 'exchangeable'; but here again a difficulty arose, since most of the eligible candidates were equally 'exchangeable'. There followed a brisk interchange of notes and appeals to other Governments and to the League of Nations. Fortunately, in the course of a short time the excitement died down, and, after Mgr. Constantine VI had announced his abdication and the Holy Synod had elected Mgr. Basil Georgiadis, Metropolitan of Nicæa, a scholar rather than a politician, peace was at last restored.

The question of the exchange of minorities also led to difficulties between Greece and Bulgaria. The Bulgarians in Greek *Greece and Bulgaria.* territory showed more eagerness to leave Greece than did the Greeks in Bulgaria to migrate into Greece. In March 1923 the Bulgarian Government appealed to the League of Nations against the treatment of their nationals in Western Thrace, while difficulties arose between Greeks and Bulgarians in Macedonia. Many Greek refugees from Asia Minor were transferred to Thrace and Macedonia, whence the Bulgarians who were due for deportation fled, without waiting for the liquidation of their property, into Bulgaria and remained in a state of destitution near the frontier, where many of the population were Greeks. This led to unfortunate incidents. The most serious of *The incident at Tarlis.* these occurred in July 1924 at Tarlis on the Greco-Bulgarian frontier near Petric, where an officer in command of a Greek detachment arrested about sixty Bulgarian inhabitants on the ground that they had co-operated with Bulgarian *comitadjis*. While they were being conveyed to a neighbouring village, thirteen of them were shot, it being alleged that they had attempted to escape. A

Commission of Inquiry exonerated the Greek Government, but censured the local authorities. As a result relations between Greece and Bulgaria were severely strained. However, at the Assembly of the Council of the League of Nations, on the initiative of Professor Gilbert Murray, the Greek and Bulgarian

The unratified Protocol. representatives, MM. Politis and Kalkoff, came to an agreement as to future procedure, and a Protocol was signed under which two members of the Mixed Commission—an Englishman and a Dutchman—were appointed to assist the Greeks and Bulgarians in the execution of the Minorities Treaty. This arrangement was welcomed at Sofia, but was less favourably received in Athens. The reason of this was that the Jugoslav Government, who denied that any of the Slavs in Jugoslavian Macedonia could possibly be Bulgarians, read into the Protocol an admission that the Slav minority in Greek Macedonia was Bulgarian, and therefore brought pressure on the Greek Government to reject the Protocol. The denunciation by Jugoslavia of the Treaty of Alliance concluded with Greece in 1913, which was announced on 15th November 1924, finally decided the Greek Government, which was anxious to preserve good relations, to refuse to ratify the Protocol, but its rejection was mitigated by an assurance that Greece was determined to carry out all her obligations under the Minorities Treaty.

Troubles, however, continued on the Macedonian frontier, which culminated in a serious affray and almost led to war

The Bulgarian Frontier Incident. between Greece and Bulgaria. On 19th October 1925 shots were exchanged between Greek and Bulgarian frontier-guards at Demir Kapu, north of Salonica, and a Greek soldier was killed. The Greek officer in command of the post arrived on the scene some hours later and gave orders to his men to cease fire ; he then advanced under a white flag and was promptly killed by a bullet. More soldiers and armed civilians came up and fighting continued on the 20th and 21st, but apparently the shooting was not very good and the casualties were not heavy. When the news reached Athens, orders were sent to the Third Army Corps at Salonica to advance into Bulgaria. The Bulgarian troops offered only slight resistance, and the Greeks occupied a considerable area of Bulgarian territory. The Bulgarian Government then appealed to the League of Nations, and the Council of the League ordered both belligerents to withdraw behind their respective frontiers. The effect of this was to stop a general offensive, for which the Greek Government had given orders and which the Bulgarians were preparing to resist. The Council then appointed a Commission under the Chairmanship of Sir Horace Rumbold, British Ambassador at Madrid, which decided that, though there was no premeditation on either side, the Bulgarians were entitled to an indemnity of £45,000 for the violation of their territory, while the Bulgarian Government was ordered to pay damages for the shooting of the Greek officer. The Commission also made recommendations, which the Council accepted, for the better organization of the frontier-guards and their supervision by two neutral officers (who were provided by the Swedish Government), one to be attached to the Greek, the other to the Bulgarian frontier-force. The Greek Government protested against the amount of the indemnity, but eventually accepted the decision of the Council. The new arrangement was tested by an incident which occurred in the following May and was satisfactorily settled.

As we have already seen, on 27th November 1924, Jugoslavia, which still felt resentment on the ground that Greece had

Greece and Jugoslavia.

failed to help her in 1915 and whose prestige and military and economic resources were now superior to those of Greece, denounced the Treaty of Alliance, the period of which had elapsed in May 1923, though it was renewable for a further year. Jugoslavia had more to offer than Greece and was thus in a position to demand concessions in the economic field.

Salonica had already been recognized in principle as the natural outlet to the Mediterranean of the trade of Southern

The question of the Port of Salonica and the Gevgeli-Salonica Railway.

Jugoslavia by the concession of a Free Zone for Jugoslavia at that port. But the Jugoslav Government was apprehensive that the facilities already offered there might prove inadequate, and the question of the access to Salonica over 48 miles of Greek railway also gave rise to a difficult problem. In January 1925 the Greek Government showed a conciliatory spirit by reducing freight-charges on the railway as well as by its refusal to ratify the Bulgarian Minorities

Protocol, to which Jugoslavia had objected. In May, however, demands were made not only for the enlargement of the Free Zone but also for its definite cession, so that it would become practically Jugoslav territory, and for the handing over of the administration of the railway to Jugoslavia. These suggestions were regarded in Greece as inconsistent with Greek sovereign rights, and on 1st June 1925 the Greek and Jugoslav delegates, who were in conference at Belgrade, decided, in view of their complete divergence of opinion, to adjourn the negotiations *sine die*. It was not until 1929 that a satisfactory settlement of these questions was eventually reached.

Abortive negotiations.

CHAPTER XIX

THE DICTATORSHIP OF GENERAL PANGALOS AND THE RETURN OF M. VENIZELOS (1925–8)

WHILE the Government was thus principally engaged in the attempted solution of foreign questions, the internal situation remained unsatisfactory and the National Assembly had not come to any decision about the new Constitution. The inefficiency and corruption of the administration showed no improvement, and discontent was rife. At the end of June 1925 the Government of M. Mikalapokoulos resigned after a minor *coup d'état* had been carried out by General Pangalos and Admiral Hadjikyriakos, who seized the National Bank and the General Post Office. General Pangalos then formed a government, in which Admiral Hadjikyriakos was included, which proceeded to dissolve the National Assembly and on 30th September published by proclamation the terms of the new Constitution. The provisions included a President, who was to be elected for a term of five years, and a Chamber and an Upper House under the title of Senate, consisting of 150 members, of whom 100 were to be elected by parliamentary vote, 30 by various professional corporations and guilds, and 20 by the Senate itself and the Chamber. Elections were to be held early in the coming year, and the new Constitution was then to be brought up for ratification.

General Pangalos as Premier.

In November MM. Rouphos and Sechiotis, both members of the Royalist Party, joined the Government, the former as Minister for Foreign Affairs, in which capacity he soon proved his ability ; and the elections for the Senate were fixed for 10th January 1926. But on 3rd January General Pangalos suddenly announced that the Government had changed its plans, that the elections for the Senate and Chamber were adjourned *sine die*, and that it had been decided that all administrative and executive power was to be transferred to the General himself ; in fact, he assumed a

General Pangalos becomes Dictator.

dictatorship with the avowed object of restoring internal harmony and national economy.

As a dictator General Pangalos was a curious phenomenon ; a military dictator, he had seized power to deal with a political situation. He had no new political doctrine to impose ; he had no desire to abolish democracy, but he wished to put an end to the pernicious activity of political partisanship which was rending the Greek nation and preventing any real national progress. He recognized that what Greece required was a settled and stable administration which would give the country peace and enable it to gain the respect of other nations. But he lacked the qualities of a genuine leader and his authority was based on force, though his violence was tempered by a certain benevolence, and his intentions were better than his performance. He was emphatically not the man whom the crisis demanded.

General Pangalos did little to improve the economic situation, though his Finance Minister resorted to the now familiar device *Internal* of a forced loan by the clipping of banknotes. *measures.* His chief expedient for curbing party passion was a campaign against the Press, which was subjected to such a rigorous censorship that the expression of public opinion was almost entirely suppressed. He went as far as to forbid the publication in the Press of manifestoes by the chief political leaders and exiled the most active of these, MM. Kaphantaris and Papanastasiou, as well as General Kondylis, to the Ægean island of Santorin. A measure which insisted that ladies' skirts must not be more than fourteen inches from the ground aroused more interest in the European press than any of the dictator's other legislative efforts.

In the sphere of Foreign Affairs negotiations were carried on during the dictatorship with Italy and Jugoslavia. Relations *Foreign Relations.* between Greece and Italy had been strained ever *Italy.* since the Corfu incident of 1923. But in March 1926 M. Rouphos visited Rome and had an interview with Signor Mussolini. These conversations resulted in a new Commercial Treaty which was signed in November. One of the questions raised by Signor Mussolini concerned the British Naval Mission, to which he objected on the ground that it would promote British naval supremacy in the Eastern Mediterranean. It was announced that the Greek Government had decided to denounce their contracts both with the French Military Mission and with the British Naval Mission, but neither of these decisions was actually put into effect.

Though relations with Jugoslavia were officially friendly, the Press of both countries indulged in mutual recriminations. *Jugoslavia.* Jugoslavia found fresh reason for complaint in the formation of a Greek Free Zone at Salonica, which was deemed likely to hamper the operation of the Jugoslav Free Zone. The question of the Gevgeli-Salonica Railway was also still unsettled. In January 1926, however, the Jugoslav Minister at Athens informed the Greek Government that his Government was disposed to consider the conclusion of a Balkan Pact, on the lines of the Locarno Pact, if outstanding problems could be solved. General Pangalos expressed himself as ready to make sacrifices in order to place the relations between the two countries on a better basis, with the result that on 17th August, after prolonged negotiations, a Treaty of Friendship was signed and satisfactory arrangements were made for the joint exploitation of the railway, which was to remain in Greek hands, and for the transport of goods to and from Salonica, and for the extension of the Jugoslav Free Zone. But before General Pangalos could carry out his intention of ratifying this Treaty by legislative decree, his Dictatorship had come to an end, and the Treaty was never ratified.

On 16th March 1926 General Pangalos announced that the new Constitution would be ready by the end of April and that *General Pangalos* it was intended that the Powers of the President *becomes* should be greatly extended on the model of *President.* those of the President of the U.S.A. ; also candidates must be between forty-five and sixty years of age, and all members of the Royal Family, and also M. Venizelos, were specially excluded from standing for election. The General said that he was uncertain whether he would himself be a candidate. All this was too much for Admiral Koundouriotis whose habitual calmness had become more and more perturbed by the General's political antics, and he resigned the Presidency on 19th March. Meanwhile the leaders of the various political parties made up their minds for once to lay aside their feuds and co-operated in nominating M. Demertzis, a moderate Royalist and an ex-minister, as their joint candidate. This alarmed the

General, who proposed to suspend the age-limit in favour of M. Zaïmis, whose candidature, he hoped, would split the vote, but who promptly refused to lend himself to this manœuvre. Thereupon General Pangalos had no expedient but to announce his own candidature and issue an election address. Just before the date of the election he declared that, owing to the fact that arrangements in twenty-three out of the thirty-three electoral divisions were incomplete, voting could only take place in the remaining ten ; whereupon the party leaders acted as apparently the General intended them to do and withdrew the candidature of M. Demertzis. Thus General Pangalos was left as the only candidate, and, as no votes were given for any one else, all the votes recorded were in his favour. He chose to regard the result of the election as a vote of confidence and took the oath as President on 18th April.

The problem which now faced the Dictator-President was to find some one who would undertake the Premiership. It was obvious that the Prime Minister would be a mere puppet, and the office was hawked about for some weeks. At last M. Eutaxias, a gentleman of advanced years who had first attained ministerial rank under M. Delyiannis in the previous century, consented to officiate, but by this time the sands were running out.

In August there were disturbances in various parts of the country, including Euboea and Crete, and on 16th August M. Kaphantaris, who had twice been arrested and exiled and then allowed to return during the dictatorship, was again arrested together with other political leaders, including General Metaxas.

The fall of General Pangalos.

On 22nd August General Kondylis, assisted by the garrison of the capital, carried out a bloodless *coup d'état* after seizing public buildings and releasing political prisoners. The Dictator was away on a summer holiday at Spetsai when the news reached him. He boarded a destroyer and attempted to escape, but off Cape Matapan he was captured by another destroyer and brought to Athens, whence he was finally transferred to a fortress in Crete.

General Pangalos failed as a dictator because he proved quite unable to deal successfully with the internal troubles of the country and had performed no services which could win the gratitude or the admiration or even the confidence of the nation. Unlike Mustapha Kemal, the saviour of Turkey, he

had not preserved Greece in the past from national peril. Her
The causes of his fall. Balkan neighbours had their own problems to deal with, and there were no outstanding questions of international relations which could not be solved by peaceful means ; Turkey, Greece's most recent enemy, was busy consolidating and organizing a new State in Asia Minor and introducing Western civilization, and was anxious to live at peace with her neighbours. A dictator may often prolong his rule by military successes which flatter the *amour propre* of his people ; but the situation offered no scope for achievements of this kind, and the disaster in Asia Minor had cured the Greeks of any desire for military adventure. Further, there is in Greece no tradition of discipline and blind obedience, and there was no external threat to induce the people to subject themselves to the will of an irresponsible ruler, whose efforts were directed to putting an end to their chief amusement in life, the game of party politics.

Though the Republican Guard under Colonel Zervas had taken part in the overthrow of General Pangalos, they had
Rioting in Athens. apparently expected to transfer their allegiance to another military dictator, and, when General Kondylis ordered their disbandment, they broke into open mutiny and were only overpowered by the calling out of other troops. There was rioting and street-fighting in which the populace took the opportunity to join. Though a good deal of blood was shed, the situation was soon in hand, and the leaders of the Republican Guard were court-martialled and sentenced to imprisonment for life.

On 22nd August Admiral Koundouriotis accepted the invitation of General Kondylis to resume the office of President of the
General Kondylis retires from public life. Republic. General Kondylis, who had assumed the Premiership, announced on 23rd September that he would retain that office until after an election had been held, when he would retire from public life and disband his party, the National Republicans. There were protests, especially from the Royalist leaders, against the decision that votes should be counted on the system of proportional representation ; but the election was carried through without disturbance and resulted in a Republican majority of thirty-four members—too few to justify the formation of a

Republican Cabinet. General Kondylis was as good as his

M. Zaïmis forms a Coalition Government. promise and resigned, and a Coalition Government was formed. Fortunately for Greece, the veteran statesman and patriot M. Alexander Zaïmis, who had always held aloof from party politics, stepped into the breach, as he had done more than once before, and consented to become Prime Minister. Among the other members of the Cabinet were the Royalists, M. Tsaldaris and General Metaxas, and the Republicans, MM. Kaphantaris, Michalakopoulos, and Papanastasiou.

On 25th September the memorial to the British soldiers who had fallen on the Macedonian front in the War of 1914–18 was consecrated at Doiran, and the British representatives took the opportunity of again acknowledging the deep debt of gratitude which the Allies owed to the gallantry of the Greek forces who had helped them to deal the first fatal blow to the Central Powers.

The first pre-occupation of the new Government was the clearing up of the financial muddle caused by the incompetence

Financial measures. of the late Dictatorship. A committee of experts was appointed to review the transactions sanctioned during the Dictatorship, and its recommendation was accepted that all contracts which had been entered upon which were not either irregular or illegal should be ratified.

On 28th February 1927 a Commercial Agreement with Bulgaria was signed, and similar Conventions were signed with Rumania on 28th March and with Italy on 1st June. On 25th August the Treaty of Alliance with Jugoslavia and the Conventions regarding the Salonica Free Zone and the Gevgeli-Salonica Railway, signed on 17th August 1926, were brought before the Chamber and rejected. On 2nd November a Commercial Agreement with Jugoslavia was signed at Athens.

During this year also the Greek Government, through its capable Finance Minister, M. Kaphantaris, took steps to deal

The settlement of the Greek War Debts. with the outstanding problem of War Debts. An Agreement for the settlement of the British War Debt was signed on 7th April, by which Greece undertook to pay nearly £21,500,000 in sixty-two annual instalments of £200,000, rising to £400,000 in 1936. On 5th December a similar Agreement was made

with the U.S.A. Government, which also granted a loan of
£2,500,000 for refugee settlement. On 14th June the Greek
Government applied to the Council of the League of Nations
for assistance in obtaining £9,000,000 for the stabilization of
the currency, for refugee settlement and for the liquidation of
the deficit, which was sanctioned in principle on 17th June.
In September the Council approved a Protocol embodying the
conditions under which the loan was to be issued and a scheme
of financial reform.

Meanwhile some impatience was being manifested at the
delay of the Coalition Government in settling the constitutional
Adoption of the question. In April the President threatened
new Constitution. resignation if postponement continued, and
General Kondylis returned to public life and
resuscitated his Republican Party in order to put pressure on the
Government to bring the Republican Constitution before the
House and also to deal with General Pangalos, on whom no
sentence had yet been passed. In May there was unrest in the
army, but the danger of military intervention was prevented by
the action of Generals Plastiras and Othonaios, who secretly
communicated with M. Venizelos, who was now in Crete, and
induced him to write and warn the Government of the danger
of too passive an attitude towards the threat of force. On
2nd June 1927 the Chamber passed the new Constitution, which
embodied provisions for the Presidency and Senate.

On 20th October the official celebration took place of the
centenary of the Battle of Navarino and gave an opportunity
Centenary of for a demonstration of Anglo-Hellenic friend-
Navarino. ship. Lieut.-General Sir A. Codrington, grand-
son of the Admiral who commanded the Allied
fleet at the battle, was sent on a battleship to represent the
British Government, and a commemorative dinner was held in
London.

The year 1928 found Greece in a more satisfactory financial
position than for many years past, but the Cabinet of M. Zaïmis,
Dissensions in which had already been reconstituted on
M. Zaïmis' 11th August 1927, when M. Tsaldaris, the
Cabinet. Royalist leader, resigned over the question of
the gold reserve of the National Bank, was again
reorganized on 3rd February 1928, when M. Papanastasiou

12

resigned owing to a disagreement about the acceptance of a tender for a scheme of road-construction. But Cabinet dissen-

Return of
M. Venizelos
to Greece.

sions continued, particularly after the return of M. Venizelos to Athens on 24th March. On 19th May M. Kaphantaris resigned his leadership of the Progressive Liberal Party and his portfolio in the Cabinet, and his action decided M. Venizelos to resume the leadership of the Party as the only organization strong enough to frustrate the threats of those who sought to profit by the present political anarchy. Called into consultation by the President, he expressed his willingness to form a Government if no satisfactory alternative could be found. On 28th May, however, M. Zaïmis succeeded in again reconstructing his Cabinet with the support of the Progressive Liberals and the moderate Royalists led by General Metaxas. It was thus a Government of the Centre, since the extreme Royalists and the left-wing Republicans held aloof. But Cabinet disagreements continued, and it had become obvious that the time had come to put an end to the Coalition Government and to restore

M. Venizelos
becomes Premier.

Party rule, and M. Venizelos was the only leader strong enough to form a united Cabinet. M. Venizelos himself recognized that it was his duty to return to active political life and assumed the office of Prime Minister on 3rd July 1928.

On 9th July M. Venizelos dissolved the Chamber and fixed 19th August as the date of the new elections. Meanwhile he persuaded the President to take the unusual step of issuing a Decree modifying the electoral law by the abolition of proportional representation, which, in his opinion, had tended to produce numerous small parties rather than decisive majorities. The election resulted in a victory for the Government, which could count on the support of two-thirds of the deputies. On 11th July the question of General Pangalos' fate was decided by releasing him from prison.

The Prime Minister recognized the expediency of continuing the task of improving the relations of Greece and her Balkan

Foreign Relations.
Italy.

and Mediterranean neighbours begun by his predecessor. By the middle of September an agreement had been reached on the terms of a Treaty of Friendship and Conciliation with Italy, which was signed on 23rd September by Signor Mussolini and M. Venizelos, who travelled to Rome for the purpose. Jugoslavia, always inclined to look at any *rapprochement* with Italy as a threat to her own security, was reassured of the friendly feelings of Greece by a personal visit of M. Venizelos to Belgrade in October,

Jugoslavia. where he received a warm welcome and signed a Protocol laying down the procedure for settling all outstanding questions regarding Salonica. There followed a prolonged period of negotiation, during which the Jugoslav Government, in view of their strained relations with Italy, showed themselves anxious to secure the goodwill of Greece and willing to forgo some of the advantages which would have accrued to them if the Agreement of 1923 had been ratified. The conversations were interrupted by the *coup d'état* of 6th January 1929 in Belgrade, which led to the establishment of a virtual dictatorship, but were soon renewed and carried to a successful conclusion on 17th March, when Protocols were signed at Geneva, which were followed on 27th March by the signature of a Pact of Friendship, Conciliation, and Judicial Settlement. The terms of the Protocols conceded most of the conditions desired by Greece : the Jugoslav Free Zone at Salonica remained under Greek sovereignty and administration, and its limits were not extended as provided for in the unratified Agreement of 1926, and the Gevgeli-Salonica Railway, the control of which had been acquired by a Jugoslav company, was ceded to the Greek Government. The satisfactory settlement of their long-outstanding difficulties by the Greek and Jugoslav Governments was no doubt due partly to the prestige which M. Venizelos still enjoyed as the creator of the Balkan Alliance of 1913, and partly to the desire of the Belgrade Government to secure the friendship of her Balkan neighbours in view of the ' forward policy ' of Italy in South-Eastern Europe.

On 1st September 1928 the Albanian National Assembly passed a resolution proclaiming Ahmed Bey Zogu King of the

Albania. Albanians, under the title of King Zog. The new régime was recognized by Greece on 4th September, and on 10th November a Commercial Treaty and Neutrality Convention were ratified between Greece and Albania.

Between Greece and Turkey there were still questions

outstanding which had been raised by the exchange of popula-
Turkey. tions, especially in connexion with the liquidation of the property of exchanged Greeks and
Turks.   M. Venizelos, on assuming office, was desirous of
resuming the negotiations which had been suspended in June, and
suggested the arrangement of a personal meeting with the
Turkish Premier, Ismet Pasha, but this proved impossible and
negotiations through diplomatic channels were resumed.

CHAPTER XX

M. VENIZELOS IN POWER AGAIN (1928–32)

THE new Constitution of 1927 had provided for the establishment of a Second Chamber, an institution which Greece had

Inauguration of the Greek Senate.

not possessed since the year 1864, but it had not yet been brought into existence. On 22nd October 1928, a Bill was introduced to establish a Senate and was passed in December after prolonged discussion. The Senate consisted of 120 members, 92 of whom were elected by the constituencies, 18 chosen by professional corporations, and 10 by the Chamber and Senate. The first election took place on 21st April 1929, and M. Zaïmis was made President, an obviously suitable choice.

M. Venizelos on assuming the Premiership could hold out no promise of any relief of taxation, but undertook to take steps

Finance and public works.

to secure a fairer incidence of the burden. He recognized that Greece was sorely in need of capital for works of development and public utility, in order to bring the country up to the level of a modern State. Political conditions since the war of 1914–18 had been unfavourable to such projects, but something had already been done. For example, in 1926 an American company had contracted to provide a proper water-supply for Athens, which had till then been dependent on an aqueduct built by the Emperor Hadrian and entirely inadequate to modern needs both for drinking purposes and sanitation and also to cope with the dust which is one of the plagues of the city. Now that Greece possessed a Government which commanded confidence abroad, it was possible to raise foreign capital, and in December 1928 a loan for public works was obtained from a banking group in London, and in January 1929 another loan for roads and drainage was raised in the U.S.A.

Vigorous steps were also taken by the Government to put down brigandage, which had become a serious menace to public security.   On one occasion two notorious highwaymen had attacked and murdered the escort of specie belonging to the National Bank ; they were captured and condemned to death.

Little progress was made with the negotiations with Turkey in 1929.   On 17th May the neutral members of the Mixed

Breakdown of negotiations with Turkey.

Commission for the exchange of populations made proposals which Greece accepted, but negotiations broke down over the question of the return to Constantinople of Greeks in possession of Turkish passports.   In August Greece proposed that all pending questions should be referred to arbitration, but Turkey refused the suggestion, and on 19th October the work of the Mixed Commission was suspended.   On 25th June 1929 a Treaty of Commerce and Navigation signed with Russia came into force.   On 25th May the Greek Government paid the first instalment due to Bulgaria in respect of the properties of exchanged nationals under the Agreement of December 1927.

On 9th December 1929 Admiral Koundouriotis, who, except for a short period during the dictatorship of General Pangalos,

M. Zaïmis succeeds Admiral Koundouriotis as President.

had been President of the Republic since its inception, was obliged by advancing years to retire.   He had filled this high office with great distinction, and though originally a prominent adherent of M. Venizelos (whom he had accompanied to Salonica, where he was one of the Triumvirate who established the Provisional Government), he had made himself acceptable to all parties by his tact and self-effacement.   A worthy substitute was found in M. Zaïmis, who, in spite of his seventy-four years was ready as ever to serve his country.   He was elected almost unanimously, his opponent, M. Kaphantaris, receiving only 22 out of 279 votes.   General Paraskevopoulos, formerly Commander-in-Chief in Asia Minor, succeeded him as President of the Senate.

Cabinet dissensions continued throughout the year, changes in the personnel of the Cabinet taking place on 7th June and

Cabinet dissensions.

5th July and again in December, when the portfolios of War, Health, and Aviation, which the Premier had hitherto himself held, were transferred to three under-secretaries, who were included in the Cabinet.   M. Venizelos found it difficult to conciliate the

Royalist Party, led by M. Tsaldaris, though he went so far as to offer that a plebiscite, to be conducted by M. Tsaldaris himself as Minister of Home Affairs, should be held to test the opinion of the people on the question of Monarchy or Republic. On 25th March 1930 celebrations were begun, which lasted for some five weeks, to mark the Centenary of the Declaration of Greek Independence. The Turkish Government was officially represented.

The year 1930 witnessed considerable progress in the regulation of the relations of Greece with her neighbours, and gave M. Venizelos further opportunities of showing his statesmanlike qualities.

The deadlock between Greece and Turkey which had arisen over the exchange of population was aggravated when in 1929 *Turkey and the question of naval parity.* the Turkish Government reconditioned the dreadnought *Goeben*, which had played such a sensational part in the war of 1914–18 by escaping into Turkish waters. This gave Turkey an advantage over Greece, whose only capital ship was the battle cruiser *Averof*, presented by the cotton-millionaire whose name it bore, which had done good service in the Balkan War by the blockade of the Dardanelles. It was suggested that Greece should steal a march on Turkey by obtaining delivery of another pre-war capital ship which had been ordered in Germany and never completed. M. Venizelos, in a speech in the Chamber on 10th February 1930, spoke against this policy and advocated the spending of the money on light naval units and aircraft, which would be more useful for defence than defiance. He declared himself convinced that Turkey had become peacefully minded and had no designs on Greek territory, and he pointed out that the League of Nations existed to settle differences if they should arise ; a much better policy, he urged, would be to resume negotiations on outstanding questions.

This policy was adopted, and the first result was the signature, on 10th June 1930, of a Convention which solved the following *Convention signed, 10th June 1930.* questions on common-sense lines : firstly, the value of the properties left behind by emigrants from Greece and Turkey ; secondly, the disposal of properties left behind by ' non-exchangeable ' nationals who had nevertheless emigrated ; thirdly, the position of Greeks in Constantinople and Moslems in Thrace who were legally 'established' and, therefore 'non-exchangeable'. The Convention was ratified by the Turkish and Greek Chambers by large majorities.

On the day on which the Convention was signed, Ismet Pasha, the Turkish Premier, invited M. Venizelos to visit Ankara
M. Venizelos visits Ankara. and discuss measures for establishing a good understanding between the two peoples. The invitation was accepted for a date in October. An incident connected with the arrangements for the visit threw an interesting light on the improved relations between the two countries. The Turks suggested that the Greek delegation should land at Haidar Pasha, the Asiatic suburb of Constantinople, but M. Venizelos expressed a preference for Ismid on the Sea of Marmara, explaining that, if he visited Constantinople, he must of necessity call on the Patriarch, and this might make a bad impression in Turkey, whereas, if he passed through without visiting the Phanar, Greek opinion would be offended. He was assured that a visit to the Patriarch would create no misunderstanding, and he accordingly passed through Haidar Pasha and visited the Patriarch on his return, receiving an enthusiastic welcome both from the Turks and from the Greeks in Constantinople.

The Greek delegation spent five days in Ankara, and great cordiality was displayed on both sides. The result was the
Treaty with Turkey. signature of three diplomatic instruments : a Treaty of Neutrality, Conciliation, and Arbitration, a Protocol for the Limitation of Naval Armaments, and a Commercial Convention. At a banquet given in his honour M. Venizelos declared that his presence in Ankara signified the end of a conflict between Greece and Turkey which had lasted for ten centuries, and he is said to have remarked to the Turkish President : ' We have agreed on the future of the Near East '. It is a curious fact that M. Venizelos had been born an Ottoman subject in Crete, which then belonged to Turkey, while Kemal was born in Salonica, which in 1930 was the second largest city of Greece.

The year 1930 also saw the end of the labours of the Refugee Settlement Commission, which concluded a Convention with the Greek Government, to whom the administration was handed

over. The Convention was approved by the Financial Committee of the League of Nations in February.
End of the Refugee Commission. Nearly a million refugees had been established
in Greece at a cost which M. Venizelos
reckoned at nearly £80,000,000. The success-
ful termination of this vast migration was a notable achievement
and gave Greece a practically homogeneous population ; in
particular, Greek Macedonia, which had contained a hotch-
potch of conflicting nationalities, was now inhabited by a
population of which 90 per cent. were Greek by race and
sentiment.

Another notable event of 1930 was the first Balkan Conference held in Athens in October. It was an unofficial meeting
The Balkan Conference of 1930. of representatives of Greece, Jugoslavia, Bulgaria,
Albania, Rumania, and Turkey, promoted by
M. Papanastasiou, an ex-premier, who presided,
and was inspired by the example of the con-
clusion of the Locarno Pact. The delegates received an enthusiastic welcome in the Greek capital. Committees were formed
to deal with political questions, economic problems, intellectual
co-operation, communications, and social questions. The
political committee adopted a resolution that the Foreign
Ministers of the Balkan States should meet yearly and exchange
views, and that a pact should be discussed, under which war
should be outlawed, disputes should be settled peaceably, and
mutual assistance should be promised. The chief importance of
the Conference was that it brought together representatives of
the six States in a friendly atmosphere and showed them that
there were many matters in which fruitful co-operation was
possible.

M. Venizelos attended the Hague Conference on Reparations
early in 1930, as representative of Greece, with satisfactory results.
After the settlement of War Debts due from Greece, a balance
was allocated to the Greek Treasury payable in sums of £706,000
for fourteen years and £344,000 for a further twenty-two years.
In March the Government was authorized to negotiate a loan of
£8,000,000 for road construction and drainage, and in April a
contract was signed with the British firm of Messrs. Henry Boot
and Son for land-reclamation and irrigation at the cost of
£6,500,000.

In April 1930 General Pangalos, the former dictator, was brought to trial for a breach of trust while a Minister of State *Trial of General Pangalos.* in connexion with the grant of a concession for a casino at Eleusis, and was sentenced to two years' imprisonment and five years' loss of civil rights. At the end of October some of his supporters planned an unsuccessful attempt to overthrow the Government during the absence of M. Venizelos in Turkey. The conspirators to the number of twenty-seven were arrested and brought to trial. There was also a threat of disturbance by Communists, whose headquarters in Athens were raided on 14th February.

During 1931 M. Venizelos maintained his authority as Premier in spite of opposition from those who criticized his *M. Venizelos justifies his policy.* methods as savouring of autocracy. He replied to his critics in a speech made at Athens in March, when he denied that he had ever acted unconstitutionally and maintained that he was carrying out a mandate entrusted to him by the electorate when he used his powers to enforce discipline. In reply to a Royalist challenge in the Chamber he stated his intention to remain in office until the legal termination of the existing Chamber in the autumn of 1932. The only open act of hostility was a rising planned by Major Katzaros and other followers of General Pangalos, who were easily arrested and brought to trial.

The finances of Greece at the beginning of the year showed a healthy condition, the budget of 1931 yielding a small surplus. *Finance and public works.* A further loan of £4,600,000 was raised for public works, which included road-construction and draining operations in the Vardar and Struma Valleys. On 3rd April an agreement was signed with the British Government which granted Imperial Airways facilities in Greece in return for permission to Greek aviation to use air-ports in Malta and Cyprus ; as a result Athens became a port of call for civil aircraft on the way to and from the East. When Great Britain went off the gold standard, the Greek Government was placed in a difficult position, since Greek currency was linked with sterling and about one quarter of her Central Bank reserve was deposited in London. In order to avoid any threat to the stability of the drachma, the Stock Exchange in Athens was closed for five days and restrictions were placed on the export of capital, but the bank rate rose from 9 to 12 per cent. Greece did not finally abandon the gold standard until April 1932, when she adopted the dollar as the basis of exchange.

Three occasions occurred during 1931 for demonstrations of Anglo-Greek friendship. On 5th April a statue of Rupert *Anglo-Greek Ceremonies.* Brooke, who had died during the war of 1914–18 on Greek soil, was unveiled on the island of Skyros in the presence of M. Venizelos. A statue of George Canning, in whose premiership the British Government recognized the Greeks as belligerents in 1823, presented by Mr. and Mrs. Charles Boot, was unveiled in Athens on 6th April. On 16th July M. Venizelos took part in the ceremony of handing over the deed of gift which conveyed Newstead Abbey, the home of Lord Byron, to the Corporation of the neighbouring city of Nottingham.

While M. Venizelos was in England he conferred with the British Government and afterwards, on his return journey, *Greece and the Hoover Moratorium.* with the French Government, in order to discuss the effect on Greek finances of the adoption of the Hoover Moratorium for war debts. A threatened annual loss of £500,000, including £266,000 due each year from Bulgaria, was a serious matter for Greece. The Greek Government suggested that this loss could be to some extent compensated if Bulgaria consented to forgo payments due under the agreement of 1927 for the compensation of exchanged populations. Eventually Greece agreed to pay half the sum due under this agreement on condition that Bulgaria paid an equal sum on account of reparations.

Greek relations with Turkey were still further strengthened when Ismet Pasha, the Turkish Premier, with the Minister of *The Turkish Premier visits Athens.* Foreign Affairs, arrived in Athens on 3rd October to return M. Venizelos' visit to Ankara. It was an occasion for the display of cordial friendship, and the enthusiasm of the Greek populace made it clear that the two countries were determined henceforward to live at peace with one another and to co-operate for their mutual advantage. Agreements were ratified which included a Treaty of Friendship, a Commercial Convention, and a Protocol for limiting naval armaments.

The Second Balkan Conference was held in Constantinople in October 1931 in a more definitely official atmosphere than the Athens Conference of the previous year. It was attended by two hundred delegates from the six states. The Greek representatives submitted the draft of a Balkan Pact, to which was annexed a proposal that provision should be made for the establishment of an Inter-Balkan Commission on Minorities. The proposal was referred to the Political Committee of the Conference, but little progress was made with its discussion. On the whole the Conference had little result to show for its activities, but the meeting of representatives of the different states in friendly discussion was all to the good.

The Second Balkan Conference.

In the autumn of 1931 a difficult situation arose, which indirectly concerned the Greek Government, when the national movement in Cyprus came to a head. The island, four-fifths of the inhabitants of which are Greeks, had been under British administration since the time of the Berlin Conference in 1878. On the outbreak of the war of 1914-18 it had been annexed by Britain by an Order in Council. As we have seen, in 1915 its cession had been offered to Greece if she gave her ally, Serbia, 'immediate and complete support', which, however, had not been forthcoming. The British sovereignty of the island had been recognized by the Treaty of Lausanne in 1923, and its administration had been assumed by the Colonial Office. Since the vast majority of the 'unredeemed' Greeks had been gradually 'redeemed' either by the acquisition of the territory in which they lived or else by migration, a strong national movement for union with Greece had for some time been gaining force among the 250,000 Cypriot Greeks and was fostered by the Church and in the schools and in athletic and social clubs all over the island. It is true that Cyprus had been admirably administered and its resources developed and exploited under the British authorities, but not unnaturally the inhabitants, though technically citizens of the British Empire, had not ceased to be Greeks in sentiment, and the desire for liberty far outweighed any gratitude for the material advantages which they had gained.

The Greeks in Cyprus.

In November 1929 a Cypriot delegation had visited London and presented a petition praying that the island should be ceded to Greece. The Colonial Secretary replied that his Majesty's

Cypriot delega-
tion in London
in 1929.

Government could not accede to this request and that the subject was definitely closed and further discussion would be unprofitable.

The outbreak of October 1931 was due to the defeat of the Greek members of the Legislative Council on two measures,

Rising in
Cyprus, Oct.
1931.

the Elementary Education Bill of 1929 and the Budget of 1931. The former took away the Control of Education from the local committees of management and aimed at preventing the use

of the schools for Nationalist propaganda. The Budget of 1931, which imposed additional taxation, was passed by the combined vote of the British official members of the Council and the Turkish members.

On 9th September the members of the Cypriot Greek National Movement resolved that a declaration should be addressed to the Cypriot people calling on them to refuse to pay taxes and to boycott British goods. On 18th October the Metropolitan of Kition, Mgr. Mylonas, who had placed himself at the head of the agitators, precipitated matters by publishing a manifesto setting forth the wrongs under which the Greeks were suffering and calling on them to resist the authorities and proclaim the union of Cyprus with her Mother-country Greece. On 21st October a public meeting was held in Nicosia, the capital, from which the demonstrators, singing the Greek National Anthem and shouting for union with Greece, marched against Government House, where the Governor, Sir Ronald Storrs, was at dinner. The house was attacked and set on fire and burnt with all its contents. The rising spread rapidly over the island and it was found necessary to summon help from abroad. On 23rd October two cruisers and two destroyers arrived from Crete and seven R.A.F. troop-carriers with 150 men from Egypt. The rising was quickly put down with few casualties. The ringleaders were deported, and the municipality of Nicosia was fined £20,000 to pay for the damage done. On 12th November it was announced in the House of Commons that Letters Patent had been approved abolishing the Legislative Council and empowering the Governor to make laws ; the future constitution of the island was to be considered in the near future.

The news of the rising caused great excitement and aroused deep sympathy in Greece, which was voiced in the Press and *Greece and the Cypriot Rising.* by public demonstrations, which had to be checked by the police and even by the military. A requiem for the Greeks who had fallen in the riots was not allowed to be held in Athens but took place outside the city, and there were further demonstrations on Armistice Day.   M. Venizelos took up a strong and statesmanlike attitude and declared that there was no Cypriot question between the Greek and British Governments, but only between the British Government and their Cypriot subjects ; agitation in the Press and elsewhere could serve no useful purpose and would have no influence on the British Government ; whatever sympathy the Greeks might feel for the aspirations of the Cypriots—and, by implication, for those of the Dodecanesans—if the Powers held that their interests demanded the continued occupation of the islands, nothing could alter their determination ; moreover, it was essential that nothing should be done to alienate the friendship of Great Britain.   He concluded, however, by confessing that he himself hoped that the idea of the cession of Cyprus to Greece need not be abandoned for all time.   The statesman-like attitude of M. Venizelos in thus boldly advocating a policy which was directly opposed to Greek national sentiment recalled the similar occasion in 1912 when he had checked the agitation for the union with Greece of his native island of Crete, which had in due time been gathered into the national fold.

The year 1932 was a troublous time for Greece both in the political and in the financial sphere.   The economic blizzard of *Economic position of Greece in 1932.* 1931 had a serious effect in Greece as in many other countries, and in view of the lessened demand for her products in the world markets, she found difficulty in meeting the service of her external loans, which had been contracted mainly for public works which were still unproductive.

Early in the year various palliative measures were introduced. The movement of capital was restricted, heavy duties were imposed on imports, exports were encouraged, and a system of barter with other countries was attempted.

In January M. Venizelos visited the European capitals in

order to try and obtain a loan which would enable Greece
Financial Difficulties. to balance her budget, pay interest on her external loans and avoid inflation. As a result Sir Otto Niemeyer was sent by the League of Nations to report on the financial position of Greece. On 5th March the Prime Minister stated that the Government could carry on if a loan of £2,500,000 was obtained and would resign rather than repudiate its public debts. The League Financial Committee recommended that Greece should meet her foreign payments due on 1st May and suspend the sinking funds, and that she should be granted a loan of £2,000,000. This did not meet the Government's minimum requirements, and M. Venizelos offered to resign in favour of a Coalition Government, but the leader of the Opposition, M. Tsaldaris, refused to co-operate, and the Government remained in office. In April M. Venizelos visited Geneva to plead before the Council of the League of Nations but failed to obtain better terms, and therefore instructed the Greek Ministers in the European capitals to approach the foreign bondholders, asking them to agree to the postponement of interest due on 1st May and the suspension of the sinking funds. The Budget introduced on 20th May made no provision for sinking funds but set aside a sum of over a million pounds for interest on loans, which, however, was to be retained for the moment in Greece. On 30th July a decree was issued under which all foreign currency deposited in the banks was converted into drachmas at the rate of 100 for the dollar and 385 for the pound. After prolonged discussion an agreement was reached with the foreign bondholders that during 1932-3 payment should be made of 30 per cent. of the amount due as interest on loans.

In the political sphere two measures proposed by the Government in May 1932 aroused bitter controversy. One was a Bill
M. Venizelos resigns and then resumes office. for the adoption of proportional representation, which was eventually passed. The other was a measure for the restriction of the Press, which was considered necessary by the Government owing to the violent tone of the Royalist papers. It met with such determined opposition that on 21st May M. Venizelos resigned. The Republican leader, M. Papanastasiou, then formed a Cabinet of his own supporters after failing to enlist the support

of the Populist Party under M. Tsaldaris, but resigned on his first appearance before the Chamber, and on 5th June M. Venizelos again assumed office.

At this juncture the army intervened, and a Military League was formed to support the Republic. It was alleged by his *The Military* opponents that M. Venizelos was responsible for *League.* this move, and he replied by challenging the leaders of the various opposition parties to give a pledge not to raise the question of the régime during the coming ten years, and by asserting that, if they did so, the Military League would disband itself. The pledge was refused, and the Chamber was dissolved on 18th August after a speech from the Prime Minister in which he reviewed the achievements of his four years of office and justified his foreign and domestic policy.

Polling for the new Chamber took place on 25th September. It produced a situation of stalemate, the Liberals obtaining *Elections of* 102 seats, the Populist Party 96, the Progressive *Sept. 1932.* Republicans 15, and the other various groups 40. An attempt was, therefore, made to form a Coalition Government of all the parties except the Communists, but it proved impossible. Eventually, on 4th November, M. Tsaldaris succeeded in forming a Cabinet by a Coalition from the various anti-Venizelist parties, MM. Venizelos, Kaphantaris, and Papanastasiou undertaking not to outvote the Government during the coming eight months. M. Tsaldaris' position, however, was difficult, since he could only muster 111 supporters against an opposition of 129 members.

On 26th September Macedonia, especially Chalcidice, and Thessaly were visited by a severe earthquake, which caused heavy casualties. The British Mediterranean fleet arrived early on the scenes with relief.

CHAPTER XXI

THE REACTION TOWARDS MONARCHISM AND THE RESTORATION OF KING GEORGE II (1933-5)

THE beginning of the year 1933 found the minority Government of M. Tsaldaris in a precarious position. During January
*Fall of
M. Tsaldaris'
Government.*
his Finance Minister, M. Angelopoulos, resigned because he disagreed with the policy of including in the Budget the funds necessary for paying 30 per cent. of the amount due to foreign bondholders. The general financial policy of the Government was attacked by M. Venizelos ; and when M. Tsaldaris asked for a vote of confidence and failed to obtain it, he resigned on 13th January and M. Venizelos formed another Cabinet, which was destined to be short-lived. The Chamber was then dissolved, and new elections were held with the result that 111 Liberals, 131 members of the Populist Party, and 6 Independents were returned.

On the evening of the Election Day, 5th March, General Plastiras, who, it will be recalled, had been at the head of the
*Attempted coup
d'état of 5th
March 1933.*
revolution of 1923, was at M. Venizelos' house listening to the results of the poll. When it became clear that the Populist Party was going to obtain a majority, he went out and seized the Ministry of War and dispatched troops and armoured cars to patrol the streets. The next day no newspapers were allowed to appear, and at midday a manifesto was issued stating that, since Parliamentary rule had broken down and a civil war was imminent, the General and his supporters had taken charge of affairs pending the appointment of a government strong enough to deal with the crisis. The *coup d'état* failed owing to lack of support from the soldiers and populace, and was put down after desultory street fighting, in which the casualties were insignificant. General Plastiras escaped and succeeded in reaching Rhodes.

After discussions had taken place between President Zaïmis,

M. Venizelos, M. Tsaldaris, and General Othonaios, the last-
named was commissioned by the President to
restore order and hand over the administration
to the party which had obtained the majority
at the election. On 10th March, therefore, M. Tsaldaris again
became Prime Minister.

M. Tsaldaris again Premier.

On 6th June in the evening M. and Mme. Venizelos were
motoring back to the capital from Kephissia followed by a
second car containing members of M. Venizelos'
bodyguard. About six miles outside the city
they were joined by another car, the occupants
of which began to fire upon them. The tyres
of the second ¯car were punctured and one of its passengers
killed. M. Venizelos' car drove on, followed by the strange car,
from which some fifty shots were fired at it, but the shooting
was poor and M. Venizelos was unharmed, though Mme
Venizelos was injured by broken glass and the chauffeur was
wounded. The would-be assassins were not arrested, and
connivance on the part of high officials of the police was suspected.

Attempted assassination of M. Venizelos.

Much time was spent in the Chamber during the rest of the
year arguing questions which arose out of the *coup d'état.* The
Government proposed that senior officers who had supported
General Plastiras should be retired from the army, and a Bill to
this effect was passed by the Chamber and, though at first rejected
by the Senate, eventually became law. Next, General Metaxas
insisted on the impeachment of M. Venizelos for complicity in
the *coup d'état.* M. Venizelos, in defending himself, spoke in
praise of General Plastiras and roused an uproar in the House ;
whereupon the Liberal deputies left the Chamber and threatened
to stay away unless the Government could guarantee the protection of members and the right of free speech. The Prime Minister
refused to allow the discussion of the motion for impeachment
in the absence of M. Venizelos and the Liberals, and when General
Metaxas insisted on his motion, he put an end to the dispute by
proclaiming an amnesty for all those who had been concerned in
the *coup d'état.* M. Tsaldaris, who genuinely wished to bring
about political appeasement and showed tact and patience in the
methods which he employed, did his best to establish a *modus
vivendi* with the Liberal Party, but found M. Venizelos quite
unwilling to compromise.

In Foreign Affairs there was some activity during the year, but no complications arose which threatened the relations of
Foreign Affairs in 1933.
Greece with other states. The Turkish Foreign Minister visited Athens in July. In September M. Tsaldaris and M. Maximos, his Foreign Minister, visited Ankara and signed a Greco-Turkish Treaty which amplified the scope of the Treaty of 1930. Negotiations with Bulgaria were begun in November to settle outstanding economic questions but made little progress. In December M. Maximos visited Zagreb, where he met King Alexander and members of the Jugoslav Cabinet, and then proceeded to Paris, Rome, and London in order to establish relations between the Greek Government and the Cabinets of those Powers, who had long been accustomed to regard M. Venizelos as the sole fountain-head of Greek policy. Trade Agreements were signed during the year with Albania and Soviet Russia.

The Fourth Balkan Conference met at Salonica in November.
Fourth Balkan Conference.
Amongst other business it repeated the resolution passed at the Third Conference held in the previous year in favour of a multi-lateral pact between the Balkan States.

The tenth anniversary of the foundation of the Republic was fêted during March 1934. Though Greece was at the
The Tenth Anniversary of the Republic.
time under a government of monarchist convictions, the Prime Minister on assuming office had undertaken not to raise the question of the régime, and so found himself unable to object to the celebrations, but the advantage was naturally taken of the occasion by the Republicans.

The political situation in 1934 was still dominated by the deadlock between the Government and the Opposition, the
The political impasse.
former having a majority in the Chamber, while the Liberals had the upper hand in the Senate and so were able to block any measure passed in the Lower House. There were several bones of contention between the Government and its opponents, of which the most serious were the question of the reform of the electoral system and the approaching election to the Presidency of the Republic. At the last general election the votes had been counted on the system of proportional representation, and

the Government now wished to revert to the majority system. M. Zaïmis' five years' tenure of the office of President was due to expire at the end of the year and the Government was anxious to see him re-elected, though he was now nearly eighty years of age, but his re-election could only be secured by the co-operation of the Liberal majority in the Senate. M. Venizelos seized the opportunity to attempt a bargain with M. Tsaldaris and offered the support of his party for the election of M. Zaïmis, if the Government would yield to his views about the electoral system and also with regard to changes in the method of superannuation in the army ; if the Government refused to compromise, he threatened to stand for the Presidency himself. M. Tsaldaris would only go as far as to declare his readiness to facilitate an agreement between the Government and the Opposition for a new electoral law, if M. Zaïmis' candidature received the general support of all parties.

Party dissensions, therefore, continued and culminated in a violent scene in the Chamber in June, when, during a passage of arms between General Kondylis, the Minister of War, and M. Papanastasiou, leader of the Socialist Party, a chair was hurled and struck the latter statesman. This precipitated a general *melée*, after which the opposition parties withdrew from the Chamber and refused to return. Finding that all attempts at compromise were useless, the Government introduced its own Electoral Bill, which was promptly thrown out by the Senate. A further dispute then arose over the article of the Constitution which provided for a joint sitting of both Houses when a Bill passed by the Chamber was rejected by the Senate, the Opposition maintaining that this procedure was obligatory, the Government that it was permissive.

A stormy scene in the Chamber.

The political deadlock now appeared to be complete, and, as the date of the Presidential election approached, it seemed that the only possible solution was to dissolve the Chamber and hold fresh elections. At the last moment, however, seventeen Liberal Senators approached the Prime Minister with an offer to support the candidature of M. Zaïmis if M. Tsaldaris would undertake to repeal the electoral law. A joint sitting of both Houses was accordingly held on 19th October and M. Zaïmis was re-elected President.

Re-election of M. Zaïmis as President.

Meanwhile those who had been guilty of the attempt on the life of M. Venizelos on 6th June 1933 were still at large. But

M. Venizelos retires to Crete.
on 3rd October M. Venizelos' private police arrested a notorious brigand, Karathanasis by name, who was under suspicion of having taken part in the outrage. This arrest by unofficial police after the failure of the official agents still further embittered the relations between the Venizelists and the Government. The Minister for Home Affairs at once resigned, and the Chiefs of the Athens Police and of the Gendarmerie were replaced ; but the trial of the accused was further postponed. M. Tsaldaris again attempted to bring about a reconciliation with M. Venizelos, but he refused to return to his duties as a deputy and retired to Crete.

The most important event affecting Greece during 1934 in the sphere of external relations was the signature of the Balkan

The Balkan Pact of 1934.
Pact. We have seen how, at the successive Balkan Conferences, progress had been made in securing co-operation in the economic and cultural fields, and how tentative suggestions had been made for joint political action. The time now seemed ripe when the Balkan States could follow the example of the Little Entente and the Baltic States by combining to safeguard the *status quo* against Treaty revision and form a block which would be able to hold its own amongst the Powers and secure its members from the interference and patronage of more powerful neighbours.

The signatories to the Pact, which was signed on 9th February 1934, were Greece, Turkey, Rumania, and Jugoslavia. Every

The attitude of Bulgaria.
attempt had been made to induce Bulgaria to join, but, though the Bulgarian Government expressed its willingness to co-operate in a Pact of Non-aggression, it refused to commit the country to any perpetuation of the existing order, that is to say, to a renunciation of claims to treaty revision.

The Pact declared that the signatory Powers wished to consolidate peace in the Balkans and were 'firmly resolved to

The provisions of the Pact.
guarantee respect for existing contractual agreements and the maintenance of the established territorial order'. They, therefore, mutually guaranteed the 'security of all the Balkan frontiers' and undertook to 'consult one another on measures to be taken, if their

interests were affected, and not to embark on political action or assume political obligations in respect of any Balkan State which was not a signatory without mutual discussion '. The adherence of the other Balkan States (Bulgaria and Albania) would be ' an object of favourable examination ' by the signatory Powers.

The signature of the Pact was unfavourably received in Bulgaria, where the assurances that it was not in any way directed against Bulgaria's interests were regarded with suspicion. Nor was there great enthusiasm for it in Greece, where the Opposition criticized it as unwise and unnecessary, and extracted an assurance from the Government that Greece would not be involved in war if any of the signatory Powers was attacked by a non-Balkan State.

A disagreement with Albania on the language question in the autumn of 1934 aroused considerable excitement in Athens.

The Greek Language Question in Albania. The action of the Albanian Government in forbidding instruction in secular schools in any language except Albanian was really inspired by a desire to discourage Italian propagandism, but it indirectly affected Greece and gave rise to protests. The Albanian Government, however, waived its insistence on the use of Albanian as the medium of instruction in Greek schools, but required that teachers in these schools should be drawn from the Greek minority in Albania and not appointed from Greece.

The economic improvement which had begun in 1933 continued in 1934. Both the revenue and the trade figures showed

The economic situation in 1934. a marked increase, and the restriction of imports and the control of the exportation of foreign currency maintained the drachma at a steady level. The cover of gold and foreign exchange reached 4000 million drachma in June 1934 as compared with 1600 million at the end of 1932.

The year 1935 opened with a promise of more harmonious relations between the political parties in the Greek Chamber.

The political situation in Jan. 1935. The joint action of the Government and the Opposition in the re-election of M. Zaïmis as President of the Republic had proved that co-operation was not impossible, and before the end of 1934 the opposition members had returned to their duties in the Chamber. Perhaps the continued absence in Crete of M. Venizelos, who refused to return to Athens until steps had been taken to bring to trial those who had been arrested on suspicion of having been implicated in the attempt on his life, contributed to a more peaceful political atmosphere. On 16th January 1935 a combined meeting of the party leaders took place at which agreement was reached on a programme of development during the coming six years, which included plans for the reorganization of the defences of the country and the construction of a large cruiser and a number of destroyers and submarines.

On 1st March, however, a military rising, which had been for some months in secret preparation, suddenly threw the country into a turmoil. In spite of assurances by M. Tsaldaris that he had no designs against the Republican régime, the extreme Republicans seem to have decided that a movement in favour of the Monarchy was making headway in the country and to have resented that a Government of Royalist sympathies should continue to direct the policy of the Republic. In particular, the more ardent Republicans among the officers of the Fleet and Army feared that, if a restoration of the Monarchy took place, they would inevitably lose their commands, and they, therefore, determined to forestall such a possibility by forcibly ejecting the existing Government. The insurgents, therefore, led by a group of retired officers seized the Military College and the barracks of the Evzones in Athens and the arsenal at Salamis. The flag-ship *Averof* and several smaller naval units put to sea and summoned the garrisons of the provinces by a wireless proclamation to join the movement to overthrow the Government. The only response from mainland Greece came from Macedonia, where General Kamenos proclaimed the Revolution and rallied a force round him. At Salonica the timely action of the Corps Commander in arresting officers suspected of complicity prevented any rising, but the rebels seized Serres, Demir-Hissar, Drama, and Cavalla ; but, when General Kondylis, the Minister of War, arrived in Macedonia and took the field against the rebels, the insurrection quickly collapsed. General Kamenos and some of the other officers who had joined him fled across the frontier

The attempted Revolution of March 1935.

Its causes.

Failure of the Revolution on the mainland.

and surrendered to the Bulgarian authorities. In Athens the movement failed to enlist the support either of the majority of the troops or of the general public, and the insurgents were soon isolated in two main groups and overpowered.

Meanwhile the *Averof* and the accompanying destroyers had made their way to Suda Bay in Crete, where M. Venizelos

The rebel fleet in the Ægean. placed himself at the head of the movement. After establishing their own nominee as Governor-General of Crete and deposing the loyal authorities the insurgents left for Samos, Chios, and Mitylene, harassed by the Greek Air Force, which had remained

Collapse of the Revolution. loyal. But the failure of the movement in the capital and on the mainland in general made further operations at sea useless, and the rebel officers decided that they had better escape while there was yet time. They, therefore, left the fleet to make its submission to the Government and fled to Italian territory in Rhodes, where M. Venizelos also arrived on 13th March. The movement collapsed because it was badly organized and led, and because public opinion was against it. M. Venizelos retired to France. His participation in the attempted revolution was almost the last and certainly the least creditable act of one who had gained a high reputation as a statesman and to whom Greece owed much in the past.

On the suppression of the rising the Government was faced with the problem of punishing the ringleaders. The Prime

The punishment of the insurgents. Minister immediately declared that exemplary punishment would be inflicted on the guilty and that the Army and Navy would be purged of officers, and the civil service of officials, who had failed in their duty to the State. A court martial at Salonica condemned one officer to death and passed severe sentences on a number of others. General Kamenos and nine other officers who had escaped into Bulgaria and eight others who had fled to Turkey were sentenced to death. On 22nd April General Papoulas, President of the Republican Defence League, was condemned to death and immediately executed. M. Venizelos was condemned to death in his absence, together with General Plastiras, who had been chosen leader of the rising but had taken no active part. M. Venizelos' son Kyriakos received a sentence of ten years' and General Gonatas of five years' imprisonment. A large number of civil servants, university professors, and schoolmasters were dismissed, and, beside those officers who had been court-martialled, some nine hundred were cashiered, suspended or placed on the retired list. These drastic measures caused some consternation not only among the public in Greece but also in foreign countries, and the British, French, and American Ministers in Athens were instructed by their Governments to recommend the Greek Government to mitigate their severity towards the rebels.

General Kondylis, whose prompt action had put down the rising, was made Deputy Premier in March. On 1st April the Chamber, which had already approved the steps taken by the Government to suppress the movement, passed measures abolishing the Senate, suspending the permanency of the judiciary and of the Civil Service, and dissolving the House. 9th June was fixed as the date of a general election, and the members then elected were to meet as a National Assembly.

Another effect of the failure of the rising was to raise in an acute form the question of the possible restoration of the mon-
The question of archy. A declaration was made at the end of
the restoration of April by General Kondylis, representing the
the Monarchy. Government, that, although all the political parties had recognized the Republic, the government would submit the question of the future régime to the nation if there was sufficient evidence for the demand for such action.

The General Election, in which the Republican Parties took no part, was held on 9th June 1935 and resulted in the return of 243 members of M. Tsaldaris' Populist Party, 37 followers of General Kondylis, 7 followers of General Metaxas, and 6 Independents.

The first meeting of the National Assembly was held on 1st July ; it voted in favour of a plebiscite, leaving the fixing of
The question of the date to the Government. Some members
the plebiscite. of the Cabinet led by General Kondylis, in view of reports that the Government meant to postpone the plebiscite, pressed M. Tsaldaris to declare his personal attitude on the question of the future régime. When he refused to do so, General Kondylis resigned, but was included in a new Cabinet immediately formed by M. Tsaldaris, in which five of the

former members were not included. After further controversy and more threats of resignation from General Kondylis, the Government issued a proclamation urging the nation to vote for the restoration of the monarchy at the plebiscite, which was fixed for 3rd November. On 10th October, however, under pressure from the extreme Royalists, M. Tsaldaris again resigned and was succeeded as Premier by General Kondylis, who formed a Cabinet in which M. Theotokis was Foreign Minister. The Government then obtained from the National Assembly a vote in favour of proclaiming Greece to be a Monarchical State, but on the understanding that the return of the King should not take place until after the plebiscite. General Kondylis was meanwhile appointed Regent, and M. Zaïmis' functions as President of the Republic automatically came to an end.

King George II of Greece, who, as we have seen, had occupied the throne from 28th September 1922 to 19th December 1923,

The return of King George II. was now forty-five years of age. On leaving Greece he had made his headquarters in London and was a well-known figure in English society. It had been obvious ever since the victory of the Royalists in the election of 9th June 1934 that sooner or later he would be called upon to return to Greece. From the first he made it clear that he would not re-ascend the throne at the invitation of a single party but only if an overwhelming majority as expressed by a plebiscite demanded his return.

The plebiscite of 3rd November 1935, which is generally believed to have been stage-managed by the army, resulted, according to the official returns, in a vote of 97 per cent. in favour of the Restoration. Thereupon the Regent and the Cabinet took the oath of allegiance to King George II, and a delegation was sent to London to invite him to return and resume the Royal functions. He left London on 14th November and, after visits to Paris and Rome *en route*, reached Athens on 25th November and was received with general rejoicings.

On the King's arrival General Kondylis submitted to him

The King insists on a General Amnesty. the resignation of the Government and was requested to carry on the administration. But difficulties soon arose between the King and his Ministers. King George, who was anxious to pursue a policy of political appeasement, insisted on the granting of an amnesty to all political offenders, while General Kondylis felt himself unable to accept an amnesty of so general and unconditional a kind. The Cabinet, therefore, resigned and was replaced by a non-Party Ministry in which M. Demertzis was Prime Minister. The General Amnesty was then proclaimed, and the King dissolved the National Assembly, and 26th January 1936 was fixed as the date of the General Election. M. Venizelos, who, on the insistence of the King, was included in the General Amnesty, recommended the Liberal Party not to oppose the new régime and expressed a hope that the King, by continuing to follow the wise path upon which he had already entered, would consolidate his position on the throne and bring unity to the nation.

In the sphere of international affairs the unprovoked invasion of Abyssinia by Italy in the summer of 1935 made it clear to

Greece and sanctions against Italy.

Greece that for the moment Italian Imperialism was not going to launch its thunders against the Balkans, and on this account there was a feeling of relief. But Greece and the other countries of the Balkan Entente, as members of the League of Nations, could not remain mere onlookers. They had soon to make up their minds whether or not to take part in the application of economic sanctions against Italy under Article 16 of the Covenant. Greece, together with the other members of the Entente and also Bulgaria, decided to join in the League Sanctions in spite of the serious loss of trade which was involved. In informing the Italian Government of their action the Greek Government took the opportunity of pointing out that their Treaty of Friendship with Italy contained a clause reserving to Greece the right to fulfil any undertakings which arose under the Covenant of the League. In December Greece, together with Jugoslavia and Turkey, took up a still more definite position when the British Government asked whether their support would be forth-coming against Italy if she took military action in retaliation for sanctions. They all replied in the affirmative. The idea that Great Britain was taking the lead in resisting Italian aggression produced a profound impression in the Near East, and a corre-sponding disillusionment ensued when Great Britain, having induced the smaller states to take a firm line, herself began to weaken in her opposition to Italy.

On 22nd August 1935 Admiral Paul Koundouriotis, the first President of the Greek Republic and the Grand Old Man of the Greek political world, died at the age of eighty years.

Death of Admiral Koundouriotis.

CHAPTER XXII

GENERAL METAXAS BECOMES DICTATOR (1936-9)

THE General Election held on 26th January 1936 only resulted in a further political deadlock. The Liberals under M. Sophoulis,

The General Election of Jan. 1936.

who had succeeded M. Venizelos as leader of the Party, secured 127 seats and had the support of the Agrarian and Republican Parties, which gave them a total of 142 votes; the Populist Party of M. Tsaldaris secured 69 seats and received the support of the 63 members of the Popular-Radical Party led by General Kondylis and M. Theotokis, 7 members of General Metaxas' party and 4 members of the Macedonian group, giving them a total strength of 143 members. The result was that the Communists with 15 members, like the Irish Nationalist members in the British Parliament of 1910, held the balance between the two groups.

On 31st January General Kondylis died suddenly of heart failure at the age of fifty-seven after a romantic career during

Deaths of General Kondylis and M. Demertzis.

which he rose from a private in the Greek Army to be General, Premier, and the 'King-maker' of 1935, and starting as a supporter of M. Venizelos became leader of the ultra-Royalists. On 7th March M. Sophoulis, who had been elected President of the Chamber, attempted to form a Cabinet but failed to secure the co-operation of M. Tsaldaris. He offered, however, to support M. Demertzis, who on 15th March formed a Cabinet in which General Metaxas was Deputy-Premier and Minister of War. But before he met the Chamber, M. Demertzis in

General Metaxas becomes Prime Minister.

his turn suddenly died on 13th April and was succeeded as Prime Minister by General Metaxas. The Chamber met at the end of April and passed a vote of confidence in the Government. It was then prorogued for five months after empowering the Government to govern by decrees subject to the approval of a

Committee of forty members which included all the Party leaders.

Death was busy amongst Greek political leaders in the year 1936. On 18th March M. Venizelos died in Paris at the age of

Death of M. Venizelos.

seventy-two. Eight times Prime Minister of Greece, he was undoubtedly the greatest statesman that Modern Greece has produced and one of the few Greeks who have become prominent figures in European politics. His chief services to Greece, which were performed in the sphere of international rather than home affairs, were his championship of the Greek cause in Crete ; his part in the formation of the Balkan Alliance, which brought Greece a great extension of territory as the result of the Balkan Wars ; the measures which he took to enable Greece to secure her interests by fighting on the side of the Allies in the war of 1914-18 ; his representation of Greece at the Peace Conference and at the Conference of Lausanne ; his settlement of the differences between Greece and Jugoslavia ; and his measures for the reconciliation of Greece and Turkey. Against these services must be set his advocacy of the unfortunate war against Turkey in Asia Minor and his participation in the abortive revolution of 1935 ; M. Venizelos was something of a political gambler, and these were ventures that failed. His methods may have sometimes been open to criticism, and he was often unhappy in his choice of lieutenants, but he was a true patriot, and, but for him, Greece to-day would bulk much less prominently on the map of Europe and the ' Great Idea ' of the consolidation of the Greek people would never have been carried into effect. King George II wisely showed his appreciation of M. Venizelos, when, in spite of his former opposition to King Constantine, he insisted that his name should be included in the amnesty of 1935 ; but even after his death, party feeling still ran so high that the suggestion that M. Venizelos should lie in state in Athens on his way to burial in his native island had to be cancelled for fear of disturbances, and his body was conveyed direct to Crete for burial.

On 16th May M. Tsaldaris, leader of the Populist Party and

Death of M. Tsaldaris.

ex-Prime Minister, died suddenly. By the deaths of General Kondylis, M. Demertzis, and M. Tsaldaris within a period of three months, three important parties were deprived of their chiefs.

The most striking event in international politics in 1936 was the Balkan Conference held at Belgrade from 4th to 6th May.

General Metaxas at the Balkan Conference of 1936. Greece was represented by General Metaxas, who with some support from the Turkish delegation exerted himself to reduce to a minimum the obligations assumed by Greece under the Balkan Pact. Greece made it clear that she had no intention of taking up arms if the opposing side included Italy as well as Bulgaria and Hungary.

In June Dr. Schacht, the astute German Minister of Economics, visited Athens and made an agreement for balancing the trading account between Greece and Germany, which, *Financial agreement with Germany.* chiefly owing to purchases of tobacco and metals, showed a large sum in favour of Greece, by extensive purchases from Germany, mainly of military material. M. Tsouderos at a meeting of the shareholders of the Bank of Greece, of which he was governor, issued a timely warning of the danger of upsetting the economic balance of the country by abandoning the cultivation of cereals in favour of luxury products, such as tobacco, which might at the moment command attractive prices abroad, but of which there might easily be a dangerous over-production.

The second half of 1936 failed to show any progress towards the unity of Greece for which King George II had hoped when he re-ascended the throne. The constant strife *The failure of Constitutional Monarchy.* between the political parties, which had little regard for the interests of the country and played each for its own hand, was carried on in the Parliamentary Committee, as before in the Chamber, and led to constant obstruction, which prevented any useful legislation. Further, the almost simultaneous death of the chief party leaders made discipline still more difficult to enforce. By the prorogation of the Chamber for five months the Communists had been deprived of their controlling vote, but they were active in promoting disorders and agitation all over the country; at Salonica, for example, a strike was fomented which was only put down after considerable bloodshed. The Cabinet realized the necessity of taking steps to deal with the situation and prepared a decree fixing minimum wages, but at the same time they exasperated the trades-unionists by advocating compulsory arbitration in labour disputes and Government control of trades-union funds.   The union leaders, therefore, replied by fixing 5th August 1936 for a general strike.

In the face of this threat General Metaxas realized that any step that had to be taken must be taken quickly.   He knew that, *General Metaxas becomes Dictator.* if the Chamber were summoned to debate what measures should be adopted, precious time would be wasted in fruitless discussion and nothing would be done to save Greece from the possible danger of following the example of Spain and plunging into civil war.   On 4th August, therefore, at the eleventh hour, he obtained King George's signature to decrees proclaiming martial law, suspending articles of the Constitution which affected the personal liberty of the subject, and dissolving the Chamber. Henceforward he ruled without a Parliament and established a Dictatorship which was to last until his death.   He himself, besides being Premier, held the portfolios of Foreign Affairs, War, the Marine, and the Air ;   the rest of his Cabinet consisted partly of specialists and partly of retired naval and military officers of tried experience and character.

There is little doubt that the *coup d'état* was the result of a sudden decision imposed by the critical position of affairs, but *His social policy.* General Metaxas soon showed that he meant to use his autocratic powers for the benefit of the community.   He drew up a programme which included sweeping social reforms, and measures for the development of industry and for the reorganization of the armed forces. Greece had become more and more the prey of social unrest and agitation.   To cure these evils, General Metaxas, by a series of decrees, introduced compulsory arbitration on labour dis-putes and collective contracts, an eight-hour day in all industries, a minimum wage for all workers, a system of health insurance and health services, holidays with pay and a Sunday rest.   He made a beginning of improved housing conditions, and he remitted about one-third of the debts of the Greek peasants, chiefly refugees from Asia Minor and Bulgaria, who had been hard hit by the fall of agricultural prices and were unable to meet their obligations to the Government, which had settled them on the land.   The administration of Athens, its suburbs, and the Peiræus was placed under the control of a Governor with

Cabinet rank assisted by a Prefect in charge of the municipal and police authorities. For the country at large he instituted a ten years' programme of development of road construction and public works. He devoted special attention to the strengthening of the army and navy and fortifying the frontiers, and he took stern measures to ban politics from the barrack-room. He inaugurated a youth movement and a Greek version of the German ' Strength through Joy ' movement.

Like other dictators, General Metaxas found that in order to secure his position he had to resort to drastic censorship of the *Measures of*   Press. He even insisted on the use of the blue *repression.*   pencil upon the Greek classics, refusing to allow a public performance of the *Antigone* of Sophocles without severe ' cuts ' of passages which savoured too much of criticism of authority, and forbidding the reading in schools of the Funeral Oration of Pericles because of its encomium on democracy. Local government, when it showed too much independence, was suspended in several towns, and the Chair of Constitutional Law in the University of Athens was abolished.

On entering upon his dictatorship General Metaxas stated that he had assumed the minimum of power necessary to face *General Metaxas*   the danger of Communism and would not *states his position.*   relinquish it until the social order had been completely stabilized ; the nation must submit to discipline, and party adherents must renounce and forget their parties which no longer existed ; no new elections would be held, since the old parliamentary system was ended ; the new Government was permanent and would apply the newly established system until it had achieved the regeneration of Greek society.

In foreign affairs he announced that there would be no change in the policy of Greece, which would continue to be based on a close understanding with Turkey and the maintenance of the Balkan Entente.

The result of General Metaxas' measures was that, outwardly at least, a tranquillity, to which Greece had long been a stranger, reigned throughout the country. The only challenge to his rule was revealed by the discovery on 1st December 1936 of a plot against the Government, which involved the arrest and

14

trial of nine persons, who were condemned to periods of imprisonment of from six months to two years.

On 15th September 1936 M. Alexander Zaïmis, ex-President of the Republic, who had been ten times Prime Minister—

*Death of
M. Zaïmis.* several times taking office at a crisis in the history of the country—for five years High Commissioner of Crete, and Governor of the Bank of Greece, passed away at the age of eighty-one years. The descendant of a family which had taken a prominent part in the War of Indepenence, he had performed inestimable services to his country. A strong, silent man—a combination of qualities rare among Greek politicians—he enjoyed the confidence of the country throughout a long career. It is said that in his will King George I advised his successor, King Constantine, always to remember that he was a constitutional monarch and to consult M. Zaïmis if ever he found himself in difficulties.

On 17th November the mortal remains of King Constantine and his wife Queen Sophia and of Queen Olga, wife of King George I, were brought back to Greece and interred at Tatoi, the royal estate in Attica.

In February 1937 the annual Balkan Conference was held at Athens and revealed the usual harmony among its members,

*Foreign Affairs
in 1937.* who also expressed their approval of the Treaty of Friendship concluded between Jugoslavia and Bulgaria. During May Ismet Inönü,[1] the Turkish Premier, visited Athens bearing cordial greetings from Kemal Ataturk, but it was understood he had the further mission of warning General Metaxas that his pro-Nazi and pro-Fascist leanings were causing some alarm among his Turkish allies. The visit was returned in the autumn by General Metaxas. King George visited London, Paris, and Rome and doubtless conveyed to the three Governments the resolve of Greece to keep on good terms with the Mediterranean Powers without identifying his country with any one of them to the exclusion of the other two. About the same time Baron von Neurath, the German Foreign Secretary, visited Athens, and Dr. Schacht also came for a second time to make arrangement for economic

[1] He had assumed the name of Inönü, just as Kemal adopted that of Ataturk, when a decree was issued in Turkey compelling all Turkish citizens to add surnames to their names.

exchanges between the two countries. An agreement was

Finance and economic affairs. concluded with the German Government for a loan of 350,000,000 drachmae at 3 per cent. interest repayable in six yearly instalments, which was used to meet the armament requirements of Greece and the early completion of her defence programme.

In April the Greek Government concluded another agreement with the British firm of Messrs. Henry Boot and Son involving a sum of more than £2,000,000 to be spent on drainage and irrigation in Thessaly and land-reclamation and flood-protection in Epirus and other work in Crete.

The question of interest on foreign loans, for which a temporary arrangement had been made in 1936, was again discussed in July and August 1937. Greece refused to pay more than 40 per cent. on the coupons due in the year ending March 1938, an offer which was refused as inadequate by the Council of Foreign Bondholders and the Loans Committee of the League of Nations.

The wheat harvest of 1936 had been a disastrous failure ; it was, therefore, necessary to import large quantities of foreign grain, which was a strain on the exchange resources of the country. On the other hand the crops of 1937 and 1938 were much above the average. Industrial activity had been on the increase for some years, and, as a result, unemployment had fallen considerably, while the standard of living had risen, though at the same time the cost of living increased. Additional taxation proved necessary to meet the increased expenditure on the public services and on re-armament, and severe measures were taken to prevent tax-evasion.

During the year 1938 the Government maintained a firm grip upon the country in spite of symptoms of unrest and

Plots against the Dictatorship. although General Metaxas showed no signs of re-establishing the constitutional régime for which he professed to be preparing the country by the stern discipline to which he was subjecting it. On 28th January it was announced that a plot against the life of the Dictator had been brought to light. Twelve party leaders, including four ex-Ministers, were arrested and sent into exile in the Ægean, and a number of Communists were seized on the charge of agitating in favour of a Popular Front. In May seventy more Communists were arrested, including four members of the dissolved Chamber. A more spectacular rising occurred in Crete, where in July M. Mitsokaitis, a former Minister and nephew of M. Venizelos, at the head of 500 armed men occupied Canea, the capital of the island, and imprisoned the Governor. The Government immediately proclaimed martial law, established the capital at Candia, and, sending units of the fleet and air force and transports with troops, quickly suppressed the rising. The ringleaders were arrested and put on trial, four of them being condemned to death, while about a hundred others were sentenced to various periods of imprisonment. The second anniversary of the establishment of the dictatorship was celebrated on 2nd August by a national fête.

At the meeting of the Council of the Balkan Entente held at Ankara in February and attended by General Metaxas as Greek *Foreign Affairs in 1938.* delegate, it was decided that the Italian sovereignty over Abyssinia, which had already been recognized by Rumania and Jugoslavia, should be recognized by the Entente as a whole, and Greece and Turkey followed the example of the other two member states. On 27th April the Turkish Premier and Foreign Minister visited Athens for the signature of a Greco-Turkish Agreement of Friendship and Neutrality, and their visit was returned by General Metaxas in November. Conferences between the Naval Staffs of Greece, Turkey, Rumania, and Jugoslavia were held in July, and between the Military General Staffs in November.

On 31st July 1938 a Treaty of Friendship and Non-aggression was signed at Salonica between the States of the Balkan Entente *Treaty between the Balkan Entente and Bulgaria.* and Bulgaria. This agreement recognized the right of Bulgaria to re-arm and abrogated the limitation of armaments clause in the Treaty of Neuilly. Bulgaria was not required to guarantee the existing frontiers but undertook not to modify them by force of arms and to submit any disputes with her neighbours to arbitration or judicial settlement. Further, the clauses of the Treaty of Lausanne which provided for the demilitarization of the frontiers between Bulgaria, Greece and Turkey in Eastern Thrace were to be allowed to lapse. It looked as if Balkan unity had at last become a reality and as if the question of Bulgarian access to the Ægean either at Salonica or Dedeagatch might be amicably arranged. Unfortunately, however, when the testing moment came, the hopes of joint Balkan action faded into thin air.

On 8th February Prince Nicholas of Greece, the third son of King George I and uncle of King George II, died at the age of sixty-six years. He had left Greece in 1917, when his brother King Constantine was deposed for the first time, and remained abroad until the restoration of King George II in 1935. During his exile he successfully developed his talent for landscape painting. His third daughter, Princess Marina, had married the Duke of Kent in 1934, and their union was hailed in Greece as another bond between the Greek and British nations.

Death of Prince Nicholas of Greece.

On Good Friday, 7th April 1939, the Italians suddenly landed troops at the Albanian ports and marched on Tirana. They met with little opposition at Durazzo and none elsewhere, and next day reached the capital, where an Italian Government was immediately set up. King Zog with Queen Geraldine, who had just given birth to an heir to the vanishing throne, fled and eventually reached Greece. The whole country was soon overrun and annexed to Italy.

Italy seizes Albania.

This act of wanton aggression forced the Balkan States to decide what their future action would be if the Italian operations were farther extended. In Greece there were rumours that an attack on Corfu was imminent, and the Greek Government hastened to communicate their apprehensions to the British Government, with whom the Italian Government had concluded an agreement which contained an undertaking that nothing would be done to modify the *status quo* in the Mediterranean. They were informed that the British Government had warned the Italian Government that they would take a serious view if any aggressive action was undertaken against Greece and had received assurances that Italy had no such intentions. On 10th April the Italian Minister in Athens visited the Greek Prime Minister and assured him that the territorial integrity and political independence of Greece would be absolutely respected. On 13th April Mr. Neville Chamberlain informed the House of Commons that the British Government, while it did not feel that there was sufficient ground for

Great Britain gives a guarantee to Greece and Rumania.

bringing the Anglo-Italian Agreement to an end, attached the greatest importance to the avoidance of any disturbance of peace in the Balkan Peninsula and had, therefore, decided that, if any action were taken which so threatened the independence of Greece or Rumania as to compel the Greek or the Rumanian Government to take military measures, the British Government would feel obliged to lend them all the support in their power. A similar declaration was made at the same time by the French Government. These unqualified and unilateral guarantees did much to calm public opinion in Greece, where it was felt that the two Western European Democracies had abandoned their policy of diplomatic retreat and intended in future to take a firm stand against aggression. Meanwhile General Metaxas took every possible military precaution short of actual mobilization and did what he could to hasten the process of re-armament ; and, when strong Italian forces made their appearance on the Greco-Albanian frontier, the Greek Government replied by strengthening its own forces in that region.

In view of possible eventualities attempts were made by the Greek Government during the year 1939 to bring about a better *Bulgaria refuses* understanding with Bulgaria, and Greece re-*to join the* newed her offer of port facilities in a Bulgarian *Balkan Entente.* Free Zone to be established at Salonica. But Bulgaria still refused to join the Balkan Entente as long as her territorial claims were unsatisfied, in particular demanding the return of the Dobrudja and the provision of an Ægean port complete with a land-corridor of approach. In fact, Bulgaria had become more rather than less insistent upon what she regarded as her legitimate aspirations, though she promised to exert herself to maintain neutrality. In March General Metaxas paid a visit to Belgrade, and in June M. Gafencu, the Rumanian Foreign Minister, visited Athens.

On 12th July 1939 an Agreement was signed in London under which Great Britain gave Greece credits for the purchase *Financial Agree-* of goods to the value of more than £2,000,000 ; *ment with* but the deadlock between the Greek Govern-*Great Britain.* ment and the Council of Foreign Bondholders on the question of the payment of interest on Greek External Loans continued, though it was arranged that a Greek economic mission should visit London early in 1940, when the question would be discussed.

On 4th August the third anniversary of the entry into office of General Metaxas was publicly celebrated. The absence in 1939 of any open opposition to the régime, such *Third Anniver-* as had occurred in 1938, might be attributed *sary of the* either to the thoroughness of the totalitarian *Dictatorship.* system as now established, or else to a recognition of the advantages of a dictatorship in the face of external dangers. But it is to be noted that, on hearing of the Italian invasion of Albania, the Greek political exiles in Paris, headed by General Plastiras, announced that, in view of the perils that threatened Greece, they withdrew their opposition to General Metaxas.

CHAPTER XXIII

THE OUTBREAK OF WAR IN 1939 AND THE ITALIAN ATTACK UPON GREECE

AS the danger of an outbreak of war between the Western Democracies and Germany grew more imminent, Greece and *The Balkan States and the threat of war.* her Balkan neighbours became more and more apprehensive of what the future might have in store for them. It seemed likely that if Germany attacked Poland, Italy might also join in and seize the opportunity for making a descent on the Balkans.

At the time of its creation and as long as no external danger threatened, the Balkan Entente seemed to give promise of co-operation by the States forming it as a solid bloc which would offer a common front against any aggressor. But, with Bulgaria holding aloof, it had tended to become a league against Bulgaria's claim for the revision of her frontiers rather than a basis for Balkan collaboration. As danger from without increased, each Balkan State feared that it might be the first victim of aggression, and the nearer it lay to the territory of a possible aggressor the more careful it must be to give no cause of offence.

Greece had long looked to Great Britain as the most reliable protector of the smaller nations, but, when she saw that the *Greece and Great Britain.* dismemberment of Czecho-slavakia had failed to rouse the British lion to more than an angry lashing of its tail, her hopes of effective aid from that quarter were somewhat dashed. But the spontaneous offer to Greece of a guarantee after the Italian seizure of Albania had shown that, though Great Britain could give nothing beyond moral support to a Central European country in its hour of need, she was ready to take a more practical interest in the fate of Greece.

Moreover, Great Britain, being essentially a Naval Power, was in a position to give effective help to a maritime country like Greece, while Greece on her part had much to offer Great

Britain in the way of harbours and sea- and air-bases, if the struggle extended to the Mediterranean. The lesson of the war of 1914–18 had not been forgotten by the Greeks. In that war small countries, such as Serbia and Rumania, had been overrun and conquered, but in the end sea-power had been the deciding factor, as it had been in the Napoleonic wars, and these countries had been restored and had received great accessions of territory, while the Allies of the Central Powers, such as Turkey and Bulgaria, who had thought themselves on the winning side, had finally been among the conquered. In any case Germany had no navy in the Mediterranean and the British Navy was likely to be more than a match for the Italian ; and on the land side there were buffer-states between Germany and Greece.

Again, her extensive sea-board and the fact that communication between Greece and the rest of Europe is by sea rather than by land, makes Greece more susceptible to Western influence than are her Balkan neighbours. Moreover, Greece has had a historic sympathy with Great Britain ever since the days of Byron and Cochrane, and this had been re-invigorated on the battle-fields of Macedonia, where the Greek troops were in closer contact with the British Army than with the forces of the other Allies.

But, whatever her sympathies might be, it behoved Greece to walk warily and to avoid provoking either Germany or Italy by identifying herself too closely with their potential enemies. Moreover, she was still economically dependent on Germany, whose policy it had long been to involve the smaller states in such a mesh of trading and barter agreements that they would naturally hesitate to adopt an openly hostile attitude towards her. Germany had become the best customer of Greece, who supplied her with tobacco and metals in return for armaments and material for railways and public works, with the result that many Greeks had become dependent for their livelihood on friendly relations with Germany.

Greece and Germany.

When the crisis over Danzig ended in the declaration of war on Germany by Great Britain and France in September 1939, Italy, contrary to the general expectation, held aloof, and Greece, to her surprise, found not only that for the time being was she left in peace but that Italy, so far from showing any inclination to

The outbreak of war.

attack her across the Albanian frontier, was actually proposing
to withdraw the troops already there. Italy
Greece and Italy. went farther and suggested a Treaty of Non-
aggression, which Greece managed to refuse without causing
any serious offence. This was followed by an exchange of
notes which expressed the hope that the two Governments
would be able to put their relations on a more definite footing
than the Pact of Friendship concluded in October 1929, but it
remained only a pious hope ; for the moment, however, Greece
and Italy were on far better terms than had seemed possible a
few months before when Italy had seized Albania.

On 19th October 1939 a Tripartite Treaty of Alliance
between Great Britain, France, and the Republic of Turkey was
Great Britain signed in Ankara and was naturally welcomed
and France make by Greece. It contained the following clause :
an Alliance ' As long as the guarantees given by France and
with Turkey. the United Kingdom to Greece and Rumania
by their respective declarations of 13th April
1939 remain in force, Turkey will co-operate effectively with
France and the United Kingdom and will lend them all aid and
assistance in its power in the event of France and the United
Kingdom being engaged in hostilities in virtue of either of the
said guarantees '.

At the beginning of 1940 Great Britain and Greece signed
War Trade Agree- a War Trade Agreement which to a large extent
ment between enabled Greece to shake off the grip which
Great Britain Germany had fastened upon her economic life
and Greece. by substituting Great Britain for Germany as
the market for Greek products.

On 2nd–4th February a meeting of the Foreign Ministers of
the four States which had signed the Balkan Pact was held at
The Balkan Belgrade. The joint communiqué which was
Foreign Ministers issued announced the extension of the Balkan
meet. Entente for a further period of seven years
from 9th February 1941, and recommended the
maintenance of close contact between the four Ministers for
Foreign Affairs until the next meeting of the Permanent Council
in February 1941 ; pronouncements were also made in favour
of strengthening the political and economic bonds between the
signatory Powers and the adoption of a joint attitude in face of

the European War. These resolutions, though, at the time they were made, they may have had a reassuring effect, proved of little real value. The Russian annexation of Bessarabia found the Balkan States quite incapable of presenting a united front and naturally encouraged Bulgaria also to hope for the fulfilment of *her* demands for frontier revision at the expense of Rumania.

Greece, however, could draw comfort from two circumstances—the firm attitude of Turkey and the presence of powerful

Relations of Greece with Great Britain and Turkey.
Allied armies in Syria, Palestine, and Egypt. These armies, with the help of the British Mediterranean fleet, might prove a very present help in trouble and were not hampered by the difficulties of transport and communications which prevented any real help being given to Poland and Finland. Further, Greece, geographically and strategically, was in a much safer position than any other Balkan State. She had no land frontier with Germany or Russia, and it seemed unlikely that Italy, if she joined in the war, would attempt an attack from Albania on Northern Epirus, where the physical conditions were such as to discourage an invader. Lastly, for the moment the policy of the Axis seemed to be to avoid any outbreak of hostilities in the Balkans, which would reduce the supplies which were being derived from that area and might increase the danger of a clash of interests between Germany and Soviet Russia.

The Nazi conquest of Norway, Denmark, Holland, and Belgium followed by the capitulation of France in June 1940

The effect of the Fall of France on the Balkan States.
caused grief and consternation in the Balkans and at the same time increased the conviction that it was essential to avoid any cause of friction with the Axis Powers. The result was that the States which felt themselves most threatened pursued whatever policy they thought most likely to enable them to save their own skins, and any thought of their common interests was abandoned ; they were united only in a strong desire not to share the fate of the smaller countries of Northern Europe. The peninsula was overrun by hordes of Germans in the guise of ' tourists ' and business men and persons vaguely attached to the diplomatic staffs, who carried on barefaced propaganda. Rumania, Bulgaria, and Jugoslavia seemed to be undecided

which way to turn, Rumania rejecting the British guarantee and tending rather towards Germany, while Bulgaria and Jugoslavia angled for possible support from Russia. Greece and Turkey observed a strict neutrality and trusted to the guarantee of Great Britain, now that the Balkan Entente was in a state of manifest dissolution.

On 20th June 1940 Italy declared war on Great Britain. The Duce thought that he saw in the fall of France and the difficulties

Italy declares war on Britain.

of Great Britain, thus left to carry the whole burden of the war, a grand opportunity to share the spoils of a victory, which he was convinced was now assured for Germany, without having to fight for them. It was a predatory attack on a State against which Italy had no real grievance and with which she had signed a Treaty which had settled all Mediterranean questions of any importance.

In his speech announcing the Italian declaration of war Mussolini took the opportunity to emphasize his peaceful

Mussolini declares his peaceful intentions towards Greece.

intentions towards the Balkan peoples. ' I solemnly declare ', he said, ' that Italy does not intend to drag other peoples who are our neighbours into the conflict. Let Switzerland, Jugoslavia, Turkey, Egypt, and Greece take note of these words of mine.'

But Greece, in spite of this assurance and of the Pact of Friendship concluded with Italy in October 1929, could not forget the Corfu incident, the annexation of Albania and the sufferings of the Greeks in the Dodecanese. Her distrust of her Western neighbour was increased by reports during the summer that 125,000 Italian troops were being concentrated in Albania, where the normal Italian garrison had been 70,000 men, and by the sinking without warning of the Greek steamer *Loula* by an Italian submarine on her way from Istanbul to Port Said.

In July rumours were abroad that the Soviet Government had sent an ultimatum to Turkey which demanded territorial

Turkey applies the Protocol of the Treaty of 1939.

concessions ; they were officially denied both in Turkey and in Russia, but considerable uncertainty remained as to what Russia might be planning, and in the circumstances the Turkish Government deemed it the safest course to put immediately into operation the Protocol of the Anglo-Franco-

Turkish Treaty of Alliance which provided that ' the obligations undertaken by Turkey . . . cannot compel that country to take action having as its effect, or involving as its consequence, entry into armed conflict with the U.S.S.R.'. This action had the important result that Turkey still remained neutral when Greece was attacked by Italy and Article 3 of the Treaty remained inoperative.

On 4th August the fourth anniversary of the establishment of the Dictatorship of General Metaxas was celebrated. Though

The Fourth Anniversary of the Dictatorship. it would be too much to say that his régime was generally popular, Venizelist and other critics for the most part refrained from expressing their sentiments, since no one else would have been inclined to assume the responsibilities which rested on his shoulders and it was generally admitted that he had done much for Greece, especially in the sphere of internal reform. Further, experience had shown that any one who voiced his criticism was liable to be relegated to exile on some Ægean island far from the cafés of the Place de la Constitution at Athens. General Metaxas had hitherto managed to steer the country along the smooth waters of neutrality without any sacrifice of national dignity or political independence, while at the same time he had refused to follow the example of Hitler and Mussolini and establish a single-party Government or poison the minds of the youth of Greece by means of a totalitarian form of education.

But action was soon to be taken by Italy which brought the crisis nearer. On 15th August the Greek cruiser *Helle*

The Italians torpedo a Greek cruiser. (2115 tons), the vessel on which King George II had returned to Greece, was torpedoed by an Italian submarine while at anchor off the mole at Tenos in the Cyclades, one of the crew being killed and twenty-six wounded, while casualties were also inflicted upon civilians on the quay. The *Helle* was on an essentially peaceful mission, being present officially in accordance with a Greek custom, decorated with bunting, in honour of the Feast of the Assumption, which is the occasion of an important pilgrimage to the island. The choice of a religious date recalled that Albania had been invaded on Good Friday. Italy's action was generally interpreted as an attempt to intimidate Greece preparatory to a demand for the cession of Corfu to Italy. On the following day two Greek destroyers on their way to Tenos were unsuccessfully bombed by Italian aeroplanes. During the previous week the Italian press had been fulminating against Greece, alleging that an Albanian, Daut Hoggia, had been murdered by the Greeks. The Italians described this man as a 'patriot', while the Greeks asserted that he was a brigand and that he had been murdered by two other Albanians who had fled to Greece for sanctuary. A Note was sent to Athens by the Italian Government demanding the extradition of the murderers and the payment of an indemnity.

In the middle of October, while Germany was strengthening her hold on Rumania, the Italian press campaign broke out again and in a still more violent form, demanding *Italian press* the cession to Albania of the Jannina district and *agitation against* of the coast of Epirus as far as Preveza. It also *Greece.* clamoured for the exclusion of British newspapers from Greece and the suppression of comment on the war in the Athens press. Germany at the same time demanded the revaluation of the drachma in her own favour and the granting of unlimited visas to German 'tourists'. General Metaxas took up a firm position and the nation supported him. Reservists were called up for practice in the new weapons and machines recently acquired by Greece, and, in view of the disappointing harvest, arrangements were made for the importation of cereals from Russia, while stocks of sugar were ordered from America.

On 27th October the Italian wireless reported clashes on the Albanian frontier and an explosion at Santi Quaranta, an Albanian port near the Greek boundary, for which 'Greek or British agents' were said to be responsible. Such accusations formed part of the usual technique and foreshadowed an immediate crisis, which came even more quickly than was anticipated—the very next morning.

At 3 a.m., 28th October 1940, the Italian Minister at Athens delivered to the Greek Government an ultima- *Italian ultima-* tum, which was to expire at 6 a.m., demand- *tum to Greece,* ing a passage for Italian troops to 'certain *28th Oct. 1940.* strategic points', which were not specified, and promising 'full respect of Greek sovereignty'. Greece was accused of having violated her neutrality by granting naval and air bases in Thessaly to the British.

Even before the ultimatum had expired, the Italians at 5.30 a.m. crossed the frontier from Albania into Greece.

General Metaxas met the Italian demands with a contemptuous refusal, exclaiming, ' This is tantamount to a declaration of

Greece accepts the challenge.

war '. He knew that he had the backing of the whole nation, and within a few hours the Greek Army, already partially mobilized, was on its way to the front. Greece had accepted the Italian challenge.

The only possible explanation of Mussolini's action—and the initiative undoubtedly came from him and not from the Italian

Why did Mussolini attack Greece ?

General Staff—is that he expected that Greece would submit without a struggle, a supposition for which he had absolutely no warrant. He evidently hoped by a quick and cheaply-won victory to restore his own prestige and that of the Fascist party ; for dictators must be always producing results, and the prospects in North Africa were not too rosy. It seems unlikely that he acted without securing the blessing of Hitler,[1] but he had probably realized that the penalty of dependence on Germany might be the exclusion of Italy from the Balkans, and that he would get nothing but what he himself might win ; if he could seize Greece, he would at least secure the command of the Adriatic, and the conquest of Greece could be represented as a valuable contribution to the Axis drive towards Syria and Egypt. He can hardly have imagined that the British Government would fail to carry out its guarantee and come to the help of Greece.

Greece was, fortunately, in a much healthier moral condition to resist an attempted invasion than the countries of Northern

Greek morale.

Europe which Germany had so easily overrun. The Greeks are intensely patriotic, and a crisis has the immediate effect of inducing national unity. It was also clear to the Greeks what subjection to the Axis had involved elsewhere, and they realized that any and every sacrifice was worth while to avoid a similar fate. Again, there was no ' fifth

[1] Editor's Note.—Cf. *Ciano's Diary*, 1939-1940 (Ed. M. Muggeridge, 1947), p. 297.

column ' in Greece to welcome the invaders and cause confusion in the country ; not only was there no German or Italian minority but the relations of Greece with the Axis Powers had been those of commerce only, and they had established no stranglehold on Greek industry which might have brought a swarm of ' technicians ' into the country to form a nucleus of pro-Axis influence. Indeed, the Greeks have always discouraged the settlement of foreign industries in their country, and such foreign capital as is invested there is mainly British.

That Greece was under the dictatorship of General Metaxas in the hour of danger had several beneficial results. Firstly,

The Dictatorship and the crisis. since Parliamentary Government had long been in abeyance, there was no question of summoning the Chamber to debate what policy the country should adopt, which in Greece would certainly have led to interminable discussions ; the Government could on its own responsibility decide immediately what action must be taken and give immediate orders for carrying it out, and, in a crisis, prompt action is of supreme importance. Secondly, being free of parliamentary control and Minister for War as well as Premier, General Metaxas had been able to build up, out of the admirable material ready to his hand, a strong and united national army without the interference of party influences ; and, himself a profound student of war and strategy—he had been known as ' the Little Moltke ' when he was a student of the Kriegsakademie in Berlin and had been Assistant-Chief-of-Staff in the Balkan Wars—he was able on his own authority to choose those who should lead the army, and his choice was soon amply justified. Lastly, the strict censorship which the Government exercised over the Press made it impossible for foreign influences to secure the control of newspapers and use them for purposes of propaganda in order to confuse or poison public opinion.

CHAPTER XXIV

THE GERMAN INVASION: THE OCCUPATION OF GREECE BY THE AXIS (1941-5)

THE months which followed the Italian invasion from Albania in October 1940 brought imperishable glory to the Greek arms. Despite their superiority in everything except courage, the Italians were quickly driven back across the frontier and subjected to relentless pressure. Some help was provided by the R.A.F., but no Allied land-troops were sent, or indeed asked for, since the Greeks were fully capable of dealing with the invaders and the terrain demanded dogged infantry work supported by mountain-batteries and supplied by pack or human transport—a type of warfare in which the Greeks excel. The unusual severity of the winter caused unspeakable suffering, which the hardy Greeks supported far better than the Italians. By the beginning of 1941 the Greeks had occupied nearly one-third of Albania and were still advancing, and by the end of February the Italian losses were estimated at 100,000 and the prisoners at 23,000.

Thus far all had gone well with the Greeks, who had proved themselves the only small Power able successfully to resist the Axis, and the collapse of Italy in Albania seemed imminent; but with the German occupation, first of Roumania and then of Bulgaria, which joined the Axis pact on 1st March, it became more and more likely that Hitler would take a hand in Greece and come to the rescue of Mussolini's craven hosts. Meanwhile the British Foreign Secretary and the G.I.G.S. had visited Athens and arranged that the help promised by Great Britain should be sent. British and Imperial troops began to arrive early in March and eventually numbered about 58,000, of whom 35,000 were combatants. An attempt by the Italian fleet to interfere with our convoys resulted in the great British victory off Matapan on 27th March 1941.

Then the blow fell. At 6.30 a.m. on 6th April the German Minister at Athens informed the Greek Premier that Germany was about to invade Greece on the ground that British troops had been landed there. On that very day the Germans crossed the frontiers of both Greece and Jugo-Slavia with overwhelming mechanized forces.

This is no place to dwell in detail on the military operations which led to the fall of Greece. For the Anglo-Greek forces they consisted in a series of rearguard actions before the superior German armament, upon which, however, heavy casualties were inflicted. The Greeks began by holding the 'Metaxas Line' along the River Mesta and the Rupel Fort on the River Struma, until these were turned by armoured divisions which descended the valleys of these rivers. Next an attempt by the Anglo-Greek forces to hold a line running north-west from Salonica was thwarted by a powerful drive across Southern Jugo-Slavia and down the Vardar Valley and the Monastir Gap, while the Adolf Hitler S.S. Armoured Division descended on the right flank of the Greek army in Albania, forcing it to capitulate on 20th April. The rest of the Anglo-Greek forces fought further rearguard actions in Thessaly and in the historic Pass of Thermopylæ. But on 21st April the Greek Government informed the British Commander that the Greeks could resist no longer and urged the withdrawal of the Expeditionary Force, the overwhelming superiority of the Germans in tanks and aircraft making further resistance profitless. The evacuation was effected from numerous small ports and beaches in Attica and the Peloponnese.

General Metaxas, who, whatever opinion may be held of his earlier career, had deserved well of his country in accepting the Italian challenge and forming a rallying point for the nation, had died on 29th January and was succeeded as Prime Minister by M. Korizis, who died by his own hand on 18th April. M. Tsouderos, a former follower of Venizelos and a well-known banker, became Premier on 20th April and accompanied King George when he transferred his Government first to Crete and then to Egypt, whither he again returned after a sojourn in London.

It was a foregone conclusion that the Germans, after over-running the Greek mainland and many of the islands, would attempt to seize the key-island of Crete. General Wavell decided that every effort should be made to hold it. At the end of April, besides eleven Greek battalions, there were some 27,000 Allied troops in the island, but many were either non-combatants or had escaped from Greece where their guns, transport, and other equipment had been lost. The civilian population put itself at the disposal of the military authorities and displayed the utmost courage. The Allies possessed three aerodromes in Crete, but these obviously would not serve to support an air force adequate to deal with an enemy who had air-bases so near at hand on the mainland and in the Dodecanese. In the middle of May aerial bombardment of the Allied positions began, followed on 20th May by the landing of parachute troops, who were soon disposed of ; but they were followed by swarms of troop-carrying planes, and the defenders, who performed miracles of bravery, mainly with the bayonet, could not deal fast enough with the invaders. The struggle, however, was kept up for some twelve days before it was decided to evacuate the island.

It has been generally recognized that the resistance offered by the Greeks and their allies in Greece and Crete, though involving a tactical defeat, made a valuable contribution to the Allied cause. It not improbably diverted the Germans from making an attempt to break through Turkey to the Caucasus ; it delayed the offensive against Russia for some vital weeks ; it destroyed air-borne troops which might have been used with effect elsewhere in the Middle East ; and it prevented Germany from sending help to the rebels in Iraq and the Vichy French in Syria. But defeat meant the crucifixion of the noble nation which had sacrificed everything in the cause of freedom.

The Germans entered Athens on 27th April, and a period of stark privation and relentless oppression began for the Greeks. On 30th April a puppet government was set up under the rene-gade Tsolakoglou, who tried unsuccessfully to follow the example of the Vichy French Government and persuade the Greeks that they had been dragged into the war by the British and then abandoned. The Germans themselves occupied key-points in Greece, such as Salonica, Crete, and Mitylene, and retained control of communications. Thessaly, Epirus, and Central and Southern Greece went to Italy, which also added most of the Ægean Islands to its command at Rhodes. The Bulgars received as their reward Greek Thrace and Eastern Macedonia, where they imposed a policy of expulsion and extermination upon the Greeks and colonization by their own nationals.

The Italians continually intrigued to oust Tsolakoglou in favour of their own nominee Kotsomanes, for whom they at one time obtained five portfolios in the Cabinet, but his shameless exploitation of the resources of the country led in 1942 to a successful general strike by the Greeks and the fall of the Cabinet, and Logothetopoulos, an ex-Professor of Obstetrics and a submissive tool of the Axis, became Premier. On 7th April 1943 the growing power of the Allies and the fear of invasion led the Germans to enlist the services of John Rallis as Premier, a better-known politician with a black record. But after the fall of Italy the Germans practically assumed the whole administration and the puppet government was powerless.

Agriculturally, Greece is a poor land, not producing enough cereals to satisfy an already low standard of living ; it, therefore, has to obtain imported foodstuffs in exchange for its own products, such as tobacco and currants. Owing to the Albanian war the seed for the 1941 crop remained unsown for lack of men and transport. The rich fields of Thessaly had been laid waste, and Macedonia and Thrace, which produced more than they consumed, had passed to Bulgaria. Industries were suppressed or working for the Axis, the roads and railways were partially destroyed, and the Greek merchant-fleet was sunk or chartered by the Allies. Moreover, a preposterous charge was levied to pay for the cost of the occupation. Thus taxation, the reckless issue of paper money, the rise of prices and the fall of production, accompanied by confiscation and looting, soon caused hopeless chaos, economic, financial and social, which resulted in a state of general starvation with its accompanying epidemics. Mortality, especially among the children, reached an appalling figure. Something was done to improve the position by imports from Turkey, which enabled the establishment of soup-kitchens, and the Swedish-Swiss Commission did splendid work, but famine and disease together wrought terrible ravages, from which the country will take many years to recover.

But their sufferings did not prevent the Greeks from keeping up a gallant and effective fight against their oppressors, through strikes and sabotage by the civilian population and armed resistance by guerilla forces, who were joined by stragglers left behind when the British withdrew. For example, a general strike induced the Germans to suspend a decree for the conscription of Greeks for labour in Germany, while destruction of administrative buildings and supply-dumps was frequent. A flourishing underground press helped to keep up the spirits of the people, guerilla forces of Greek patriots were active, especially in Crete, Thessaly, Epirus, and Western Macedonia. Many trains were wrecked, communications cut, and isolated enemy units exterminated, with the result of weakening enemy morale and obliging the Axis to keep a large army of occupation. But resistance brought a heavy penalty upon the population in the murder of countless hostages and the destruction of villages and crops.

Unfortunately, as in the War of Independence, differences arose between the various guerilla bands and became acute in the spring of 1943. One of the chief causes of friction was the question of the future régime. The largest partisan force was the E.L.A.S. (National Popular Army of Liberation), directed by a political organization, the E.A.M. (National Liberation Front),[1] which owed its origin to resistance against the Metaxist dictatorship and contained a strong Communist element. The chief rival force was the E.D.E.S. (Greek Republican Liberation League) led by General Zervas, who claimed to be republican and a follower of the exiled General Plastiras, the leader of the military revolt in 1922. Allied liaison officers had by this time been attached to the guerillas and did their best to compose their differences, and later in the year six of the guerilla leaders were sent on a mission to Egypt, where the Greek Government was now established, to discuss military co-operation with the Allies. They took the opportunity to air their political views and, in particular, it was urged that King George II, since he had allowed the suspension of parliamentary government and the four years of the Metaxist dictatorship, should not return to Greece before the people had been given the opportunity of deciding what

---

[1] In the following account the E.A.M. will usually be mentioned when political action is referred to, the E.L.A.S. when military operations are in question.

régime they preferred. The raising of this question was the occasion of misleading rumours, emanating from unfriendly sources, that the British Government would insist on the return of King George.

After the collapse of Italy fresh quarrels broke out between the E.L.A.S. and the E.D.E.S. over the partition of the material of war which the Italians had handed over to the guerillas rather than to the Germans. These disputes again took a political turn, the E.L.A.S. accusing the E.D.E.S. of Fascist leanings and a desire to re-establish privilege and even dictatorship in Greece, while the E.D.E.S. charged their opponents with terrorization. All this provided excellent material for German propaganda.

The elimination of Italy from the war aroused in Greece the hope of an early liberation, the delay of which caused a national disappointment ; also the feeling arose that the Government in Cairo had been too complaisant in accepting the idea of Italian co-belligerency. The loss of the islands of Leros, Cos, and Samos, which had been seized by the British, was a further cause of disillusionment. On 21st December the Greek Premier in a broadcast from Cairo appealed to the guerillas to reconcile their differences and combine against the common foe, or else to lay down their arms, since their quarrels were only benefiting the enemy.

Early in 1944 the factions, especially the E.A.M., intensified their political activities and demanded representation in the Greek Cabinet at Cairo. The Government replied that they should first lay aside their quarrels, but promised that their claim should be considered. Finding that they were not to receive immediate satisfaction, the E.A.M. set up a political committee at the E.L.A.S. headquarters in ostensible rivalry with the Cairo Government. This step awakened the sympathy of many of the Greeks who were serving in the Allied forces, and mutinies broke out on several Greek warships in the Middle East and in the 1st Greek Brigade, which was under orders to proceed to Italy. Discipline was soon restored by the British Authorities.

Meanwhile M. Tsouderos had resigned the premiership, and the King had invited Colonel Venizelos, son of the famous statesman, to form a cabinet. When he failed, his place was taken on 26th April by M. Papandreou, leader of the Social Democratic Party, who had recently escaped from Greece. He declared that his mission was the creation of a government of National Unity, in which all parties should share. He received a message of encouragement from Mr. Churchill, who promised British support and suggested that his three objectives should be the union of all against the common foe, the cleansing of Greece from foreign occupation, and the free choice by the Greeks of the régime under which they wished to live.

In May the new Prime Minister summoned a conference of representatives of all the political parties to meet in the Lebanon, at which the following programme was adopted : (1) The re-organization of the Greek armed forces in the Middle East under the Greek flag, (2) the unification of the resistance forces under the orders of the Government, (3) the suppression of terrorism and the guarantee of political liberty when Greece was freed, (4) the provision of food and medicines, (5) the guarantee of order and personal security after the liberation, so that the people might be free to express their will about the future régime, (6) the punishment of those who had betrayed their country and exploited its miseries, and (7) the satisfaction of the national claims of Greece. On 22nd May M. Papandreou formed his Government of National Unity and sent a message to Mr. Churchill that the delegates at the Conference had decided to forget their differences and to work together for the liberation of Greece. The new Government made clear its view that until the liberation of Greece the King remained the Chief of the Greek State and was responsible, in collaboration with the Allies, for securing its interests, but that, when freedom came, the people would be given an opportunity of expressing its will about its future government.

In spite of the apparent unity which had been secured, difficulties soon arose. The E.A.M., who had been invited to participate in the Government, failed to arrange for their representation, and, while discussions were still proceeding, it was reported that hostilities had again broken out between the E.L.A.S. and the E.D.E.S. The Premier stated that the E.A.M. were demanding seven places in the cabinet of fifteen and that the E.L.A.S. refused to submit to the control of the Government. Speaking in the House of Commons on 27th July, Mr. Eden stated that the British Government was giving M. Papandreou full support in his efforts to carry out the Lebanon Agreement, which had the approval of the great majority of the Greeks, and that the E.A.M. were making demands which were not justified by their numerical strength. In August, however, the E.A.M. decided to send representatives to Cairo and agreed to join the Government on condition that five portfolios were allotted to them. The Cabinet was then reconstituted and, in view of the expected liberation of Greece, the Government was transferred in September from Cairo to Naples.

By the beginning of October 1944 it was becoming obvious that events elsewhere in Europe would soon oblige the Germans to withdraw their forces from Greece. The action to be taken by the Allies in these circumstances had been discussed by Mr. Churchill and President Roosevelt at the Quebec Conference, and they were agreed that it might be necessary to send troops to Athens to save the country from starvation and anarchy. As a result the British and U.S. Chiefs of Staff arranged for the despatch, if circumstances demanded it, of a British Expeditionary Force.

Editor's Notes.

(1) It has never been satisfactorily explained why E.A.M. agreed to attend the Lebanon Conference. This party had certainly not renounced its policy of gaining control of Greece. It is possible that it foresaw the Allies would free Greece and that it calculated that it would be to the party's ultimate advantage to have some place in the Government. Later, E.A.M. agreed to join the Government and at the Caserta Conference Sarafis (E.A.M.–E.L.A.S.) and Zervas (E.D.E.S.) agreed to place their forces under the control of the Government, which in turn placed them under the Allied Commander (Major-General Scobie).

(2) It is often said that the Greek resistance movement was a negligible contribution to the war efforts of the Allies. But although the results were limited, the movement itself had some importance and would have been of great importance if, as they contemplated, the Allies had made an attack on Europe through the Balkans. In any case the Greek *andartes,* besides destroying an amount of enemy manpower and materials, threatened the German line of communications and tied down two German divisions, which, if used in Italy, might have had serious consequences for the British.

CHAPTER XXV

THE LIBERATION OF GREECE : THE CIVIL WAR OF 1944-5

ON 12th October Athens and Peiræus were reported to have been liberated by the Greeks themselves, and on the 14th, British troops landed under Major-General Scobie, who assumed the command of the Allied Forces in Greece. Later in the month Mr. Eden, Lord Moyne, Resident Minister in the Near East, General Maitland Wilson, and Admiral Cunningham arrived in Athens, and steps were begun to deal with the food supply and the currency question.

M. Papandreou, the Greek Premier, who reached Athens on 18th October, issued an urgent appeal to the people to abstain from political strife and return to their ordinary avocations and work for the restoration of their country. But his words fell for the most part on deaf ears and clashes frequently occurred between bodies of guerillas. The E.L.A.S. in particular showed a disposition to use their arms against their political opponents rather than against the remnants of the Germans who were still retiring from Greece. The most pressing problem, therefore, was to induce the various guerilla organizations to disarm. Negotiations for disbanding both the E.L.A.S. and the E.D.E.S. were progressing favourably, until on 9th November the Greek Mountain Brigade arrived from Italy and were given a great reception in Athens. Thereupon the Left extremists demanded that both this force and the Sacred Battalion, which was fighting in Crete, should also be disbanded, on the ground that they were also volunteers and tainted with royalist sentiments. To deal with this situation General Scobie announced that both the E.L.A.S. and the E.D.E.S. were to give up their arms by 10th December. When the Decree embodying this order, which also included a provision that Greek military formations on service abroad should be demobilized on their return to Greece, came up for signature by the Cabinet, the E.A.M. representatives refused to consent and resigned in protest.

Meanwhile more and more E.A.M. supporters were reaching Athens, and on 3rd December an organized demonstration occurred which was fired upon by the police, who inflicted and sustained casualties. Other armed partisans who reached Athens next day were disarmed by the British. Clashes also took place between the E.L.A.S. and the E.D.E.S. in other parts of Greece. It is generally agreed that it was the intention of the E.A.M. to seize the capital and establish themselves in power by force of arms. By 4th December the E.L.A.S. forces were in strength within a mile of the Government headquarters and the British Embassy and had occupied nearly all the police buildings and killed most of the police. Orders were therefore sent by the British Government to General Scobie to assume control of Athens and the immediate neighbourhood, and he proceeded to take steps to restore order in the city. This soon led to clashes between the British troops and the E.L.A.S., and there were losses on both sides. The disturbances inevitably led to the suspension of measures of relief, and the bakeries were unable to issue the bread ration. On 8th December General Scobie reported that the rebels were still flocking into Athens and keeping up a fierce resistance, and the following day 10,000 E.L.A.S. troops were in the neighbourhood of Athens where they were attacked by the R.A.F. On 20th December the E.L.A.S. achieved a success in the capture of the R.A.F. Headquarters at Kephissia near Athens.

On 13th December General Plastiras, the former Liberal Prime Minister, who had gone into exile when General Metaxas became Dictator, returned to Athens at the request of M. Papandreou. He appealed to the insurgents to lay aside civil strife and devote themselves to restoring order and reorganizing the army to take its part in the last and hardest phase of the war against the common enemy. As the month went on the British forces gradually gained ground, expelling the E.L.A.S. troops from their positions south of Athens and recapturing the Peiræus station. On 21st December M. Papandreou expressed the gratitude of the Greek people for the service rendered by British arms in protecting the defenceless Government from an armed minority which sought to impose a political tyranny. He protested that events at Athens were being misrepresented by certain sections of the British and U.S.A. press ; in particular, he denied that any Right Wing Party existed which was trying to impose its policy against the will of the people.

On 25th December, to the surprise of the whole world, Mr. Churchill and Mr. Eden suddenly arrived in Greece. They immediately reached an agreement with the Greek Premier that a meeting should be called of delegates of the various parties to suggest steps for putting an end to civil strife and make it possible for Greece to play her part worthily among the United Nations. This meeting was held under the presidency of Archbishop Damaskinos of Athens and was addressed by Mr. Churchill, who stated that the Greek Premier had accepted his suggestion of an all-party conference. He stated that the British troops had come to Greece with the approval of President Roosevelt and Marshal Stalin, and had become involved in the troubles through doing what they regarded as their duty—a duty which they would continue to discharge. In a statement to the Press he expressed his conviction that, if the British had not intervened, there would have been a very serious massacre in Athens, and he denied that there was any foundation whatever for rumours that the British wished to impose any particular régime upon Greece. ' We need nothing,' he said, ' from Greece but her friendship.' The Conference met and agreed on the necessity of appointing a Regent. To this the King was persuaded by Mr. Churchill to consent, and he declared at the same time that he was resolved not to return to Greece unless summoned by the free and fair expression of the national will. Archbishop Damaskinos was appointed Regent.

By the end of the year the British, using tanks and aeroplanes, had cleared the greater part of Athens and the Peiræus, but organized resistance lasted for some little time afterwards. Meanwhile the E.L.A.S. had seized a large number of hostages and carried them away to the mountains.

On 31st December M. Papandreou resigned the Premiership, and the Regent invited General Plastiras to take his place. Having formed his Cabinet the new Premier announced that his policy would be to restore order, to punish those who had collaborated with the enemy, to satisfy the urgent needs of the people and to stabilize the currency. He appealed to those who had been misled to return to their duty.

On 11th January General Scobie entered into fresh communications with emissaries of the E.L.A.S. with a view to a truce. They expressed their willingness to withdraw from Athens, Patras, Salonica, and other areas to be agreed upon and to exchange prisoners of war, but refused to release the hostages whom they had seized. However, an agreement was reached providing for a cessation of hostilities in order that discussions might be held for the settlement of outstanding questions, and after further negotiations the E.L.A.S. agreed to release all hostages except those guilty of criminal acts and those who had collaborated with the enemy. A large demonstration was held in Athens and was addressed by General Scobie, who declared that the British intended to protect the liberties of the people from whatever quarter they were attacked ; he hoped that the demonstration would have an effect on public opinion, which had been grossly misinformed about Greek affairs.

On 22nd January a British T.U.C. delegation, under the leadership of Sir Walter Citrine, reached Athens to report on the situation. They talked with members of the Government, labour leaders, and British soldiers, and were shown evidence of the atrocities committed by the E.L.A.S. on civilian hostages. They found a very different state of affairs from that presented by some organs of the British Press. Amongst other statements Sir Walter Citrine said : ' One thing is apparent beyond any shadow of doubt : in this country there has been deliberate, cold-blooded, organized, systematic murder. . . . I am quite certain that it is utterly impossible for the British Government to discontinue its responsibility in this country until conditions of normality have been brought about. I have no doubt that this is the wish of the Greek people themselves.' An official statement of the Ministry of Justice announced that the bodies of 1218 persons put to death by the E.A.M. and E.L.A.S. had been exhumed in Athens during December 1944 and January 1945, of whom four-fifths were civilians, including 168 women.

In the early part of February negotiations were in progress between the Government and the E.A.M. to decide what form of amnesty should be granted as a necessary preliminary to negotiations for a political peace. The Government agreed that the act of bearing arms against the State should not be regarded as a crime, and that only those guilty of violations of criminal and military law should be liable to punishment. The Conference met on 6th February and was attended by Mr. Harold Macmillan, Resident Minister in the Near East, the British Ambassador, three members of the Government, and three members of the E.A.M. The agreement which was reached was published on 13th February. The following were the main points : (1) the democratic liberties of the people were to be restored, (2) martial law was to be gradually relaxed, (3) there was to be an amnesty for political crimes committed since 3rd December, but those who did not lay down their arms by 10th March and those guilty of crimes against common law were excluded, (4) all hostages were to be released by the E.L.A.S., (5) a national army was to be formed, (6) all E.L.A.S. forces were to be disbanded within fourteen days, (7) civil administration was to be re-established, (8) there was to be a ' probe ' into civil servants of three categories, those who held office under Metaxas, those who functioned during the occupation, and those who took part in the revolt on the side of the E.A.M., (9) a plebiscite was to be held to decide on the future régime and a general election during the present year, and Allied observers were to be invited to attend on both these occasions. The agreement was generally welcomed in Greece and met with approval elsewhere.

On 14th February Mr. Churchill and Mr. Eden again made a surprise landing in Athens on their way back from the Crimea Conference and received a tumultuous welcome. On his return to England, Mr. Churchill, speaking of the British intervention in Greece, said : ' I am sure that we rescued Athens from a horrible fate. I believe that the Greek people will long acclaim our action, both military and political. Peace without vengeance has been achieved.' He added that a great deal remained to be done which must be the task of the Greeks themselves.

During March, British troops progressively occupied more and more areas of the country hitherto controlled by the E.L.A.S. and collected the surrendered arms and, under an agreement between the Government and U.N.R.R.A., arrangements were made for the delivery of food and clothing to every part of Greece.

Thus, thanks to outside intervention, what had practically amounted to civil war was brought to an end, but it left very bitter feelings behind it, and those who know the Greeks cannot help regarding the present condition of affairs as a truce rather than as a final reconciliation. The Agreement[1] of 13th February 1945 was in a sense a victory of the Right over the Left and led to a reaction further towards the Right, which brought about the fall of the Plastiras Cabinet early in April after three months of office.

Editor's Note.

The real issue of the civil war of 1944-5 was not one between Monarchy and Republicanism as it appeared at the time to many in England and America. The real issue was whether Greece should or should not become a communist-dominated state. It is true that only a small proportion of E.L.A.S. was communist, but E.L.A.S. was directed by E.A.M., which in turn was dominated by K.K.E. (Greek Communist Party). Those who question this view, however, pertinently ask why E.A.M. did not seize power, as they could easily have done, before the British arrived in Greece. The probable explanation is that at this stage the Russians, having no wish to antagonise the British, did not instruct K.K.E. to seize the government; and that K.K.E. itself, in the erroneous belief that strong British combat forces would be sent to Greece, did not think it would be possible to seize and hold Athens. When, however, K.K.E., which greatly resented the arrival of the royalist Greek mountain brigade, saw that the British troops were hardly a combat force, it was both incited and encouraged to attempt to seize power in Greece. That K.K.E. had such an aim seems to be evident from the story of its next attempt to seize power during the civil war of 1946-9.

[1] The Varkiza agreement.

CHAPTER XXVI

THE RECONSTRUCTION OF GREECE DURING THE POST-WAR YEARS : GREECE AND EUROPE, 1945-56

THAT the Varkiza agreement of 13th February 1945 was merely a truce, and not a final reconciliation, was made evident in the years that followed. Although great numbers of Greeks welcomed the opportunity to dissociate themselves from E.A.M., the hard core of the movement, K.K.E., still existed and was to make yet another attempt to seize the government. Three conditions favoured its efforts : the instability of Greek political life ; the appalling social and economic chaos that reigned in Greece ; and the assistance and encouragement that the Greek communists received from the Soviet Satellites, Bulgaria, Jugoslavia and Albania. Had the Greeks been left to themselves, they could hardly have warded off the threat. Happily for them, first the British and then the Americans came to their assistance ; and, if they did not achieve all that they wished to, they at least saved the inhabitants from ruin and starvation.

The Paris Reparations Conference estimated the war devastation in Greece at $8,500m. Two thousand villages and one-quarter of all buildings had been destroyed ; three-quarters of the Greek Mercantile Marine, two-thirds of the motor vehicles and nine-tenths of the locomotives had disappeared ; the larger road bridges had been demolished ; the Corinth canal had been blocked ; the telegraphs and ports had been badly damaged ; vast areas of olive groves, vineyards and forests had been laid waste ; and the number of cattle and sheep had been greatly diminished. Throughout the war people had existed on a semi-starvation diet ; thousands died ; and many more thousands would have perished but for the food sent by friends of Greece through the International Red Cross. When Greece was liberated, immediate relief was carried out by B.M.L. (British Military Liaison) in readiness for U.N.R.R.A. to take over. Altogether U.N.R.R.A. imported 2,667,500 tons of foods into Greece up to 30th June 1947. This relief probably delayed somewhat the production programme and certainly gave rise to a black market ; but it saved Greece from collapse and set going a partial recovery.

It soon became clear, however, that Greece needed assistance on a very large scale to enable her to become a viable State.

American Aid to Greece. The sums of money needed were far beyond the resources of Britain, who informed the U.S.A. that her economic commitments in Greece must end on 31st March 1947. Fortunately for the Greeks, the American State Department, which had hitherto regarded Greece as the special concern of Britain, decided to act ; and on 12th March 1947 President Truman sent to Congress a special message asking for a grant of $400m. to provide assistance to Greece and Turkey. Three-quarters of this sum went to Greece. Half of the $300m. was devoted to military purposes and the other half to economic aid. Later the economic commitments were handed over, under the Marshall Plan, to E.C.A.[1] Between 1944 and June 1953, Greece received military and economic aid to the extent of $743m. and $1,829m. respectively. Of the total of $2,572m., approximately $344m. came from British sources. American military aid amounted to about $529m. ; U.N.R.R.A.'s contribution was $416m. and American economic aid after 1947 came to nearly $1,200m. Wisely the Americans realised that it was not sufficient merely to restore the Greek pre-war economy with its serious limitations. Hence they planned five major power plants, a factory for making diesel engines, a small steel industry (for making steel from scrap), extension of the cement industry and an increased output of bauxite. They also planned much roadbuilding and the accumulation of rolling stock with a view to attracting tourists. Again, they hoped to increase agricultural production by importing tractors and other types of machinery, by increasing storage facilities for fruit and grain, by extending the use of fertilisers, and by providing instruction in husbandry for the agrarian population. Finally they drew up a housing programme and planned an improvement of the country's medical arrangements.

Unfortunately it was not possible to carry out all this programme. First of all the civil war of 1946–49 delayed the

[1] Economic Co-operation Administration.

recovery. Next, the Americans reduced considerably their assistance. By 1950 they were committed to the great expense of the war in Korea : they were moreover somewhat exasperated by the instability of Greek governments and by a considerable degree of Greek administrative inefficiency, above all by the failure to prevent tax evasion. In 1951 they decided not to finance any project not already started. Marshall aid was reduced in 1950–51 from $277.5m. to $206.8m., to $182m. in 1951–2, and to $80m. in 1952–3. Nevertheless the achievement was considerable. The production of grain, tobacco and cotton was by 1953 well above the pre-war level, as was also the output of textiles, chemicals and other industries. The olive groves and vineyards had been restored, and the increase in the numbers of livestock, which, however, remained below the 1939 figure, was most encouraging.

During this time the numbers of Greeks employed in agriculture fell considerably, the displaced persons being absorbed by industry, by the army and by the growing administration. But among the industrial and blackcoated workers there was much unemployment. In the overcrowded professions there was much under-employment, which was again to be found among the agricultural workers, whose average holding is very small. Both unemployment and under-employment have no doubt contributed to the political instability of Greece, as has also the lag in wages behind prices. The peasants and industrial workers, and those with fixed incomes have found it increasingly hard to live in post-war Greece ; and these classes stand out in sharp contrast to those who live easily, spending on luxuries what they ought to be paying in taxes.

The political instability arising from these economic conditions was much increased by the Greek multi-party system which gives rise to short-lived governments consisting of unstable coalitions. For the first seven post-war years Greece witnessed frequent changes of government, and first the British and then the Americans had to face the difficulty of dealing with a constantly changing personnel in charge of the various ministries and departments. Such a situation was all the more unfortunate because on most major issues the Greeks were fundamentally united. The vast majority of Greeks were opposed to K.K.E., whose numerical strength was never very great. They were

16

also generally agreed on foreign policy—alliance with the Western powers and the realisation of national aims. There was, moreover, a substantial majority in favour of the monarchy, the future of which had at one time seemed in doubt.

Whether the king should, or should not, return was, according to the Varkiza agreement, a question to be decided by a plebiscite *The question of* under Allied scrutiny. This plebiscite was to *the monarchy.* precede a general election. In view, however, of the chaotic state of Greece in 1945 it was obviously unwise to hold either the plebiscite or the elections until some degree of stability had been attained. On the other hand, the delay meant a series of governments which had no constitutional sanction and which the British had the unpopular task of supporting. After the fall of the Plastiras Government in April 1945, Admiral Voulgaris formed a " service " ministry which included the economic expert, Professor Varvaressos. But this administration was attacked by almost all parties, in particular by K.K.E., which organised strikes, and even by monarchists working through an organisation known as " X " (*Chi*). In August Voulgaris resigned, and, until Mr. Kanellopoulos was able at length to form a government, the Regent, Archbishop Damaskinos, assumed the functions of Prime Minister. In view of this unsatisfactory situation, which was likely to recur at any moment, the British, French and American governments agreed that a general election should precede the plebiscite and should take place in January 1946. This decision annoyed both the monarchist Populist party and the Liberals, who threatened to abstain from taking part. As a result, however, of Mr. Hector McNeil's[1] visit to Athens in November 1945 it was agreed that a coalition government should be formed by the elder statesman Sophoulis and should hold elections before 1st March. The elections finally took place on 31st March. E.A.M./K.K.E., which had already withdrawn support from the Government, refused to take part, for to have done so would have displayed the numerical weakness of the Left. Sophoulis proceeded without the Left Wing parties. Out of 354 seats Populists and other Royalists obtained 231. The centre parties of Papandreou, Venizelos and Kanellopoulos (they were prepared to accept monarchy if the majority desired it)

[1] British Under-Secretary of State for Foreign Affairs.

obtained 67; and the uncompromising Republicans obtained only 51. Of the electorate only 49% voted. K.K.E., which had earlier declared that the voting registers were entirely false, naïvely claimed the 51% which had abstained from voting.

The new government, which was formed by Constantine Tsaldaris, was, as would be expected, anxious to hold the plebiscite as soon as possible and obtained the agreement of the British that it should take place on 1st September. As far as one can judge (Allied observers supervised the formation of the registers but not the voting) this plebiscite was properly conducted. Of those entitled to vote, 80% registered, and 1,700,000 votes approximately were recorded. Of these 69% were cast for the mcnarchy and 31% against. Many former republicans seem to have voted for the King, who returned to Greece on 27th September. Attempts to form a coalition Government failed and Tsaldaris again took office.

By this time rebel bands of K.K.E. under the leadership of Markos Vafiades had become active in Northern Greece and *The civil war of 1946–9.* even in the Peloponnese, where supplies from behind the Iron Curtain were dropped by aircraft. On 3rd October 1946 Greece complained to the Security Council that the rebels were being trained on foreign soil and that fugitives were allowed to cross the frontiers into Albania, Bulgaria and Jugoslavia. In the debate that followed Soviet Russia, who had already demanded that the British should withdraw from Greece, argued that the satellites were hardly intervening in Greece as much as the Western powers. The argument was typical and thoroughly cynical. The British were intervening to uphold a lawful government and to set a stricken country on its feet. The powers behind the Iron Curtain were endeavouring to retard the recovery of Greece and were supporting a rebel minority, which had already attempted to seize power by force. In spite of Russia's attitude, the United Nations appointed a Commission of Investigation, which, in its report of May 1947, stated that it had found evidence of the subversive activities of Greece's northern neighbours. In the debate that followed there arose a deadlock in the Security Council, which referred the matter to the General Assembly of the United Nations. The Assembly appointed yet another Committee of Investigation (U.N.S.C.O.B.), which arrived in

Greece in November. Its report confirmed the findings of the earlier Committee of Investigation. This report, however, was rejected completely by the Soviet representative, Vishinsky, who went on to denounce Greece as having become an American colony.

The developing threat from K.K.E. had enabled the King to obtain, early in January 1947, a coalition government under Maximos. This government, which included Papandreou, Venizelos, Kanellopoulos and Zervas, was still in being when the Americans, in fulfilment of the Truman doctrine, took over from the British the task of saving Greece from economic collapse and civil war. To defeat the rebels, who had a 600-mile frontier over which they could retreat, the Greek Government had to employ large forces ; and by the winter of 1948–9 there were five divisions in the field. Although the rebels were probably never much greater than 25,000 in effectives, they were well armed and well trained in guerrilla tactics. They could choose their time and place of operations, strike quickly and disappear, only to strike again in some other quarter. They were not easily defeated. Indeed, had they been content to pursue these tactics only, they could probably have gone on indefinitely. But their political aims required that they should seize a town and set up a rival government. This was a much more difficult undertaking. Between May 1947 and February 1949 they failed twice at Florina, twice at Konitsa and once at both Grevena and Karpenisi. In these encounters they suffered heavy losses.

Three other developments contributed to their final defeat. When in the summer of 1948 Jugoslavia left the Cominform, the rebels operating from Albania were isolated from those operating from Bulgaria. Then again, when the Cominform announced in February 1949 its intention to create an independent Macedonia, which would have included a large and productive area of Greece, many of the rebels, who were nationalists before communists, withdrew their support from K.K.E. General Markos himself gave up the leadership, his place being taken by Zachariades.[1] Finally, there was the appointment by the Greek Government of General Papagos as commander-in-chief in place of a war council which had hitherto directed military

[1] The Secretary of K.K.E.

operations. General Papagos was very popular with the troops, whose morale improved. He was, moreover, highly acceptable to the Americans, who were now able, through the creation of a joint Greek-American general staff, to impart a greater efficiency to the military operations. In the final offensive against the rebels in the Mount Grammos area in the summer and early autumn of 1949, the Greek Army carried all before it and captured the headquarters of Zachariades. Already, before this final operation took place, the Russians, realising the rebels were facing defeat, proposed for Greece free elections. in which the rebels should play a part, the supervision of the elections by the powers (which in 1946 Russia had denounced as interference) and the withdrawal of all foreign troops from Greece. This proposal, which had already been rejected by Great Britain and the U.S.A., received from the United Nations the contempt it deserved.

The civil war of 1946–9 was very costly and could not have been fought without American financial aid. As already mentioned, this civil war retarded the economic recovery of Greece ; and it also brought further devastation to a country that had suffered so much. Many towns and villages were destroyed or damaged ; 700,000 persons (a tenth of the population) were displaced and some 25,000 children were abducted by Greece's northern neighbours. It says much, however, for the Greek Government and for Greek society in general that, in the midst of all this turmoil, civil liberty and democratic principles were maintained. Not until 1947 were the communist newspapers suppressed and K.K.E. itself was not outlawed until the end of that same year. Altogether the Greek Government executed just over 1,000 subversive persons, some of them for crimes committed during the German occupation. The less malignant persons—those who were misled—were treated with clemency. After a period of detention and instruction, they were released and many of them served in the army against the rebels.

The retention of civil and political liberty meant that Greek party politics ran their usual course. On 24th August the Maximos coalition broke up and, much to the *The Greek Rally*. annoyance of the Americans, Tsaldaris formed a Populist ministry, which was likely to put its party interest before the national interest. American pressure, however, caused this government to be reconstructed under the aged Sophoulis who included in it a few Liberals.   In January 1949 Sophoulis, faced with much internal dissension in his government, tendered his resignation.   At this point King Paul (who had in April 1947 succeeded to the throne on the death of his brother, George II) intervened and threatened " a different solution " if the parties would not sink their differences.   Sophoulis again took office.   Represented in the new government was the new party of Markezinis, a young and forceful politician who seemed at that time to have a future before him.   It was he who persuaded Papagos to accept appointment as commander-in-chief.

In June 1949 Sophoulis died.   Tsaldaris failed to form a ministry but agreed to serve in a coalition as deputy of Diomedes.   But with the end of the civil war in sight, Greek politicians had no wish to continue coalitions of this kind : rather there was a general feeling that new elections should be held.   Markezinis, now outside the government, canvassed the idea of a provisional government under Papagos, but the Commander-in-chief (now a Field-Marshal) made it quite clear that he had no wish to take part in politics.   In January 1950 Diomedes resigned ;   Theotokis formed a caretaker government ;   and a general election, under the system of proportional representation employed in 1946, was held in March.

Out of 250 seats (a new electoral law had reduced the number) 62 went to the Populists ;   56 to the Liberals ;   45 to a coalition party, E.P.E.K. (National Progressive Union of the Centre), under Plastiras ;   35 to Papandreou's Democratic Socialists ; and 18 to the Democratic Front (the Left).   Zervas's National Party had only 7 seats and the new Markezinis Party only one. This election showed a very decisive swing from the Right to the Centre, but it created a situation in which no government could command support in Parliament.   After some four unstable governments it was decided to hold further elections in September 1951 under a new system of proportional representation designed to reduce the lesser parties.   However, five weeks before polling began Papagos assumed the mantle of General de Gaulle, entered the arena with a new party, the Greek Rally, and, strongly supported by the Athenian Press, attacked the old regime of parties.   Joined by followers of Kanellopoulos and Markezinis, at the polls he captured the votes of the Populists, who were now reduced to two parliamentary members. Out of 258 seats the Greek Rally obtained 114, E.P.E.K., 74, and the Liberals, 57. Papagos refused to enter any coalition. Hence Plastiras formed a government, which lasted till October 1952. At new elections held in November under a straight ballot system the Greek Rally obtained 239 seats and E.P.E.K. 61. The Liberals and the parties to the Left had no candidates returned.

In the new Papagos ministry Markezinis became Minister of Economic Co-ordination and in December announced a realistic economic programme rather on the lines of that earlier proposed by Professor Varvaressos. Administrative costs and welfare services were to be reduced, and foreign capital was to be encouraged to replace the diminishing American aid. Much progress was made, but in August 1953 the catastrophic earthquake in the Ionian Islands placed a great strain on Greek resources. Further affliction came in like manner to Thessaly in April 1954 and to Volos in April 1955. Fortunately 21 countries subscribed generously towards the relief of the victims and U.S.A. came forward with a special grant of over $19m.

Although the Greek Rally provided a government with a stable parliamentary position, there were signs of dissension within the ministry and a decline of its popularity in the country. Markezinis withdrew in April 1954 and his friends, Kapsalis and Papayanis, in the following November. In February 1955 Markezinis announced that he had founded a new party of progressives whose parliamentary members numbered twenty-two. In October 1955 Field Marshal Papagos died. Karamanlis formed a new cabinet which was designed to preserve the unity of the Greek Rally, but, owing to differences within the party and to attacks from outside, the new Prime Minister agreed to hold a general election before April. Prior to the election he formed a new party, the National Radical Union of which just over half the parliamentary candidates belonged to the Greek Rally. This party was joined by certain Liberals. Other Liberals under Papandreou and Venizelos, the Populists under Tsaldaris and E.P.E.K. formed a coalition, the Democratic Union, with the extreme leftist party (itself a coalition), E.D.A.[1] The main purpose however of this " unholy alliance " of the centre parties with the extreme Left was not to produce a

[1] United Democratic Left.

coalition government but to defeat the Radical Union, to repeal the existing electoral law (a curious mixture of different systems for different areas) and to hold yet further elections under a system of proportional representation. Also in the field were the party of Markezinis and a new Popular Social Party led by the former deputy Prime Minister of the Greek Rally, Stephanopoulos.

The elections were held on 19th February 1956. Out of 300 seats, the National Radical Union obtained 165, though the Democratic Union had a slightly greater number of votes. This result certainly followed the aim of the electoral law to provide a government with a majority and a strong opposition. It also answered the gloomy forecasts by foreigners that Greece was about to swing decisively to the Left.

On forming his new government on 29th February, Karamanlis announced that his economic policy would be to raise the standard of living, to encourage foreign investments and, by a high rate of interest, to promote saving. There are signs that this policy is having some effect. By August 1956 foreign investments amounted to $50m., unemployment was diminishing and various new industrial developments were in progress. Private deposits in the banks had increased, thus enabling credit facilities to be extended. Greek shipping (over 12m. tons under 15 different flags at the end of 1955) continued to flourish.

As the internal affairs of Greece became more settled, questions of foreign policy began to occupy more attention. At the end

Greek National Claims. of the civil war of 1946–9 there was a wide demand that Greece should occupy what the Greeks call Northern Epirus (Southern Albania).

The claim to that territory had already been unsuccessfully made by Tsaldaris at the Paris Peace Conference in 1946. At that same conference Greece also (unsuccessfully) made claim to a more northerly frontier in Western Thrace—a frontier including the passes of Kovelik-Balkan and Kresna instead of following the more southerly slopes of the Rhodope mountains. Had Greece obtained this frontier rectification she would have found it easier to deal with the rebels who between 1946–9 operated from Bulgarian bases. The failure to improve her northern frontiers was a great disappointment to Greece. On the other hand, at the Treaty of Paris of 15th February 1947, she obtained

the Dodecanese from Italy, who also agreed to pay Greece
$105m. as reparations.

Of all the problems of Greek foreign policy the most difficult
is that of Cyprus. This problem has not only threatened the
Greece and   solidarity of the Balkan Pact (which Greece had
Cyprus.   concluded with Jugoslavia and Turkey and
               which in 1954 was converted into a military
alliance) but it has led to a deterioration in Greek relations with
her old and faithful ally, Great Britain. There has even arisen in
Greece a demand that Greece should withdraw from N.A.T.O.
which she had joined in the autumn of 1951. Finally, in its
handling of the Cyprus question, first the government of
Papagos and later the government of Karamanlis came in for
fierce and somewhat irresponsible criticism from the opposition
parties.

Cyprus has a population of just over 360,000 Greeks and
just over 80,000 Turks. Passing under British control in 1878
and formally annexed by Great Britain in 1914, in 1925 Cyprus
became a Crown Colony. As we have seen, in 1915 Britain
offered Cyprus to Greece in an attempt to win over the Greeks
to the Allied cause.[1] At all other times Britain has opposed the
enosis (union) of Cyprus with Greece—a demand revived shortly
after the British occupation. The Greek claim, and the demand
of the Cypriots too, are based on the religious, linguistic, racial
and cultural affinity between Cyprus and Greece. Both Greeks
and Greek Cypriots argue that just as the Ionian Islands, Crete,
Thrace and the Dodecanese have rightly become parts of Greece,
so too should Cyprus which is culturally similar to these other
territories. They add, quite rightly, that the argument that
Cyprus has never been part of Modern Greece is quite irrelevant.

Although British rule in Cyprus is open to criticism, it has
been much better than Britain's enemies and misinformed friends
would have us believe ; and its material benefits (which have
been all too few) have nevertheless been such that many Cypriots
(like many of the Ionians in 1864) would lose considerably
through *enosis* with Greece. But the feeling of brotherhood
among Greeks (despite their fratricidal struggles) is a strong
one ; and the right to self-determination and national unity is a
principle which elsewhere Britain has generally upheld. She

[1] See above, pp. 176-8, in which is described the Cyprus problem in 1931.

16*

has by patient and liberal administration brought many peoples to a condition which fitted them for self-government and independence. The Cypriots, moreover, are not an immature people ; great numbers of them (thanks to British administration) are more sophisticated and better citizens than many of the mainland Greeks. They are certainly capable of self-government and of deciding whether or not they wish for *enosis* with Greece.

Unfortunately for Greece and the Cypriots, the problem of Cyprus is not a simple one. The world to-day is very different from that of 1864 when Britain belatedly but graciously handed over to Greece the Ionian Islands. These islands were of limited strategic importance. But Cyprus, especially after the British withdrawal from Egypt, has become a military base which is vital to British interests. What is more, British policy in the Middle East is based on friendship with Turkey who prefers that the Turkish Cypriots should remain under British rule. The Greeks argue that the Turkish minority in Cyprus would have nothing to fear if the island became part of Greece, and they can proudly and justifiably call attention to Thrace where the Moslem minority enjoys religious liberty and shares in the political life of Greece. The Greek reply to British strategic demands is also very plausible. The Greeks point out that Cyprus can remain a British military base, which would be all the more valuable if the civil population were friendly and that Greece is prepared, and has indeed offered, to provide further bases on the soil of Greece. But the British, bearing in mind what has happened elsewhere, have firmly contended that they cannot fulfil their international obligations and safeguard their own essential interests unless they can have complete and un-disputed control of Cyprus. They are prepared to give the island a constitution but are determined, so long as the inter-national situation requires it, to retain the legal and effective control of Cyprus.

The offer of a constitution unaccompanied by a promise of a plebiscite at a definite date seems not to have much attraction for the Cypriots. When in October 1946 the British Colonial Office invited various bodies in Cyprus to form a consultative assembly to advise the British Government on a constitution, many of these bodies refused to co-operate ; and A.K.E.L. (the Communist Party of Cyprus) seized the occasion to demand self-government.   Subsequently this party changed its policy and demanded *enosis* with Greece—a demand also supported by the Orthodox Church under the leadership of Archbishop Makarios.   In January 1950 the Church in Cyprus held an unofficial plebiscite, it being claimed that 215,108 out of 224,757 entitled to vote had declared for *enosis*.   But this manoeuvre had no effect whatever on the British Government, which was prepared to go no further than to grant a constitution.

To the Greeks the British attitude seemed most unreasonable and they have placed their governments under constant pressure on the Cyprus issue.   No Greek government, even if it wanted to, can ignore the demand for *enosis*.   To come out openly, however, in favour of *enosis* renders the Greek Government vulnerable to the British accusation of seeking territorial gain regardless of the defences of the Middle East.   Hence official Greek policy has been to express sympathy with the desire for *enosis* but, in pressing for a solution, to demand only the human rights of the United Nations' Charter, including the right to self-determination.   As late as March 1954 Field-Marshal Papagos could say that the Greek Government's Cyprus policy was one of firmness and compromise best calculated to serve Eastern Mediterranean security and Anglo-Greek ties.   But before long he was obliged to state that if Britain failed to find a solution the only recourse was an appeal to the United Nations.

Events in Cyprus from this time onwards aggravated the situation.   In July 1954 Archbishop Makarios urged the Cypriots to reject the British offer of a constitution and to form a national assembly.   The next month he led his congregation in a demonstration demanding *enosis*.   From December 1954 onwards there were many demonstrations in Cyprus and in April 1955 there began a series of bomb outrages organised by E.O.K.A. (National Organisation of Cypriot Fighters).   The British took stern measures and, when terrorist activities showed no signs of diminishing, in September 1955 proscribed E.O.K.A. and sent military reinforcements to the island.

Already, as early as April 1954, there had been demonstrations in Greece in favour of *enosis* and it was these together with pressure from certain members of the Greek Rally which forced Papagos to take a firmer line on Cyprus.   That same month the Greek Foreign Office stated that if by 22nd August Britain had not agreed to hold bi-lateral talks on Cyprus (talks excluding Turkey) or if such talks failed, Greece would bring the Cyprus question before the General Assembly of the United Nations. As the British proved unbending, on 20th August 1954 Papagos requested that Cyprus should be placed on the General Assembly's agenda. Despite British protests, the Assembly's steering committee decided 9 to 3 in favour of Greece. Greece then demanded a plebiscite for Cyprus under the auspices of U.N.O. But that was as far as the matter went, for in December a New Zealand resolution not to consider further, for the time being, the Greek request was carried 50 to nil (8 abstaining). This decision (which ought to have been anticipated) caused the Greeks much disappointment and there followed in Greece angry demonstrations against both Britain and America. King Paul, in a broadcast, appealed to his people to remain faithful to their old friends, America and Britain ; to remember that without their aid Greece and Cyprus might no longer have existed ; and not to let disappointment obscure the larger problems.

In June 1955 Britain invited both Greece and Turkey to talks in London on Mediterranean defence, including Cyprus. This move was denounced by Makarios who in July visited Athens and requested the Greek Government to send a further appeal to the United Nations in case the tripartite talks should fail. The Foreign Minister, Stephanopoulos, refused to do this, saying that such a measure would prejudice the talks which were planned for August. In a Press Conference the Archbishop stated he disapproved of the Greek Government's tactics and he himself sent a telegram to U.N.O. protesting against British security measures in Cyprus. This combined with internal pressure caused the Greek Government to act : on 21st July Stephanopoulos announced that Greece had asked that Cyprus should be placed on the Agenda of the General Assembly of the United Nations.

The tripartite talks began in London on 29th August. Mr. Macmillan's offer of a constitution to Cyprus was refused. While the talks were in progress Greek-Turkish relations deteriorated. Greek attacks on the Turkish consulate of Salonica were followed by anti-Greek riots in Istanbul and Smyrna. The Greek Government cancelled Greek participation in N.A.T.O.'s military exercises and even hinted that Greece might withdraw from the Atlantic Treaty. Opposition parties in Greece attacked the government, complaining of its servile and undignified attitude to Turkish provocations, and called for an emergency session of Parliament to debate the possible re-alignment of Greek Foreign policy. But the Greek Government stood firm and continued negotiations with Great Britain. This was indeed the only way open to it, for the second Greek appeal to U.N.O. had, like the first, met with no success.

On 22nd September 1955 Makarios announced that, in view of the situation, he would summon the Cypriots to enter a new stage of passive resistance. He later explained that he envisaged the withdrawal of Cypriots from the municipal and village bodies in Cyprus. He did not, it would seem, envisage a cessation of terrorism, for, as far as is known, he did not use his influence to put an end to E.O.K.A.'s outrages. In point of fact, E.O.K.A. increased its subversive actions. Such was the situation when, on 3rd October 1955, the new Governor, Field-Marshal Sir John Harding arrived in Cyprus. Shortly after his arrival he had several talks with Makarios who later informed the Press that he had offered to co-operate with the new Governor on the basis of a plan which admitted self-determination for the Cypriots. When offered the Macmillan proposals, the Archbishop replied that they had been rejected by the Government of Greece and were therefore unacceptable.

Meanwhile, despite anti-British demonstrations in Greece and inflammatory broadcasts to Cyprus from Athens against which the British protested, the Anglo-Greek negotiations continued. On 5th December 1955 Mr. Macmillan stated that the gap to be bridged was narrow and he hinted that a compromise might be found. He explained however that sinister forces were at work and as much as said that Makarios was one of the chief obstacles to a settlement. In February 1956, however, Makarios is said to have accepted in principle the British offer of a constitution as an interim solution. With Mr. F. Noel-Baker, M.P., acting as mediator, negotiations continued into early March, but these broke down on the refusal of the British to agree to a Greek-elected majority in the proposed legislature. Following this breakdown in negotiations, the British Government removed Makarios from Cyprus, having come to doubt his sincerity and having become convinced that he was encouraging the terrorism of E.O.K.A. This measure caused a great outcry, not only in Cyprus but also in Greece. The Greek Government not only withdrew its Ambassador from London but, under popular pressure, lodged yet another appeal to the United Nations. It stated that it would resume negotiations on the four following conditions : (1) the return of Makarios to Cyprus ; (2) the recognition of the Cypriot people's right to self-determination ; (3) the establishment of self-government based on full constitutional guarantees ; (4) a general amnesty to detained Cypriot patriots. It would seem that the Greek Government had in mind a definite period of between five and ten years for the phase of self-government and that the date fixed for the recognition of self-determination should not be made dependent on British strategic requirements.

In August 1956 E.O.K.A. declared a truce. The Cyprus Government, however, took the occasion not to speed up negotiations but to make to E.O.K.A. the offer of an unconditional surrender. Needless to say, E.O.K.A. renewed the struggle, which continued with increasing bitterness to the end of the year. In October the Greek Government succeeded in placing the Cyprus question on the agenda of the General Assembly of the United Nations. But though the Greeks received some sympathy they obtained no tangible result. Meanwhile the British Government had sent Lord Radcliffe to Cyprus to study the problem and to draft a constitution to be offered to the Cypriots. Lord Radcliffe's proposals were published as a White Paper on 19th December 1956. They provide for a dyarchy in Cyprus ; the British Governor is to be vested with the legislative and executive power in his reserved fields of external affairs, defence and internal security : the Local Legislature with Ministers responsible to it is to have the control of its own field, the Governor however being the final judge as to the exact limits of that field. The Legislature is to consist of 36 members—24 elected Greek Cypriots, 6 elected Turkish Cypriots, and 6 nominated members. The proposals go on to provide ingenious and elaborate methods of safeguarding minority rights. All this may be admirable, but the Greeks are bitterly disappointed with the basic structure of the proposed constitution, as also with the suggestion of partition as a possible ultimate solution.

At the end of March 1957, the British Government, following a marked decline in the activities of E.O.K.A. and following the United Nations' resolution of the 22nd February that negotiations should be continued to find a just settlement, released Archbishop Makarios from detention.   This act, although marred by the continuation of the Archbishop's exile (he was not allowed to return to Cyprus), gave much satisfaction to the Greeks and also to their friends in Britain.   But an immediate settlement was not forthcoming.   The Archbishop had already made it clear upon his release that he would not negotiate unless he were allowed to return to Cyprus.   He rejected outright the plan of partition, denied the right of the Turks to have a part in negotiations, and defined the just settlement as the application of the principle of self determination.   In making these pronouncements he has the support of the Greeks and it is difficult to see how a Greek Government can possibly negotiate on different principles. Such was the position in May 1956 : it can only be hoped that a reasonable solution can soon be found and complete Anglo-Greek friendship restored.

CHAPTER XXVII

THE GREEKS OF TO-DAY[1]

THE question is often asked : How far can the modern Greeks be regarded as the descendants of the ancient inhabitants of their land ? Now that the British and Greeks have been fighting side by side, we, as well as they, like to recall the military glories of ancient Greece, the victories of Marathon, Salamis, and Platæa, and to claim that our allies are the representatives of the nation which invented the arts of peace and war and laid the foundations of modern literature and science. But the claim of the modern Greeks to Hellenic descent has often been contested. For example, Fallmerayer, the German historian of medieval Greece, writing in 1830, when the Greeks had lately vindicated their freedom in the War of Independence, affirmed that the modern Greeks were an almost purely Slavonic race. This judgement seemed to the Greeks of that day, and to the foreign Philhellenes who had aided them, to be rank heresy, and they would have none of such theories ; and indeed a study of the history, language, customs, and characteristics of the Greeks tends to confirm the belief that their claim to Hellenic descent has at least a considerable basis of truth.

Greeks ancient and modern.

Down to the middle of the sixth century A.D., in spite of the inroads of northern barbarians, the population of Greece seems to have remained as Greek as in the classical period ; but in A.D. 577 there was a formidable Slav invasion, which, however, mainly affected Northern Greece. In the eighth century, after the terrible plague of A.D. 746-7, much of the open country was colonized by Slavs, who acquired a firm footing in the Peloponnese. But the fact remains that the Slavonic element was

Slavonic element in Greece.

[1] See Editor's Preface to the Third Edition. For a recent account of economic conditions, see Sweet-Escott's excellent study, *Greece. A Political and Economic Survey, 1939-53* (1954).

244

absorbed and has left practically no trace in the language and
very little in the place-names of the country. One sometimes,
however, comes across individuals, particularly in the Peloponnese,
who have the round face and flat features which are characteristic
of the Slav.

Another non-Greek element are the Albanians, probably
sprung from the ancient Illyrians, who began to descend into
The Albanians.   Greece in the fourteenth century, but, like the
Slavs, they were Hellenized and, unlike many of
their brethren in Albania proper, who became Moslems, they
remained true to the Christian faith after the Turkish conquest.
A further Albanian element was added, when Albanian troops
were employed by the Turks to suppress the abortive rising of
1770. Many of them settled in the country, especially in Attica
and the Argolid islands, and were assimilated, and, when Greece
rose against her oppressors, they provided some of the most
brilliant chiefs and the toughest soldiers and fully earned their
right to share in the dearly-won liberty of Greece. Some of
Greece's most prominent leaders, for example, Admiral Koundouriotis and M. Zaïmis, the two Presidents of the Republic,
have belonged to families of Albanian extraction. The picturesque
Albanian dress with its pleated *fustanella* has been adopted as the
Greek national costume and is worn by the Evzones of the
Greek Army. Under King Otho prominent statesmen wore
the *fustanella*, and M. Gennadius, for so long the Greek Minister
at the Court of St. James, maintained that it was the proper
dress of a Greek diplomatist abroad ; as late as 1900 the Deputy
for Tripolitsa appeared in the Chamber in the national garb.

Other elements in the population of Greece are the Wallachians
or Vlachs, the Turks, and the Jews, but they have never been
numerous enough to have any ethnological significance and
have never intermingled with the Greeks.

The Wallachians are a curious nomadic race, whose language
belongs to the Latin family and is akin to Rumanian. They
The Wallachians.   are a pastoral people settled in Northern Greece,
who spend the summer in the mountains and
the winter in the plains. Their summer encampments consist
of beehive-like huts, which are placed, if possible, in woods or
in depressions on the mountains—a practice originally adopted
to escape the attentions of Turkish tax-collectors. They are a

thrifty but generous race. One of the richest modern millionaires, M. Averof, who presented Greece with her only battle-cruiser, which bears his name, and who reseated the Stadium at Athens in marble, belonged to this race.

Owing to the exchange of populations the Turks have practically disappeared from Greece. Formerly they were to *Turks.* be found in small numbers in Northern Greece and even returned a few Turkish Deputies, who, it was noted, characteristically followed the line of least resistance and always voted with the party in power.

The Jews are rare in Old Greece, since a Greek is quite a match for the Jew in business acumen, but they form a large *Jews.* element in the population of Salonica where they were given a home by the Turks when they were driven out of Spain by Ferdinand and Isabella. The most highly educated Jews are said to speak Castilian but the lower classes speak a language which bears the same relation to Spanish as Yiddish bears to German with the admixture of some Turkish words. They not only carry on businesses of every kind but also form the lowest class of casual labourers. The Chief Rabbi of Salonica is one of the great personages of the Jewish world owing to the size and wealth of the Jewish community. An amusing incident was the acceptance by the then holder of the office of the Greek Order of the Saviour for services rendered in the war of 1914–18.

The enormous influx of refugees into Greece has probably introduced a new element of purer Hellenic stock than many of *Refugees.* the older inhabitants, since the Greek communities outside Greece, especially in Asia Minor, being surrounded by men of non-European race and of a different religion, to a great extent escaped admixture of blood.

Language is no infallible criterion of race ; but the fact that one of the oldest of languages, that of Homer, Sophocles, Plato, *The Greek language.* and the New Testament, is still a living speech is surely one of the most remarbable phenomena in the history of philology. It has naturally undergone changes, but it is no exaggeration to say that the difference between Homeric and modern Greek is no greater than that between Middle English and the English of to-day. The spoken language has of course changed more than the written, which is much nearer to ancient Greek ; in fact, any one acquainted with classical Greek can read a leading article in the Greek press. There is a much more striking difference between the popular and the official language than in most countries, and the rivalry between the ' demotic ', which contains a good many Turkish and Italian words, and the ' purified ' language has often become a serious political question. In literature also two opposing forces are at work, one of which has led to an exaggerated rusticity, the other to an unnatural reaction in the direction of ancient Greek. It often amuses the foreigner to hear Greek children calling one another by the names of great men and women of antiquity, such as Sophocles, Themistocles, Plato, Antigone, and Aspasia.

In his strong sense of nationality the modern Greek resembles the ancient, who divided the world into Greeks and barbarians.

Greek National-ist feeling. Wherever the Greek is, he always remains a Greek. There are Greeks to be met with scattered all over the globe ; for example, there are flourishing Greek communities at Manchester, Alexandria, and Marseilles and in India, and, until immigration was restricted, countless Greeks migrated to the U.S.A., where they sold fruit and confectionery in the larger cities, working and saving money in order to return to Greece and live the rest of their lives in idleness. Many of the restaurants in Canada are kept by Greeks, who are also to be found in large numbers in the Transvaal and at Melbourne. Many of the finest houses in Athens belong to Greeks who have made fortunes abroad in shipping or Egyptian cotton ; and immense sums have been lavished by Greeks who made their money abroad on the foundation of schools, hospitals, and libraries in their native places. The strong bond of nationality was never better shown than in the splendid spirit of brotherhood and self-sacrifice in which the Greeks dealt with the difficult problem of settling the hundreds of thousands of refugees who poured into Greece in the years following the war of 1914–18, as a result of the exchange of population with Turkey and Bulgaria.

Politically, too, there are striking points of resemblance between the modern and the ancient Greeks.

Strong interest in politics. Politics are the primary interest of the modern Greek. Before the establishment of the dictatorship, if he was not discussing some real or imaginary business transaction in the street or a café, the Greek was sure to be talking politics. There are innumerable daily papers in Athens, and political questions were formerly apt to split the nation into two parts, just as in antiquity they divided the Greek city-states into two irreconcilable factions, but talking and writing on political topics became dangerous under the restrictions of the dictatorship. The modern Greeks, too, have shown all the political instability of the ancients. The changes backwards and forwards from Monarchy to Republicanism in the last twenty-five years are a striking example of this.

The average Greek of to-day is at heart a democrat and an individualist, and it is difficult not to believe that, like the ancient Greek, he is also by nature a republican. The long reign of King George I may seem to contradict this, but it must be remembered that Greece was under the tutelage of the Powers and King George, as brother-in-law of King Edward VII and uncle of the Czar Nicholas, was an invaluable asset in international politics. Also his ultra-constitutional attitude on all occasions enabled him to weather the storm, though more than once the Greek Royal Family had their baggage ready packed to leave Greece on a British man-of-war. There has seldom been a more democratic king than George I. He strolled about unattended and engaged in conversation with people whom he met. In his reign court balls were extremely democratic functions ; it used to be said that if you wanted to hire a carriage to take you to the Palace, you must order it early, as the proprietor might wish to return and dress in order to be present himself. King George I was never really appreciated until his subjects realized their loss when he was assassinated in Salonica whither he had gone after its capture in the First Balkan War to assert the claim of Greece to the newly-conquered Macedonia.

Democracy and Republicanism.

There is no titled aristocracy in Greece. Many Greeks of the old Phanariot families who ruled the Christian provinces under the Turks were granted the hereditary title of Prince, but they are not allowed to use such titles in Greece and can only assume them when they go abroad. The Venetian rule in the Ionian Islands resulted in the bestowal of titles on numerous Greek families, who made it a

Social Classes.

condition of their adherence to the Greek kingdom that they might retain their titles, but they are not allowed to use them except in their own islands, where these Italian noblemen are as common as blackberries. It is of course unavoidable that Athenian society should have its social distinctions, but one of the chief claims is descent from the heroes of the War of Independence.

The democratic character of the Greek State has led, as often, to an extreme form of bureaucracy, a large fraction of the population *Bureaucracy.* being in Government employment at miserable salaries. Things, however, have greatly improved in recent years. In former days one encountered inefficiency everywhere. For example, one would find that the General Post Office at Athens had run out of the most common denominations of postage-stamps. Formerly, too, the ' spoils system ' existed, under which each new Government installed its own nominees in every kind of official position. The present writer remembers congratulating the nephew of a newly-appointed Prime Minister on his uncle's accession to power ; he replied that it made no difference to him, as he already had a good post in a bank.[1]

A striking and most agreeable quality which the modern Greek shares with the ancient is hospitality. Travelling about *Greek hospitality.* in the country districts, especially if one speaks the language and does not take a dragoman, one is welcomed wherever one goes. If there is no inn, the most substantial villager entertains the traveller. To take the stranger in—in the best sense of the phrase—is a sacred duty. When the traveller arrives in the village the mayor, or perhaps the schoolmaster, installs him in his best room, a sanctuary only entered on special occasions, and kills a lamb and gets out his best wines. He will accept no payment, though you can ' tip ' his servant, if he has one. The arrival of a stranger in a remote Greek village is quite an event and leads to a great assemblage of the notables of the place—including

[1] On another occasion the present writer, visiting Athens after an absence of some years, inquired after a lady who had given him lessons in Modern Greek. He found that, though she had no special qualifications, she had been appointed headmistress of a large girls' secondary school. Her cousin had become Minister of Education.

often a returned emigrant from America, who seizes the opportunity to air his efficiency, or inefficiency, in speaking English— and a great consumption of liquid refreshment. Occasions of this kind give the modern Greek an opportunity of displaying another characteristic, which he shares with the ancient Greek. Like the Homeric hero he wants to know all about you and does not scruple to ask questions : ' What is your name and age ? ' ' Why have you come to Greece ? ' ' What is your income ' ? They also expect you to know personally any friend of theirs who is or has been in England : ' Do you ever go to London ? If so, you must have met my second cousin, Anastasios Papadopoulos who is a waiter in Soho.' If you are unmarried, they will ask you what dowry you will expect with the lady you marry. Another common type of question concerns the wages and salaries of persons of every class in England from agricultural labourers to Prime Ministers and even the Sovereign. A story is told of a villager who inquired the annual revenue enjoyed by the King of England and, on being given a somewhat vague answer in millions of drachmas, remarked : ' I suppose he could afford to eat tinned meat ' (which is regarded as a first-class luxury) ' twice a day if he wanted to '. An evening spent in a Greek country café is a somewhat exhausting experience.

The mention of cafés, where one seldom meets any one but men, leads on to another point of resemblance between modern and ancient Greeks, the position of women. *Position of women.* Naturally in the upper strata of society in Athens and the larger cities, the position of women is the same as in other European cities. Elsewhere, however, the place of woman is in the home—and nowhere else. The lack of influence of women in affairs outside the home is, however, amply compensated by the respect and consideration which their husbands and children show to them as wives and mothers. The women do their full share of work in the field and make all the family clothing, including the spinning and weaving of the materials. Marriages are a matter of arrangement and the bride must bring a dowry suitable to her position in life and an ample supply of family linen as well as her trousseau. The position of women is also reflected in the attitude towards children. The boys are the favourites and girls are little accounted and only tolerated. When the present writer was once travelling in Laconia, his host in one village gave him an introduction to a relative in a village some miles away but solemnly warned him not to ask his cousin how many children he had, since he was in the horrible predicament of possessing eleven daughters ' and nothing male at all.'

The main occupations of the modern Greeks are the same as those of the ancients—agriculture, seafaring, and fishing. In *Agriculture.* many parts of Greece the methods of agriculture are still primitive, though modern machinery has been introduced in the great plains of Thessaly and scientific farming has been introduced in Boeotia by the British Lake Copais Co. Ploughing is usually carried on with a wooden plough drawn by oxen. Olives, figs, oranges, almonds, wine, and the small grape which is grown chiefly on the south coast of the Corinthian Gulf and derives its name of currant from the city of Corinth, are important products ; but the chief crop now is that of tobacco, on the successful harvesting and disposal of which the economic life of Greece may almost be said to depend. The sea carrying trade of Greece is one of the most *Shipping.* important industries. Developed originally in the islands, it has become one of the greatest sources of profit to Greece. During the war of 1914–18 large fortunes were made by Greeks who sold their vessels to the Allies when the submarine menace was making havoc of shipping. In 1834 the site of the Peiræus, the port of Athens, was marked by a single building, the remains of the Turkish custom-house ; now it is the third largest port in the Mediterranean and the place of call of the greater part of about five million tons of shipping, which enter and leave the harbours of Greece. Its population in 1938 numbered 198,771. Fishing is also extensively carried on, by methods which have made little progress since antiquity. The catching of tunny is still practised on the principles described by Strabo, small platforms being erected out at sea, where the fishermen look out for shoals and warn their companions when a shoal is in sight. The drag-net is also a popular method of fishing ; and spearing of fish from a boat with a flare at night is also practised. Sponge-fishing by divers is a profitable industry in some of the islands.

Hitherto we have spoken mainly about the country Greeks, who form the bulk of the population and show the character-

istics of the race in the most marked degree, since the urban
population is much the same in all countries.
Growth of cities.
The present century has witnessed an immense
development of Athens and the Peiræus, which with Salonica
are the only really large towns in Greece. In 1900 there was
still a stretch of several miles of agricultural land between Athens
and its port, but this is now covered with factories and works ;
in fact, the industrial revolution has at last reached Greece.
Athens is now the largest city in South-east Europe, having even
outstripped Constantinople, and the Acropolis towers over a
great modern town which, with its suburbs and the Peiræus,
contains a population of little less than one million souls. One
looks back with regret to the time within recent memory when
the city was about the size of an average English county town
with scarcely any industry and with a commerce almost entirely
limited to importations.

The modern, like the ancient, Greeks are great believers in
education, which is entirely free. Secondary schools have been
established in all the large centres, and the
Education.
pupils of these ' gymnasia ' are a familiar sight
with their blue uniforms and peaked caps. The University of
Athens was founded in the earliest days of the Greek kingdom
and celebrated its centenary four years ago, and a second university
was established at Salonica in 1927. Women were first admitted
to the University in 1890. The thirst for education is apt to
lead to the training for the learned professions of more men
than can find reasonably good employment. There are thus
superfluous professionally qualified men, who join the ranks of
the unemployed and tend to become political agitators and
hangers-on of the chiefs of the political factions. In 1927 a
public school on English lines was founded at Spetsai on the
initiative of M. Venizelos, in the hope that, adorned with the
old school tie, the ex-pupils would turn out to be reliable public
servants and administrators.

A remarkable feature of the streets of Athens is the so-called
' Loustros ' or shoe-blacks. The Greek considers well-polished
footgear to be the hall-mark of a civilized gentleman and has a
mania for having his shoes polished at any odd moment of the
day. Even so, the boot-blacking industry seems to be rather
overstaffed. The reason is that it is the ambition of every Greek

boy of intelligence to migrate to Athens, where he blacks boots in the day and attends night schools and is housed in hostels provided for him by the charitable. Many of these boys have reached positions of eminence in after life ; there are said to have been instances of their becoming Cabinet Ministers, but this is easier in Greece than in most countries, since Ministries are continually changing. Meanwhile they are employed not only as boot-blacks but also as messengers and errand-boys and, in emergencies, as domestic helps. They are trustworthy and intelligent and form an attractive feature of the street-life of Athens.

Until recent years athletics did not play such an important part in modern Greek life as they played in antiquity. The revival of the Olympic Games was largely due to Greek initiative, but the movement was originally inspired more by a desire on the part of the Greeks to parade their Hellenic descent than from a love of athletics. At the First Olympic Games the Greeks, through lack of foreign competitors, won most of the prizes. In particular, the race from Marathon to Athens was won by a native, who at the time was suspected by his rivals of cheating. However, so the story goes, he proved himself so admirable a long-distance runner when he led the van of the retreating Greek Army after its defeat in Thessaly in the campaign against Turkey in 1897 that he completely cleared his character.[1] Of late years, however, particularly under the recent dictatorship, there has been a marked development of sport, especially football, and University students are said to have turned their attention from politics to the safer pursuit of athletics.

One respect in which the modern Greeks fall short of the Greeks of the classical age is in their achievement in art and architecture. Like the Italians they rely on the *Art and architecture.* ancients to provide artistic attractions for visitors. They have produced no great painter and only mediocre sculptors,[2] and the architecture of modern

---

[1] Some thirty years ago the present writer attended the Panhellenic Games at Athens, which were confined to Greek athletes. In the walking race the man who came in *last* was declared winner by the English umpire ; he was the only competitor who did not *run*.

[2] Michael Tombros, the sculptor of the memorial to Rupert Brooke set up on the island of Skyros, is perhaps an exception.

17

Athens presents few features of interest. In the early days of
the kingdom the inspiration, such as it was, came with King Otho
from Bavaria and produced the vast, barrack-like old Royal
Palace and pseudo-classical buildings like the University and
the National Library. Modern ecclesiastical architecture is
feeble and uninteresting. The Cathedral at Athens is devoid
of architectural merit ; yet, to provide the material for it, a
number of Byzantine buildings of real artistic beauty were
destroyed. Of recent years, however, a movement for the
preservation and study of popular art has grown up, and an
increasing interest in painting, sculpture, and architecture has
led to the production of some good work on modern lines, and
art exhibitions in Athens attract numerous exhibitors and are
well patronized by the public.

The modern Greeks have shown little capacity for engineering. Their railways are slow and cover only a small area of the
Engineering.   country, and the tracks are so badly laid that
they are often damaged by storm or flood.
There has been a great improvement, however, in the roads of
the country since the introduction of mechanical transport, and
travelling has thus been rendered much easier. There is at least
one modern achievement in engineering which the ancients had
projected but never carried out, the canal through the Isthmus
of Corinth ; but it is too small for large vessels, and the dues
charged to foreign ships passing through are almost prohibitive,
so that the canal is little used except by small Greek steamers.
For the extensive public works carried out in Greece in recent
years the help of foreign engineers and contractors has usually
been called in ; they have found valuable co-operation in the
Greek labourer, who is an industrious and intelligent worker.

The Greeks are essentially a young nation and are still at an
earlier stage of development than many of the peoples of Europe ;
but no one who has visited Greece can fail to have been struck
by the life and energy displayed in all the departments of their
national life, in spite of the fact that circumstances in recent years
have not been very favourable. The years of war from 1913 to
1922, followed by a period of intense political dissension and the
strain of assimilating the hundreds of thousands of refugees who
flocked into the country, did not exhaust the forces of this
energetic and quick-witted people. In face of the Italian attack

of 1940 and the German invasion of 1941 they showed to the world that courage and tenacity can make up for the lack of material advantages and that brave men fighting for their national independence can hold at bay treacherous invaders who attacked without provocation or warning with all the resources of mechanical warfare launched from behind a screen of hypocrisy and misrepresentation. Their courage during the dark years of 1940–44 was astounding and their reconstruction of their country on democratic principles in the years that followed was an achievement of the highest order and worthy of the traditions of their country.

ΖΗΤΩ Η ΕΛΛΑΣ.

BIBLIOGRAPHY

ABBOTT, G. F. *Greece and the Allies* (1914–22). London 1922.
ABOUT, E. *La Grèce contemporaine.* Paris 1855.
ANDRÉADÈS, A. *Les Effets économiques et sociales de la guerre en Grèce.* Paris 1929.
ANDREW, PRINCE, OF GREECE. *Towards Disaster.* London 1930.
ANON. *The Greek Army and the Recent Offensive.* London 1919.
BICKFORD-SMITH, R. A. H. *Greece under King George.* London 1893.
BIRTLES, B. *Exiles in the Ægean.* London 1938.
BOWER, L., and BOLITHO, G. *Otho I, King of Greece.* London 1939.
BRAILSFORD, H. N. *Macedonia : its Races and its Future.* London 1906.
BROWN, ASHLEY. *Greece, Old and New.* London 1927.
BUCKLEY, C. *Greece and Crete, 1941.* London 1952.
COSMETATOS, S. P. P. *The Tragedy of Greece.* London 1928.
CRAWLEY, C. W. *The Question of Greek Independence* (1821–33). Cambridge 1930.
CHRISTMAS, W. *The Life of King George of Greece.* London 1914.
DAKIN, D. *British and American Philhellenes during the war of Greek Independence, 1821–1833.* Thessaloniki 1955.
DRAKOULIS, P. E. *Neo-Hellenic Literature and Language.* Oxford 1897.
ELIOT, SIR C. *Turkey in Europe.* London 1908.
ELLIADI, M. N. *Crete, Past and Present.* London 1933.
EPSTEIN, E. (Editor). *The Annual Register.* London (Annual Publication).
FALLS, CAPTAIN C. *Military Operations in Macedonia.* London 1933, 1935.
FINLAY, G. *History of Greece.* Vols. VI and VII. Oxford 1877.
HAMSON, D. *We fell among Greeks.* London 1946
FORBES, N., and OTHERS. *The Balkans.* Oxford 1915.
HASLUCK, F. W. *Christianity and Islam under the Sultans.* Oxford 1929.
HOLLAND, T. E. *The European Concert and the Eastern Question.* Oxford 1885.
HUDSON, G. F. *Turkey, Greece, and the Eastern Mediterranean.* Oxford 1939.
GAUVIN, A. *The Greek Question.* New York 1918.
GORDON, T. *History of the Greek Revolution.* Edinburgh 1832.
JEBB, SIR R. *Modern Greece.* London 1880.
KEROFILAS, C. *Eleftherios Venizelos.* London 1915.
LADAS, S. P. *The Exchange of Minorities of Bulgaria, Greece, and Turkey.* New York 1932.
LAWSON, J. C. *Tales of Ægean Intrigue.* London 1920.
LEEPER, SIR R. *When Greek Meets Greek.* London 1950.

MACKENZIE, COMPTON. *First Athenian Memories.* London 1931.
    Greek Memories. London 1939.
    Ægean Memories. London 1940.
    Wind of Freedom. London 1943.
MCNEIL, W. H. *The Greek Dilemma.* London 1947.
MARRIOT, J. A. R. *The Eastern Question.* Oxford 1917.
MAVROGORDATO, J. *Modern Greece, 1800–1931.* London 1931.
MILLER, WILLIAM. *Greek Life in Town and Country.* London 1905.
    The Latins in the Levant. London 1908.
    The Balkans. London 1922.
    A History of the Greek People, 1821–31. New York 1922.
    Greece. London 1928.
    The Ottoman Empire and its Successors. Cambridge 1928.
NEWBIGGIN, MARION L. *Geographical Aspects of Balkan Problems.* London 1915.
NICHOLAS, PRINCE, OF GREECE. *My Fifty Years.* London 1926.
    Political Memoirs. London (1928).
NOEL-BAKER, F. *Greece : the whole story.* London 1946.
OWEN, H. COLLINSON. *Salonica and After.* London 1919.
PALLIS, A. A. *Greece's Anatolian Venture—and after.* London 1937.
PHILLIPS, W. ALISON. *The War of Greek Independence.* London 1897.
PLATYKAS, R. D. *La Grèce pendant la guerre de 1914–18.* Berne 1918.
' POLYBIUS '. *Greece before the Conference.* London (no date).
PROTONOTARIOS, E. B. *The Macedonian Tragedy* (in Greek). Salonica 1916.
RANKIN, SIR R., BART. *The Inner History of the Balkan War.* London 1914.
SARRAIL, GENERAL P. *Mon Commandement en Orient.* Paris 1820.
SERGEANT, LEWIS. *Greece in the Nineteenth Century.* London 1878.
SETON-WATSON, R. W. *The Rise of Nationality in the Balkans.* London 1917.
SPENCER, FLOYD A. *War and Post-War Greece : an Analysis based on Greek Writings.* Washington 1952.
SPENCER, T. B. *Fair Greece Sad Relic.* London 1954.
STAVRIANOS, L. G. *Greece : American Dilemma and Opportunity.* Chicago 1952.
STEEVENS, G. W. *With the Conquering Turk.* London 1897.
STRATFORD DE REDCLIFFE, LORD. *The Eastern Question.* London 1881.
SWEET-ESCOTT, B. *Greece. A Political and Economic Survey, 1939–1953.* London and New York 1954.
THOMSON, SIR BASIL. *The Allied Secret Service in Greece.* London 1931.
TOYNBEE, A. J. *Greek Policy since 1882.* Oxford 1914.
    The Western Question in Greece and Turkey. Oxford 1922.
TSOUDEROS, E. J. *Le Relèvement économique de la Grèce.* Paris 1919.

VAKA, DEMETRA (Mrs. Kenneth Brown). *Les Intrigues Germaniques en Grèce.* Paris 1918.
VENIZELOS, E. *The Vindication of Greek National Policy.* London 1918.
VILLARI, L. *The Macedonian Campaign.* London 1922.
WILLMORE, J. S. *The Story of King Constantine.* London 1919.
WILSON, FIELD MARSHAL LORD. *Eight Years Overseas.* London 1949.
WOODHOUSE, C. M. *Apple of Discord.* London 1948.
The Greek War of Independence. London 1952.

Greek ' White Book '. Athens 1917.
League of Nations, Greek Refugee Settlement. Geneva 1926.
Publications of the Institute of International Affairs.

INDEX

GREECE

English Miles

0 10 20 40 60 80 100

Railways +++++++++++